A Clinician's Guide to
READING FREUD

A Clinician's Guide to

READING FREUD

Peter L. Giovacchini, M.D.

ARONSON
New York & London

Library of Congress Cataloging in Publication Data

Giovacchini, Peter L.
  A Clinician's Guide to Reading Freud.

  Bibliography: p. 233
  Includes index.
  1. Freud, Sigmund, 1856–1939. 2. Psychoanalysis.
I. Title. [DNLM: 1. Psychoanalytic theory. WM 460
G512]
BF173.F85G525   150.19'52   82-14891
ISBN 0-87668-484-3   AACR2

Manufactured in the United States of America.

Contents

Preface

Sigmund Freud (1856–1939), along with Darwin and Einstein, is one of those who have done the most to change the course of our civilization. His discoveries, as he himself once stated, have disturbed the sleep of the world. The viewpoints he has brought to the study of the operations of the mind are captivating as well as clinically and therapeutically innovative.

Freud discovered psychoanalysis. To read him is to learn about the development of psychoanalytic principles from their very beginning and about the conditions under which they evolved. Though considerable additions have been made to Freud's basic postulates, they still must be understood as the fundamental scaffold around which modern Freudian theory has been and continues to be constructed. The serious student of psychoanalysis should know Freud's works as thoroughly as possible, perhaps better than Freud understood them himself.

Freud was a prodigious writer. The *Standard Edition* of *the Complete Psychological Works of Sigmund Freud* consists of 23 volumes plus another volume that contains a comprehensive index. This is an excellent translation and the only one I can wholeheartedly recommend. Aside from reading the original German, the student can do no better. In fact, at times it is better than the original in that the translators have clarified or simplified an occasional ponderous passage. Since I have read both the German and English editions of Freud's complete works, I will emphasize the very rare discrepancies in translations that affect the original meaning.

Holt (Rothgeb 1973) wrote a fascinating exposition of Freud's writing style, emphasizing Freud's receptivity to ideas and tolerance of ambiguity, as well as his simultaneous involvement in artistic, humanistic, and scientific areas. He warned against pulling statements out of context and searching for definitions. Quite correctly, Holt emphasized that sometimes Freud used a term as it would be used in ordinary usage but at other times dealt with the same word as a technical concept. He agreed that to fully understand Freud, all of his major works have to be read.

From the above, the reader can predict that our approach to Freud will be compulsive. That is correct; it will also be Talmudic, in that to understand the evolution of Freud's ideas and to capture their excitement, they have to be understood in a developmental and historical context. To ponder, often over just a sentence, can be exciting and rewarding.

Freud's writings have considerable literary merit. He could be dramatic and poetic, and his case histories, as he recognized, read like novelettes. Reading Freud haphazardly or even chronologically, however, may lead to considerable confusion. Without some background or guidance, Freud can be frustrating. His premises may sound weak and his conclusions absurd, but these reactions are the expedient consequences of lack of comprehension. Cavalier dismissal would be a tremendous loss for the serious student of the behavioral sciences.

In this volume Freud's writings are arranged in a deliberate fashion that is not strictly chronological. I have picked a sequence of articles and sections from books that expounds the evolution of Freud's ideas. Only then can the theories be viewed in their proper context, from which their relevance to modern clinical theory and technique becomes surprisingly and gratifyingly clear. Here, perhaps, lies the essence of our excitement about Freud as he represents the classical psychoanalytic literature. His hypotheses and clinical observations can lead us to exhilarating discoveries and formulations that apply to our patients.

We can achieve new dimensions of comprehension as we gather our clinical data and put them alongside some early psychoanalytic concepts that have been discarded as outmoded. This is an interesting scientific paradox. Reviewing Freud's early concepts often highlights subtle and hidden nuances that are remarkably applicable to our formulations of patients suffering from character defects—patients who, on the surface, seem to be much different from those Freud studied to structure his metapsychological constructs. Thus, Freud's earliest ideas can frequently be integrated into modern theory.

It may seem that I am idealizing Freud, and to some extent I am. I justify this by pointing out that Freud has introduced us to an entirely new frame of reference and provided us with a methodological approach that also proves to be therapeutic. He is a pioneer, but pioneers are not infallible. There is much to be criticized in Freud, and this book in no way attempts to avoid doing so. Modern-day ego psychology opens up vistas that help us understand the psychic processes of primitive mental states and promise to enlighten us as to how psychic structure is acquired. Freud did not deal with these areas, but then he could not deal with everything. On the other hand, Freud is, in some ways, very much connected to the questions and problems we face today.

The book begins with Freud's "The Unconscious" (1915c) and then moves on to *Studies on Hysteria* (Breuer and Freud 1895). We will then deal with a variety of articles and monographs of that period dealing with the traumatic theory and sexual etiology of the neuroses. In the appendix, the reader will find a course outline covering the material in this book.

The sophisticated reader will note that in the articles selected here I elaborate the development of Freud's instinct theories. The only work not written by Freud is a scholarly article by Bibring (1941), which presents a relatively pithy and masterly summary of Freud's ideas up to 1920. Although the development of instinct theory is the main thread running through this book, many other interrelated themes are emphasized, which usually culminate in the discussion of some technical treatment issue.

Reading this book is no substitute for reading Freud. The book is intended to be a guide, a systematic approach, to his work. I hope that some of the difficulties inherent in Freud's expositions will be made manifest and, inasmuch as what is being discussed follows a developmental continuum, that contradictions and inconsistencies will not be as elusive as they might have been out of context.

This volume summarizes the dialogues and ideas that were stimulated in the discussions of a seminar group devoted to studying the writings of Freud. Although the book covers limited terrain, it does so in depth, in keeping with our slow and thorough approach to what might be called the microscopic elements of Freud's ideas. Both myself and the seminar participants have found this pace rewarding, particularly when we were able to use our understanding of classical theory to expand our insights into structural psychopathology and to enlarge our conceptual system, which is primarily that of ego psychology.

I have tried to retain the flavor of the seminar but also to minimize its chaos. Each session of the seminar was tape-recorded. I listened to the tapes and dictated from them into another tape recorder. In so doing, I edited the sessions, trying to translate what was said into comprehensible English. Sometimes I added a question that should have been asked. My orally edited tapes were typed, and the typescripts were then edited again by Mrs. Sandra Roberts. My wife, Louise Post Giovacchini, painstakingly typed the manuscript from the second tape.

Introduction

Two courses are essential in psychoanalytic training. First, in order to understand psychoanalysis, a student needs as complete and thorough a knowledge of Freud as possible. *Freud is psychoanalysis.* The other course, which is essential not only during training but also throughout the course of one's professional life, is a clinical seminar in which patients are discussed.

After one year of residency in psychiatry, I served in the army, where I had plenty of opportunity to read Freud. I had the *Collected Papers*, then four volumes, some monographs, *Beyond the Pleasure Principle,* "The Ego and the Id," *Introductory* and *New Introductory Lectures,* and several other works. I was not absolutely enchanted with Freud's writings. Some I found too vague and lacking in scientific perspective, but others were charming and had considerable literary merit. These mixed reactions were the outcome of the way I read the various volumes. Freud's *Collected Papers* I–IV are arranged chronologically, and I read them in sequence. The brief references made to psychoanalysis in undergraduate psychology courses gave me the impression that it was fanciful and absurd. My first reading did not stimulate my interest in depth psychology, but I knew I had to learn Freud, and so I pursued my studies. During my two years in the Army, I read everything by Freud that had been translated into English.

Upon returning to my residency, I asked one of my instructors, Heinz Kohut, what he recommended I read. He said, "Read Freud." I said, "I read Freud." He replied, "Read him again." I followed his advice and found that reading the same work innumerable times gave me a different perspective and appreciation. No matter how often I read a paper—"On Narcissism," for example—some new adjective, passage, or descriptive phrase struck me each time. One of the beauties of Freud's work is that it grows on you.

In presenting psychoanalytic theory, we will compare the relevance of Freud's ideas to current ideas and determine which of his ideas are still relevant and which are not. We will find some ideas that are obsolete in terms of modern clinical conceptual systems, but in order to understand the newest ideas in psychoanalysis, their origins must be known. In some ways, comparing ego psychology or structural psychology to Freudian psychology is comparable to the comparison of quantum or relativity theory to Newtonian mechanics.

Freud published his first two papers in 1877, at the age of 21. One of these was on the origin of the posterior nerve routes of the spinal cord of amnoceotes (the larval form of the lamprey eel), and the other on observations of the gross and microscopic structure of the organs that were thought to be the testes of the eel. The young Freud, the future discoverer of the castration complex, sought genital organs that had not yet been discovered, and found them.

From 1877 to 1887 Freud published papers on neuroanatomy, histological techniques, and cocaine. In 1880 he translated John Stuart Mills' work on the enfranchisement of women. It was unusual that Freud should become involved with such a topic, inasmuch as amid all those papers with hard scientific approaches he considered women to be castrated males.

In the late 1700s, three men—Tuke at the York retreat in England, Chiarugi at St. Boniface in Florence, and Pinel at the Bicêtre in Paris—literally released patients from their shackles, which introduced a humanistic approach to the treatment of the mentally ill. Up to this time the insane had been viewed either with awe or with contempt and disgust. These three men related to emotionally ill persons (mainly psychotics) as people rather than animals. This new attitude was responsible for the investigation of psychic phenomena in a scientific frame of reference.

These early investigators were fascinated with the manifestations of emotional illness. Their model was primarily medical. First, they had to define the entity, the diagnostic approach, and this meant that patient's behavior needed to be understood systematically. At the outset, the psychiatric approach was phenomenological. These observers were strikingly acute. Some of their reports sound as if they were written by Sherlock Holmes. The slightest gesture or the most fleeting expression did not escape them, and they were able to perceive phenomenological clusters and construct diagnostic categories. They focused at first on psychotic patients. In the mid-nineteenth century, Morel described young schizophrenic patients in considerable detail and coined the diagnostic category *dementia praecox* (demènce precôce). He believed he was observing a precocious dementing process that explained psychotic symptoms. Next, Kahlbaum postulated the condition of *catatonia*, an entity that we still consider valid today. Kahlbaum's student Hecker described *hebephrenia*. They both attempted causal explanations based upon organic factors supported by few demonstrable data. Finally, the great Kraepelin formulated a comprehensible classification which, in essence, is still the outline for our present diagnostic categories. However, again it was purely descriptive. Bleuler, another master of observation, introduced such variables as constitutional and environmental factors. None of these approaches had much to do with treatment, except in a palliative fashion.

During the mid 19th century neurologists in France worked with patients who were considered to be psychoneurotic and who had somatic, rather than psychotic, symptoms, and they called these patients *hysterics*. They believed that hysteria was the outcome of a weak psychic organization, a theory that carried moralistic overtones. There were two major groups of clinicians, one in Paris, led by Charcot and Janet, and the other in Nancy, represented by Liébault and Bernheim. They did not seem fundamentally different except that the Nancy school was much less flamboyant and melodramatic. Charcot and Liebault hypnotized their patients to suggest away symptoms, and Charcot concluded that hysteria was an artificial hypnotic state, or that hypnosis was an artificial hysteria.

In 1886, after he had done research at Brücke's Laboratory for eight years, Freud decided to improve his financial status in order to marry. He realized that he did not have adequate knowledge for a practice with emotionally disturbed patients. He had heard of Charcot and was intrigued by the fact that his treatment method occasionally achieved dramatic symptomatic improvement. This appealed to him more than the then popular method of electrical (Faradic) stimulation, bath, and massage. He obtained a grant from the Vienna Medical Society that enabled him to study under Charcot for about a year. He was fascinated by what he saw and was particularly impressed by Bernheim illustrating posthypnotic suggestion at Nancy. (Bernheim's experiment was instrumental in Freud's subsequent postulation of the existence of a dynamic unconscious.)

Freud returned to Vienna looking forward enthusiastically to the prospect of treating neurotic patients. There he translated a book commissioned by Charcot. However, Freud could not resist making annotations, footnotes, and comments on Charcot's ideas. Freud must have had doubts about some of the master's opinions, and Charcot was not particularly grateful for his help. Freud also wrote articles in French on diagnostic concepts about hysteria, especially hysterical paralysis as differentiated from organic and hysterical stigmata. He reported his findings to the Vienna Medical Society and was quite bitter about their reaction to his experiences and ideas, although Ellenberger, in *The Discovery of the Unconscious* (1970), reported that the reactions of the medical society were nowhere near as intense as Freud believed.

Before going to Paris, Freud had met Josef Breuer, a successful internist who also practiced hypnosis. Breuer's theory was that there is a traumatic moment in the development of hysteria in which the affect of anxiety or fright cannot be discharged. He considered that the ego was in a hypnoidal or split state and that the affect became encapsulated or dammed-up in the split-off portion. This affect, with symbolic manipulation, led to the formation of symptoms. Breuer developed a rationale for therapy founded on an etiologically based psychodynamic theory. His treatment consisted of hypnotizing and regressing the patient back to the ego state characteristic of the traumatic moment. By reliving the trauma, the affect could now be discharged. His famous patient, Anna O.—in reality Bertha Pappenheim—became one of the founders of the social work movement.

Janet and Charcot saw hysteria as a splitting of consciousness due to weakness. The French school disdainfully and condescendingly looked upon hysteria as a degenerative disease. We still see traces of that viewpoint today.

Freud, however, was fascinated with Breuer's theory, although he found the hypnoidal split theory too anatomical and rather similar to the theory of ego weakness postulated by the French school. Freud preferred to think in terms of opposing forces—the *dynamic unconscious,* which was one of the most unique and magnificent findings of psychoanalysis. The dynamic unconscious refers to forces within the individual that he or she is not aware of, and that these forces have effects upon behavior and cause hysteria and other emotional illnesses. The unconscious has been known to exist for centuries. Hippocrates, for instance, knew a great deal about it. But the fact that the unconscious can profoundly affect behavior and feelings and can create symptoms was not known. Even as recently as three or four years ago, at a meeting of the Illinois Psychiatric Society, a psychiatrist stated that there is no proof of the existence of the unconscious, and some people still deny its existence. Freud is still far ahead of some contemporary psychiatrists who limit their understanding of patients to descriptive classification. He insisted on knowing his patients in depth and on the basis of causal factors. This was his unique contribution.

A Clinician's Guide to
READING FREUD

1

"The Unconscious" (1915)

SYNOPSIS

In this paper Freud provided his most comprehensive discussion of what he considered to be his most important discovery, the unconscious mind. He assembled both descriptive and dynamic concepts about processes that reside below the sphere of conscious awareness.

Freud began by presenting data to justify and support his proposition that the dynamic unconscious exists as a powerful element of the mind and that it determines ordinary as well as pathological behavior. Next, he broadened the metapsychological edifice by introducing the topographical hypothesis. He postulated three psychic systems: the unconscious (Ucs), the preconscious (Pcs), and conscious (Cs). He discussed these in an anatomical sense, as opposed to qualities attributed to mental content and processes, expanding his earlier discussion of them in *The Interpretation of Dreams*.

How can unconscious feelings be explained? Is this a contradiction inasmuch as "feelings" imply that they are consciously felt? Freud's explanations depend upon the assumption of structural hierarchies: when feelings become unconscious they lose their consciously felt organization but regain this if and when they again become conscious. A feeling loses its conscious status when it is displaced to other thoughts than those it is initially associated with. The feeling or affect remains conscious but its significance does not.

In the next section, Freud provided an extensive and detailed discussion of the mechanism of repression as he investigated the relationships between the unconscious and the conscious. Repression is also the exclusive topic of another paper, "Repression," written in the same year (Freud 1915a). Freud also provided valuable clinical insights about phobias and anxiety neuroses. In fact, he came close to formulating his second anxiety theory, which proved so useful for understanding of the psychoneuroses, and which he completed in *The Problem of Anxiety* (1926a).

In examining other aspects of the relationship between consciousness and the unconscious, Freud postulated the existence of a censor between the preconscious and the conscious as well as between the unconscious and the preconscious. This point is not often referred to in the psychoanalytic literature, and Freud never brought up this topic again. Nevertheless, this concept is valuable in dealing with patients suffering from severe psychopathology involving structural defects.

In the final section of this work, Freud investigated primitive mental states as he focused upon the formation of psychic structure and the fixations of schizophrenic patients. He discussed the progression from concrete to abstract thought, the latter being associated with the acquisition of language. Early in the development of language, words are symbols for concrete objects; the unconscious, a primitive psychic system, treats the word as if it were, in itself, a concrete object, a "thing," as Freud stated. This is also characteristic of primary process and schizophrenic thinking.

It has been well established that Freud had been thinking in terms of an unconscious for some time before he wrote "The Unconscious." Ernest Jones speculated that, as an undergraduate student, Freud was familiar with the writings of the psychologist Herbart, who wrote about unconscious processes. Freud felt that mental phenomena could not be explained in terms of conscious motivation. He noted gaps in chains of associations. He assumed that these gaps could be filled in with repressed memories.

Freud thought in such terms very early in his clinical work. In a footnote to the case of Emmy von N. (Breuer and Freud 1895), he first used the word unconscious, but at this time he was trying to explain mental phenomena in terms of neural circuits. In 1895 Waelder discovered the neuron, which fit in very well with what Freud was saying about cathexes of nerve fibers. However, Freud was not able to arrive at satisfactory conceptualizations based upon neuroanatomy and neurophysiology. By 1900, as evidenced in *The Interpretation of Dreams*, he had completely given up constructing a neurological model and had abandoned attempts to explain mental phenomena in neurological terms.

In Chapter 7 of *The Interpretation of Dreams*, Freud devised a fairly comprehensible outline of the unconscious—the topographical hypothesis. In 1912, a few years before "The Unconscious" was written Freud described the unconscious from both a descriptive and a dynamic viewpoint and as a separate system of the psychic apparatus. He elaborated upon Bernheim's experiments with post-hypnotic suggestion. In "The Ego and the Id" (1923), Freud replaced the topographical with the structural hypothesis. Instead of unconscious, preconscious, and conscious, he substituted id and ego and then added superego. In 1933, he amplified these concepts further in *New Introductory Lectures in Psychoanalysis*.

At first, the concept of the unconscious was quite controversial. Today most of us accept it without too much protest, although there are still people who argue against it. I do not believe we have to take them too seriously unless we are behaviorists. Freud's postulating that man was not in control of his destiny, that there were forces inside him that could influence him, forces he was not in control of, or perhaps not even aware of, was a fairly startling, and threatening, hypothesis.

At the request of H. W. Meyers, Freud presented "A Note on the Concept of the Unconscious in Psychoanalysis" (1912a) to a British group of academic psychologists. At this time academic psychologists, especially British ones, tended to reject his ideas.

In his short introduction to "The Unconscious," Freud described repression, a mechanism that prevents an idea from becoming conscious. He postulated that an idea can exist in either a conscious or an unconscious state. Even if an idea is in an unconscious state, it still produces effects. The only way to know what is unconscious is to translate or transform it into something conscious. This task is difficult because resistance will invariably be encountered. Repressed elements belong to the unconscious, but there is more to the unconscious than what has been repressed.

What are these other elements in the unconscious? Freud postulated that there are elements in the unconscious that were never conscious, that is, they could not have been repressed. He was referring to instincts, about which there is still much to explore. It is important to recognize that Freud formulated that instincts are on the borderland between the biological and psychological and are never capable of becoming conscious. Freud was concerned with the biological aspects of instincts, which are not capable of mental representation and, therefore, cannot become conscious. For example, a metabolic process, such as a chloride shift, cannot achieve mentation and consciousness.

Justification of the Concept of the Unconscious

This is the first section of "The Unconscious." Freud believed that the concept of the unconscious would aid understanding of what he called gaps in psychic acts. People sometimes behave in certain unexplainable ways or say things that make no sense unless one assumes there were other unobservable acts or ideas interpolated between what can be seen and what cannot. In this connection, Freud was referring to obsessional ideas and phenomena that forcefully and inexplicably intrude in activity and thought. He also called attention to parapraxes, such as slips of the tongue, dreams, and the symptoms of mental illness, and he was particularly impressed with post-hypnotic phenomena. None of these can be explained solely by the concept of consciousness. Freud then pointed out that consciousness contains only a small amount of mental content. It was thus necessary to postulate that most of the material available to consciousness has to be in a latent state.

At this point, Freud used phenomena from four different frames of reference to support the concept of the dynamic unconscious: an unconscious that has its effects on behavior. Listed in descending order of conviction, he described: post-hypnotic phenomena, parapraxes, symptoms, and dreams. The first, post-hypnotic phenomena, require fewer assumptions and offer the most convincing evidence for the dynamic unconscious, whereas the last, dreams, require more assumptions, so the data they offer are less supportive.

Post-hypnotic phenomena convincingly support the hypotheses of a dynamic unconscious. Freud described in detail Bernheim's work on post-hypnotic suggestion in his 1912 paper, "A Note on the Concept of the Unconscious in Psychoanalysis." Bernheim hypnotized a patient and during the trance instructed him to carry out a simple act on given a particular signal when awake. The patient would have no idea why he performed the task. He reacted as instructed, which we now know is characteristic of hypnosis. This experiment practically defines the dynamic unconscious, since all we have to do is restate the observed phenomena to formulate the concept. For example, the patient is given instructions while hypnotized. When awake, he is not aware of these instructions. He has either forgotten them to the point that they are psychically extinct or, if retained within the psyche, they must be unconscious. The fact that the patient carries out the instructions indicates that they have not become psychically extinct, and inasmuch as they could affect conscious behavior, they must have been dynamically residing in an unconscious state. This is precisely what is meant by the dynamic unconscious. The other frames of reference require certain suppositions that post-hypnotic phenomena do not.

A fifth frame of reference, which was not separately considered by Freud, but which he did, on occasion, include among the parapraxes, is forgetting. Not all experiences become memories that can easily be brought into conscious awareness. Some memories, although forgotten, are capable of being recalled. If so, such experiences or memories were not lost, but continued residing within the psyche. Thus, they must have been unconscious.

Are all life's experiences stored in the psyche? Is everything that cannot be remembered repressed? I prefer to think that some things are actually forgotten. To use Freud's terms, they either have not been sufficiently cathected (energized), or their cathexes have not been sustained. Consequently, they lose their intrapsychic structure and integration, and simply vanish. Not all the incidents that happened on the fourth of February in the third grade are retained; if some are, it is because they became hypercathected and associated with some meaningful unconscious constellation. If such an incident can be easily recalled, it belongs to a special type of unconscious, something that is descriptively unconscious but has a different location than the system unconscious.

According to Freud, we attribute our psychic constitution to inanimate objects and to others. If acts and feelings in oneself that cannot be explained or linked with the rest of mental life are attributed to someone else, then it becomes easy to understand and explain them. We can interpret in other people what we cannot understand within ourselves, what, in ourselves is unconscious. Freud did not, however, specifically mention projection in this article.

Freud explained that inferences about the self may not reveal an unconscious but rather the existence of a second conscious. As so often happens with Freud, he postulated a thesis so that he could systematically demolish it. Here he raised three objections: (1) He questioned the feasibility of postulating a second consciousness about which the observer knows nothing; (2) His analyses have shown that latent thoughts can be quite independent of each other, which would require formulating a third, fourth and even more consciouses. (3) These latent thoughts follow laws of their own, which are quite different from laws governing conscious thoughts.

There seems to be a tendency in the living organism for synthesis and cohesiveness. The nonbiological concept of a second conscious requires conceptualizing multiple perceptual systems under no central dominance. Clincally, this makes it difficult to explain personalities that do not operate primarily on the basis of splitting mechanisms. Such a hypothesis might explain the hypnoidal states Breuer described and certain character disorders where splitting mechanisms are prevalent. However, for ordinary psychic states, the concept of more than one conscious is confusing, and from a scientific viewpoint, it is not economical.

The crucial point is that latent thoughts have characteristics that are alien to consciousness. They have laws of their own and qualify as a separate system rather than another conscious. They operate on the basis of different principles than do conscious elements.

Primary process is the characteristic mode of operation of the unconscious. Although it is related to consciousness, primary process is an operation that identifies the unconscious. Freud first discussed primary process in Chapter 7 of *The Interpretation of Dreams* (1900). He also discussed it in "Formulations on the Two Principles of Mental Functioning" (Freud 1911). The idea that certain unconscious processes occur at ego levels and come close to consciousness was finally elaborated upon in 1923 in "The Ego and the Id," when Freud introduced the structural hypothesis as a model to explain phenomena that the topographical hypothesis, the model he constructed in "The Unconscious," could not.

I wish to emphasize that rereading Freud has caused me to view the unconscious from yet another perspective. Freud stimulates something new in me each time I read this article. I am referring to his pithy remarks at the end of this first section. He admits that we do not know very much about another person's reality, but we claim to know a good deal about his unconscious. When we consider the way a person views the world, we are dealing with highly individualized matters, the products of many experiences and integrations.

Our perceptual systems, as directed toward the outer world, are organized differently than our views of the unconscious. For example, there are many different ways of reacting to a work of art, but we feel and react to pain in the stomach in pretty much the same way. The further back we go into the psychic apparatus, the more primitive the levels we experience, the more commonality we have. Although we cannot have too much faith in our ability to know what others perceive, we can have much greater faith in our knowledge about how they react at deeper levels of the personality; we move from lesser to greater specificity. In the clinical realm this should demonstrate the futility of trying to teach the patient what reality is. The reality he needs, one consonant with inner needs, would be the extension of a continuum with the inner recesses of the psyche. Another person's reality may be vastly different from ours, and we may never be able to comprehend it.

The Multiplicity of the Unconscious and the Topographical Viewpoint

In the next section, Freud postulated that there are psychic elements which are unconscious but are easily capable of becoming conscious. Freud called these elements *preconscious*, and distinguished these from other latent thoughts that are repressed and not capable of becoming conscious. Thus, he distinguished the unconscious both descriptively and as a system. The system unconscious, the system preconscious, and the conscious apparatus represent the topographical hypothesis. Heretofore, Freud considered psychoanalysis as a dynamic system and had introduced an energic hypothesis, psychoeconomics (Freud 1900, 1905). Now, however, he explicitly wrote of a topographical viewpoint, what we might consider to be an anatomical perspective, and was formally adding dimensions to his metapsychology.

The introduction of this viewpoint raised the question of how a psychical act becomes transposed from one system to another. Freud considered two possibilities. The first involved a "second registration" in a new psychic locality; at the same time, the original unconscious registration may continue to exist in the same locale. The other possibility was that the idea remains where it is but undergoes a change. Freud preferred the first explanation, although toward the end of this article he resolved the question by showing that these are not particularly meaningful distinctions if considered in a larger context. Freud's immediate purpose was to apply these theoretical possibilities to the psychoanalytic treatment situation.

An interpretation of a repressed idea that the analyst but not the patient has discovered, as sometimes occurs in treatment, will be registered in the patient's preconscious, but this will not have any effect. It does not remove the repression; it may even strengthen it. The idea now exists in two different places, the unconscious and the preconsicous, but there is still no connection between the two. Only after the resistance between the preconscious and the unconscious has been removed can the two come together and form true insight. Freud summarized this concept very well by stating that to have heard something and to experience it are two different things, even though the content is identical.

Before going on, I wish to comment on the relationship of psychical processes and anatomy. In his early work, Freud seemed to reject making anatomical localizations, and simply described mental processes. Later, he wrote about the mental apparatus as if it were specifically situated somewhere in the body. I do not believe that this is a particularly significant distinction. Actually, Freud was torn between his desire for a completely psychological system and his desire, based somewhat upon his neuro-anatomical background, to construct a spatial model. Later, he constructed a model, founded on what is known as the structural hypothesis, that located various psychic systems—id, ego, superego—relative to each other. However, he was always aware that he was dealing with metaphors.

It is difficult to think in terms of moving ideas from one system to another. An idea consists of a fairly complex organization not compatible with a freely mobile cathexis—the energy of the unconscious. However, Freud was not necessarily referring to ideas. The German word Freud used is *vorstellung*, which is usually translated as "presentation" and which is closer to a visual representation than to an idea. Vorstellung also means performance, like a scene on stage, so it is more than a simple image; it is an entire constellation. Still, for the reasons mentioned above, I do not believe Freud wanted to attach too much organized psychic energy—what he called secondary process (Freud 1900, 1911)—to *vorstellung*. Images, in contrast to thoughts or verbal presentations, can be manipulated in a primary process fashion, they can be moved about in different systems without losing their distinctiveness, their entity-like status.

Unconscious Emotions

In the third section, Freud discussed emotions as opposed to unconscious ideas. He raised the question of whether unconscious ideas exist and, if so, in what sense, and he pointed out that an instinct is represented in the unconscious by an idea. To understand this, we may find it useful to think of an instinct as a mechanism that does not yet have the organization of a mental process, something in the physical or physiological realm, as for example, the chloride shift. An instinct is a borderland concept between the physiological and psychological. Actually, Freud used the word *trieb*, which would be better translated as *drive*: it is felt and has impetus, but something within the organism, a physiological or biochemical process, is responsible for its formation. Only the idea that represents the instinct can become conscious.

Freud was referring specifically to unconscious emotions, but emotions belong to the conscious sphere. Still, clinically, we speak of unconscious love, hate, guilt, and even anxiety. Freud solved this apparent paradox by stating that an affect is perceived but misconstrued, becoming connected with another idea, with which it can enter consciousness. In other words, it becomes displaced.

Freud then described the vicissitudes of emotion. He felt that an affect can remain as it is, can become qualitatively different, or can be repressed. What did he mean when he wrote about a qualitative transformation of a quota of affect? On page 178 of "The Unconscious," Freud said, "either the affect remains wholly or in part, as it is: or it is transformed into a qualitatively different quota of affect, above all into anxiety . . ." Qualitative and quota do not seem to go together. He then described the differences between an unconscious idea and an unconscious affect. An idea, after undergoing repression, continues to exist as a structure in the system unconscious, whereas an affect exists as a potential beginning. An idea is a cathexis of memory traces, whereas an affect can be considered the result of a discharge process.

After these formulations it seems confusing that Freud should next state that there are no unconscious affects, only unconscious ideas. The difficulty, however, is semantic. An affect is a feeling. An unconscious feeling is a contradiction in terms; a feeling must be felt, and to feel something is to be aware of it. Freud knew from clinical experience that things happen to affects. He thought of repressed affects as being misconstrued as they are displaced and become attached to ideational representations different from the original one.

We can also think in terms of a hierarchy. A feeling has origins. At the beginning of its developmental path it has not yet become fully grown; this occurs at the level of conscious awareness. If we consider affects in terms of a developmental progression, we can then conceptualize their precursors. We can view affects as being inhibited in their development and postulate an unconscious state of latent affect that has the potential for forming affect. Although Freud did not apply these concepts to clinical phenomena, inhibition of affect or the lack of development of feelings can be the result of severe characterologic psychopathology or primitive fixations.

The concept of inhibition of affects is meaningful if we relate it to developmental fixations. Inhibition refers to incompletely developed affects, which commonly occur in patients suffering from severe structural problems. I have had patients who do not even know how or what they feel. All they are capable of feeling is terror. The inability to feel anything can be a very frightening experience. Other patients are not able to construct any kind of affect other than what we might consider global affect, which does not permit them to make sensitive discriminations. Some patients do not know whether they want to urinate, defecate, eat, or have sexual relationships. They have just one general feeling, which is impossible to describe. One patient depicted this feeling through colors: yellow referred to a general amorphous feeling. She saw yellow as the dominant color of all body fluids; Urine, lymph, menstrual blood, and bile, were all mixed up in her mind. During therapy, she was able to structure some affects and make some distinctions, and she eventually experienced anger as red. During regression, however, red reverted to yellow.

We can explain the relationship between the development of a structured affect and what Freud called discharge of affect. In a historical context Freud used a tension-discharge model following Helmholtz's physiology, and dealt exclusively with hydrodynamic concepts which emphasize discharge processes.

Today, many of us view affects in terms of structure, function, and adaptive significance rather than only as a discharge process. Freud, however, emphasized the achievement of psychic equilibrium through discharge of accumulated energy. This discharge is experienced as the affect of anxiety. If a sexual instinct cannot be discharged, it is deflected away from mentational elements. This happens when there are no opportunities for sexual gratification, as in prison or any other situation of forced abstinence. The mentational elements are psychic representations of methods of gratification. However, if there is no situation in the external world that would allow such modes to be operative, then they are not cathected. Sexual tension is deflected into physiological channels, and its discharge is perceived as anxiety. This, in essence, is the conversion theory of anxiety.

Is anxiety a primitve affect? Is it not, in a sense, a pre-affect from which more complex affects are derived?

Much later, Freud (1926a) described anxiety as a fundamental signal that sets defensive processes in motion. Anxiety, however, has considerable organization. There are feeling states that are considerably more primitive than anxiety—inchoate terror, for example. Undoubtedly some complex moods are capable of being reduced to fundamental affects, but Freud was not involved with such questions; he was still establishing the groundwork of classical theory. He was very much involved with the difficult topic of repression, which becomes especially complex when we attempt to conceptualize repressed affects. All of the problems previously discussed regarding unconscious affects are also relevant to repression.

At the end of this section, Freud tentatively introduces us to what might be considered a rudimentary ego psychology. He points out that the system conscious is dominant and determines whether affects will be discharged as well as controls motility.

Topography and the Dynamics of Repression

Freud conceptualized two types of repression: primal repression and repression proper. (Primal repression is *not* primary repression, and there is no such thing as secondary repression.) In repression or repression proper, an impulse seeks access to consciousness. If it is unacceptable, it is ousted or barred admission. Energic factors become important: The impulse striving for recognition and gratification has energy attached to it; it is cathected. As the impulse reaches the border of the preconscious, the preconscious somehow appropriates part of the energy of the aberrant impulse, decathecting it. The energy thus acquired is used as an anti-cathexis to force the impulse out of the preconscious and back into the system unconscious.

The decathected impulse gives up preconscious or perhaps even conscious cathexis. Although Freud did not emphasize it in this article, he implied that the act of becoming conscious involves hypercathexis. The ideational representation acquires cathexis from these higher systems. During repression it loses this cathexis, which then is added to the repressive forces as anticathexis. The initial impulse, however, retains the energy that was supplied to it by the unconscious, which caused it to push its way upward in the psychic apparatus. Without a steady expenditure of anticathexis—what Freud calls afterpressure (*Nachdrängung*)—the impulse would repeat the process of striving toward consciousness and being driven back into the unconscious.

What is the relationship between libido and cathexis? Cathexis means energy charge so we can rephrase this question to ask, what is the relationship between libido and psychic energy? Libido is defined as the energy of the sexual instincts. Quite clearly when Freud wrote about impulses and ideational representations, he was referring to components of sexual instincts. These are the objects of repression, so, in effect, libido and psychic energy can be equated when discussing the theory of repression. Primal repression is more difficult to understand and accept than is repression proper. According to Freud, the unconscious has what might be considered a pulling force, something similar to magnetic attraction. There are elements residing within the system unconscious that can never gain conscious awareness. These elements, in turn, exert an attracting force on preconscious factors associatively connected with them, and draw these elements into the unconscious. Supposedly, this is how repression begins, the repressing force initially emanating from the unconscious rather than the preconscious.

But how can the unconscious draw something into itself? Freud said that the unconscious was a seething cauldron, a reservoir of explosive forces, which has to be held in check by the more structured parts of the personality. He stated there are elements in the unconscious that never have been, or never can be, conscious. How can we know if they really exist? This cannot be tested, so we have a meaningless hypothesis. However, we might be able to infer their existence from their effects. In science, existence of molecules and atoms was postulated long before electronic microscopes and cloud chambers were available. Still, Freud was inconsistent in defining his concepts, such as the id being a seething cauldron and, at the same time, having magnetic-like forces. Can the same factors be involved in an explosion and an implosion at the same time? Still, as is so often the case with Freud, his formulations capture our fancy because they seem to be aptly suited to certain clinical situations.

The following vignette from my practice makes the concept of primal repression appealing, although it has not modified my views about it.

During analysis, a 27-year-old woman patient of mine dreamed that she was at a dance. The setting was hazy, but she was able to see the gray suit worn by a man who asked her to dance. They danced around the room, and suddenly her partner steered her to a corner and pressed himself against her. She could feel his erect penis. Inasmuch as I often wore gray suits and the transference was clearly erotic, I believed this dream was an obvious allusion to her sexual feelings toward me. I also knew she was struggling with and defending herself against her impulses. Wishing to pursue this theme, I asked her to free-associate to the dream because she was inclined to pursue other seemingly unrelated topics. She hesitantly considered some of the dream elements, such as its haziness. I then directed her attention to the man in the gray suit. She was silent for approximately a minute and then became, what seemed to me, tremendously anxious. She finally reported a sensation of intense dizziness, feeling that the couch was spinning furiously. Gradually these feelings subsided and she continued talking but make no reference whatsoever to the dream. I became immensely curious and had to interrupt her and ask her about the dream. She naively answered; "What dream?" To my astonishment, she had forgotten it completely. I then repeated the dream to her and was able to help her remember it. Once again I brought her attention to the man in the gray suit, and once more she felt the couch spinning and totally wiped the dream from her memory. I tried a third time and with the same results. As she experienced these spinning sensations, she described a vortex that was sucking her thoughts into it. Certainly the memory of her dream seemed to be pulled into the hidden recesses of her mind. This could be understood as an example of primal repression.

In this article Freud is constructing a *metapsychology*. He first coined this term in 1901 and he referred to it again in his discussion of primal repression, in which he stated that in addition to the psychodynamic and topographical, he was introducing the psychoeconomic hypothesis through his discussion of repression.

Regardless of the inconsistencies involved, some of these ideas are clinically relevant. Repression means that the psyche is protecting itself against anxiety. We can then start thinking in terms of psychopathology. Freud began by discussing the anxiety neurosis and ended up discussing phobias. The discussion of these clinical entities follows his discussion of repression. We have reached a point where we can establish a continuum between some clinical states.

We can view the *anxiety neurosis* as the beginning of a continuum. In the anxiety neurosis, libido is blocked and discharged as anxiety. If the libido is allowed to progress a little further, it will settle on the peripheral border of the ego—the soma—and then we have *conversion hysteria*. If the libido goes beyond the soma and the boundaries of the ego to the outer world it causes *phobias* at the other end of the continuum. In terms of movement of libido, we can postulate a continuum between anxiety neurosis, conversion hysteria and phobias. Here, phobia is synonymous with anxiety hysteria.

Freud concentrated on phobias and used the case of Little Hans (Freud 1909) to provide clinical data. Hans' central problem was oedipal, although Freud did not stress this here. He mentioned Hans' sexual attachment to the mother and his death wish toward his father, which expressed itself in the interesting manner of a fear of horses. The unacceptable hostile impulse toward the father (unacceptable because Hans was afraid of retaliation) was displaced onto a substitute object. Hans' feeling of wanting to kill and get rid of his father was repressed because his father was usually present and because Hans was dependent on as well as generally fond of him. Hans displaced his feelings onto a horse. He avoided horses rather than suffer inner turmoil, and through projection, was able to displace his fears onto outside, remote situations from which he could remain distant.

We can carry these processes one step further. The phobic patient can avoid the retaliatory punishment of the superego by projecting punitive • forces onto external objects. This converts an intrapsychic conflict into a conflict between the ego and some segment of the outer world.

Are there any laws or mechanisms that determine the choice of the substitutive object? The substitutive object has to have an associational connection with the original object; symbolic, contiguity, or something should have happened to or with the original object when the substitutive one was present. In the case of Little Hans, the horse stood for the father. It is big and powerful, and the external genitals are large and visible. Freud talked a great deal about this type of symbolization as early as *Studies on Hysteria* (Breuer and Freud 1895). If the substitutive object does not have one of these associations, it will not be chosen. This is extremely important because it distinguishes hysterical symptoms and phobias from other types of somatic disturbances. The latter are conditions that have been studied from a psychosomatic viewpoint.

The phobic object or situation resides in the outside world but how do we distinguish between "inside" and "outside"? Is not everything inside, even though we may perceive it as outside? Internal situations are projected and perceived as outside. I use such vague and broad terms as situations because Freud was not precise here, although he wrote of the projection of anxiety and the projection of impulses in other works. When Freud referred to the projection of impulses, he was basically speaking of paranoid mechanisms. Little Hans believed that the horse would bite him, castrate him. It may seem that anxiety is transformed into fear, since fear is supposedly a reaction to a realistic external danger. In a phobia, however, the danger is external but not realistic, thus it is still anxiety.

However, his mother did, in fact, make a castration threat as punishment for masturbation, so Little Hans learned that there are situations in the outside world that can be relatively dangerous. Hans had impulses that could evoke punishment. Presumably, these are oedipal wishes toward the mother which manifest themselves in his general curiosity and erotic orientation. Hans' sexual feelings led to the fear of castration. His mother may have actually made the threat, but because of rivalry he was afraid of his father. As stated, he projected the danger and displaced it from his father to the horse, because to some extent, the danger was internalized. He carried the prohibitions within himself and attached them to his father. Undoubtedly, he received some external reinforcement from his father as he did from his mother.

How could such a young child know the horse could be avoided? Why did the horse function as a displacement instead of some other object that is rarely encountered? Could an unfamiliar object be considered more appropriate because it is harder to generalize from that object to other objects? Freud, after all, wrote that the phobia can spread and become paralyzing.

These issues can not presently be resolved because the question of choice of neurosis is involved. The horse is apparently more primary process than a cow, a rabbit, or even a rocking horse. The horse is more elemental and better fits the bestiality of the primary process and primitive impulses. The choice of the phobic object seems to be more understandable in other phobias, such as the fear of heights, of falling, of flying, or the fear of open spaces, agoraphobia. In these we think of helplessness and vulnerability, the lack of an anchor or attachment to an external object. In claustrophobia, the fear of being crushed, of being inundated by inner impulses, comes to mind. We can make very quick connections between these phobias and the fundamental conflict.

For Little Hans, many factors converge on the horse. Hans saw horses falling, for example, and viewed this as similar to his own act of stamping his feet when defecating. The horse acted out Hans' impulses and was overdetermined. The halter depicted the father's moustache and glasses. Hans viewed horses as dependable, powerful, and capable of carrying heavy burdens.

Freud pointed out that certain objects have an innate symbolic connotation and cannot be further reduced, such as snakes or mice. Fear of such objects seems to be universal, regardless of psychopathology or even cultural background. These common revulsions can not be explained by innate destructive qualities. Freud further stated that the anxiety reaches the peripherey of a series of external objects that are associatively connected to the primary phobic object; in Little Hans' case, the horse.

This part of the paper foreshadows forthcoming important formulations. As the phobia generalizes, the anxiety that is projected is not as strong as that attached to the first substitutive object. There is less cathexis involved, and the spread to other objects presents less of a danger. Anxiety is produced in an attempt to avoid stronger anxiety; it is produced on the periphery of stronger anxiety. This is very similar to the concept of signal anxiety. In "Inhibitions, Symptoms and Anxiety" (1926a), Freud again used the case of Little Hans to work out his second and final anxiety theory.

Special Characteristics of the System Unconscious

The formulations in this fifth section are not gratuitous theory-building; they are based upon clinical observations. With the exception of the Wolf Man, Freud's major case histories were already written. Freud began here by describing the unconscious as consisting of impulses seeking discharge. Impulses exist side by side. Contradictory impulses do not influence each other but sometimes there is a compromise if two impulses are activated at the same time. Freud then went on to say that there is no negation, doubt, or degree of certainty in the unconscious. He conceptualized disparate structures without cohesive elements in the unconscious in which there can be no negation because there is no affirmation. Freud barely mentioned negation here, although later he devoted a whole article to this defense (Freud 1925); in which he considered negation a fairly high level defense because the unconscious thought being defended against gains access to the conscious sphere and is consciously acknowledged and then negated. For instance, a patient states that the therapist believes the patient had a certain thought, but then insists that the thought had never before occurred to him. This is especially striking since the analyst has not made any such suggestion. Freud believed, however, that repression is a higher-level defense. There are several variables that determine whether a defense is high or low level. This topic will be explored when we discuss the hierarchy of defenses in "Further Remarks on the Defence Neuro-Psychoses" (Freud 1896).

We can observe uncoordinated activities during early levels of development. In transference regressions, individual parts of the ego may seem to operate independently of each other. Further organization results in splitting, but this type of uncoordination antedates splitting, which assumes that some cohesion has been achieved. Glover (1930) wrote about various areas of the ego operating independently of each other and postulated the existence of ego nuclei.

This lack of cohesiveness extends to the time sense. Young children often use verb tenses incorrectly. They confuse past and present and have an insufficiently developed concept of the future. The timelessness of the unconscious is a well accepted feature.

Unconscious processes are impressively mobile. The characteristic tendency to displace cathexis from one ideational context to another contributes to the seemingly irrational manifestations of the system unconscious. The fact that displacement can be recognized as a mechanism means that there is a rationale. The unconscious follows laws called primary process. These laws do not conform to the usual rules of logic, which dominate preconscious and conscious spheres and which are referred to as secondary process.

Regarding the irrational, two statements, one about particular impulses not being subject to contradiction, and the other about forming compromises, seem inconsistent. Freud states that contradictory impulses can exist side by side, as would happen in a state of unorganization. But what about the compromise? Compromise is the result of the demands of a higher organization. As impulses strive to reach higher psychic states such as consciousness, contradictions have to be dealt with. Freud, however, did not refer to higher levels of organization. He stated that impulses can fuse in the system unconscious but can also exist side by side. I cannot resolve this contradiction.

We can think in terms of instinctual impulses and defending forces. It is the defending forces that cannot stand contradictions and which demand compromise. The compromise would have to take place in the preconscious. The lack of organization of the unconscious does not permit impulses to have enough structure to take definitive stands, so contradiction can become explicit only in a higher psychic system. Here we see the importance of stressing structural hierarchies. This can be confusing because some of the members of the seminar believed that displacement, and condensation, which involves bringing together psychic elements and includes compromise occur in the unconscious without having to come into conflict with the preconscious.

The mechanism of condensation is a primary process phenomenon, but it may become involved in secondary process activity. The latter would help construct the product of the condensation. This occurs with regularity during creative activity.

The topographical hypothesis could not completely resolve the above issues, so Freud constructed the structural hypothesis (Freud 1923). Various psychic systems, within themselves, had both primitive and structured elements. There was little delineation between one system and another; Freud traced a hierarchal continuum, in which the ego had both unconscious and conscious elements, operating with both primary and secondary process. The unconscious part of the ego, inasmuch as the ego is also organized, cannot tolerate contradiction, in contrast to the system unconscious, which can. The id (Freud's new term for the system unconscious) is simply a reservoir.* When the ego dips into it, some of the requirements of logical operations, such as the resolution of contradictions, are introduced. One system gradually blends into another. Freud stressed that the unconscious is subordinated to the pleasure principle. He also described this principle some years earlier, comparing it with the reality principle (Freud 1911). Briefly, a psyche that operates according to the pleasure principle strives for immediate gratification, ignoring the demands and inhibitory elements of reality. According to Freud, the unconscious replaces external reality with psychic reality. (I am struck by the way Freud phrased this, because psychoanalytic treatment could be described in a similar fashion.)

The unconscious does not make itself known directly. Freud used dreams, neuroses, and regressed states to explore this area of the mind. He was always impressed by the fact that unconscious mental processes

---

*In his writings, Freud repeatedly referred to the ego as being the reservoir of libido, but in "The Ego and the Id" (Freud 1923), he made the id the reservoir. In later papers he again assigned this function to the ego. This is thoroughly discussed in Appendix B (pp. 63–66) of "The Ego and the Id."

continually press for discharge. As the controversial psychoeconomic hypothesis emphasizes, discharges of unconscious energy also occur in the soma. These are often visceral discharges, which are experienced as affects. In order to effect a discharge that results in motility and action, higher systems have to become involved.

Unlike the unconscious, the preconscious inhibits discharge. Whatever displacements occur in this area are slight. The unconscious and preconscious handle psychic energy differently. Breuer postulated a bound tonic energy and an unbound, mobile, easily displaceable energy striving for discharge, the former characteristic of the preconscious and the latter typical of the unconscious (Breuer and Freud 1895). Consider these two types of energy as being similar to potential and kinetic energy. Although this is not an absolutely accurate analogy, it emphasizes that one type of energy is freely mobile and can jump from one idea to another, from one system to another. The other type of energy is tonically bound to an ideational representation. It cannot be used freely to cathect remote or unrelated elements. For example, as you the reader are sitting here looking at this book, your energy is tonically bound to it. You are not thinking in terms of sexual orgies, orgasmic releases, or if you are, you are not going to get very far with it. Your cathexis is tied to Freud, and the energy level here is balanced, in no way turbulent or threatening to get out of control. These energies are not qualitatively different—they are different energy states.

The preconscious orders its elements in a time sequence. These elements, unlike those of the unconscious, influence each other. They are subject to the restraints of reality testing and the reality principle. Here Freud made an important point that is seldom referred to. He frequently wrote about a censor (the later superego) between the preconscious and the unconscious. Now he postulated the existence of a censor between the preconscious and consciousness. Apparently this second censor is not as strict as the first one, but it is still selective as to what it chooses to permit into consciousness. It may seem superfluous and conceptually inconsistent to bring in a second censor, but, Freud was emphasizing some general structural principles, and in effect postulated multiple censors. As the psyche develops from a relatively amorphous state to a more structured, discrete entity, primary process becomes secondary process, unbound energy becomes bound, discharge involves smaller quantities of displaceable energy; in other words, the psyche achieves restraint and selectivity as the reality principle dominates. Higher structures control lower structures. Inasmuch as they may delay and integrate the demands of primitive impulses as they strive for discharge, the higher levels of the psyche censor the lower ones. Thus, from this viewpoint, the concept of multiple censors makes sense.

Communication between the Two Systems

The unconscious can not be considered a finished product or entity, is not at rest, and is not just a repository for repressed impulses from the preconscious. It can cooperate with the preconscious and be influenced by it. Freud asserted that the unconscious is alive and capable of development. He was apparently saying that structuralization can take place within the system unconscious. (Perhaps he meant a *limited* amount of structuralization can occur, because if it progresses beyond a certain point it would enter the realm of the preconscious.)

The theoretical implications are obvious. The important questions from the clinical viewpoint are: How do elements belonging to the primitive unconscious, in which there are no word cathexes, emerge in an analytic relationship (or any relationship) if they antedate the formation of concepts and words? How can these be experienced and communicated? If the patient's material is vague and disconnected, it could belong to preverbal stages characteristic of the unconscious, but if it is well structured, then it is likely to belong to a later developmental stage that contains more of the preconscious and can operate in terms of verbal concepts.

At what point does the system unconscious begin to blend with the system preconscious? Where does id become ego? How may dreams provide some insight about the blending of the unconscious and the preconscious? Is poorly structured dream material more likely to contain preverbal elements? Inasmuch as dreams are predominantly visual, a modality that has been considered to be a more primitive mode of perception than the auditory, they may be considered to have predominantly unconscious elements. It is difficult, of course, to be certain as to whether the visual modality is more primitive than the auditory. However, it is possible that the structure of the dream may not be parallel with the level of organization of the latent or manifest dream material. It could be very primitive and perhaps preverbal. Dream organization could be the outcome of reporting it, a subsequent phenomenon not related directly to the dream content. Possibly, this applies to every dream. If a needle could be inserted into the visual area of the cortex when someone dreams and then could be hooked into a television screen, it is hard to say what we would see. In this fanciful experiment, I am assuming that our needle would be capable of reproducing how the patient perceives without adding any organization of its own. Perhaps, there would be nothing to see, just fluctuating electrical currents on which images are superimposed on awakening.

There is no clear-cut point at which unconscious becomes preconscious. Unconscious elements gain accretions as they push forward and reach conscious levels. For example, a patient I saw some years ago relived fundamental terror and helplessness during a session, feelings she had never been able to communicate or express. She had begun to feel restless, and started thrashing around on the couch. To her surprise, she had an orgasm, during which she felt both erotic waves and terror. She then connected the experience to the previous material, which pointed to a state of fundamental helplessness. The orgasm was a breaking-through of an early ego state of helpless vulnerability.

Freud warned not to expect smooth separations between the unconscious and the preconscious. He seemed dissatisfied with the vagueness of his concepts. Freud's dilemma was illustrated by his contradictory discussion of unconscious fantasies. He stated that these are highly organized psychic constructions, free of contradiction, that have all the characteristics of the system conscious. On the other hand, they are unconscious and incapable of becoming conscious. If the unconscious is defined by its primary process orientation, then this formulation is inconsistent. Freud's struggle to construct a consistent conceptual system is also reflected in his discussion of multiple censors, which has already been covered. In emphasizing a structural hierarchy, Freud was getting closer to the concept of the structural hypothesis (Freud 1923), which resolved some of the problems inherent in the topographical hypothesis.

Although Freud viewed the psychic apparatus as a totality he paid comparatively little attention to the higher systems. He may have written a paper on consciousness, but if so it has been lost. He was interested in consciousness in terms of its functions, one of which is attention. He made some remarks about attention here that are related to both consciousness and the preconscious. Freud mentioned attention several times, in his writings, but not often. I believe the last time was in 1925 in his paper on the mystic writing pad (Freud 1925). Freud viewed attention as being something like pseudopodias—memory traces that correspond to external experiences—from the preconscious that reach into consciousness. (Do not confuse this metaphor with his famous metaphor of an amoeba extending pseudopodia, which illustrates primary and secondary narcissism [Freud 1914].) Consciousness receives impressions, stimuli from the outside world. The pseudopodia come into contact with the external stimuli. As Freud put it, they meet halfway. When I enter a classroom and look at my students, I do not initially see them as strangers or think: Who are they? Where have I seen them before? I know immediately who they are, because my memory traces come forward and meet the stimuli.

This concept fits well with the model of the mystic writing pad. The memory trace is an indentation on the wax-like portion of the pad. There are two layers over this wax layer. The outer one is thin and protective. As the stylus presses on these layers, it makes an indentation on the waxed surface, which is perceived on the layer immediately next to it. This layer, when pulled away from the waxed surface, loses what has been traced on it, but the tracing remains on the waxed surface. In the same way, a memory trace is registered in the preconscious. The tracing of the stylus on the layer next to the waxed surface represents the conscious perception of the external stimulus. The analogy cannot be carried further, because to do so would require that on a future occasion the stylus would have to write on exactly the same spot where the indentation meets the next layer; it would have to trace the indentation.

These higher processes are not well suited for the study of the unconscious. On the whole, consciousness and the preconscious are essentially similar. The greatest differences are between the unconscious and the preconscious.

Returning to the topic of communication between various systems, Freud described that an unconscious derivative can bypass the first censor between the unconscious and the preconscious. It undergoes organization in the preconscious and receives further cathexis there. When the cathexis goes beyond a certain level, that is when the derivative becomes hypercathected, it moves toward consciousness. If the derivative is unacceptable for whatever reason, consciousness sets up a censor between itself and the preconscious, causing the derivative to be repressed. Psychoanalytic treatment supplies us with incontravertible evidence for the existence of this second censor. Freud referred to his early experiments on free association, which will be discussed again in Chapter 2, when we review the *Studies on Hysteria* (Breuer and Freud 1895). Here he reminded us that making something that was preconscious conscious is not a simple act of perception. When the patient is instructed to relax all conscious controls and not withhold anything that comes to mind, he still does. Once again the act of becoming conscious involves hypercathexis, but Freud did not distinguish between repression, an unconscious process, and suppression (deliberate withholding).

Psychic processes can be viewed as being initially formed in the unconscious. Some reach the highest conscious levels, while other impulses are held back in the unconscious. The unconscious is also affected by stimuli that emanate from the outer world. In the normal person all paths from the outer world are open to the unconscious, but in repression, the opposite is not true, the connections between the unconscious and external reality are blocked.

Freud made the interesting observation that some people can react to another person's unconscious bypassing consciousness. There is a direct connection between the two unconscious systems and even preconscious participation is excluded. Is not the paranoid patient especially sensitive in this fashion? Clinical experience seems to confirm this. It may be that the paranoid's vigilant attitude makes him particularly astute in sensing hostility, as he constantly seeks appropriate external objects for his projections.

The content of the preconscious and consciousness stems in part from the unconscious and its drives, and in part from external perceptions. It is unclear how much preconscious processes affect the unconscious, but Freud believed that an exaggerated independence of the preconscious and unconscious is characteristic of psychopathology.

Repressive forces are undone when unconscious strivings are similar to or compatible with dominant preconscious impulses. In these instances the unconscious elements are considered ego syntonic but nevertheless betray their origins by their intolerance of contradiction and their relentless striving for discharge; they behave similarly to compulsions.

At the end of this section, Freud demonstrated his Lamarckian orientation. He considered the primitive elements of the unconscious as stemming from a prehistoric past. These are inherited and are passed along from generation to generation, but gaining accretions throughout time. Although he did not refer to Jung, he seemed to have accepted Jung's concept of the collective unconscious, which postulates that conscious experiences are passed along to future generations as part of the unconscious. Freud postulated that a sharp division between the unconscious and preconscious does not occur until puberty.

The Assessment of the Unconscious

Freud equated the study of the narcissistic neuroses with the study of the unconscious. He believed that the more we learn about these neuroses, the closer we come to understanding the unconscious. This is interesting because what Freud had learned about the unconscious was the outcome of his work on dreams and his treatment of the transference neuroses, which he now contrasted with the narcissistic neuroses. His formulations about psychosexual development came mainly from the study of hysteria, a transference neurosis. In "On Narcissism: An Introduction" (1914), he viewed narcissistic neuroses as entities that would give us information about the ego, but stated that they teach us considerably about the unconscious. Freud also postulated that narcissistic neuroses illustrate dichotomies between the ego and the external world. This is really object-relations theory or what we might call ego psychology, but he did not pursue the topic further at this point. He was specifically referring to Bleuler's concept of schizophrenia. (Bleuler coined the term schizophrenia.)

Here, Freud assumes we know what the narcissistic neuroses are since he had mentioned them in previous writings.

What are the narcissistic neuroses? Freud included schizophrenic, psychotic, and borderline states in the category of narcissistic neuroses, although the last term was not coined until the 1950s by Knight (1953). Freud did not classify psychoses per se under the rubric of narcissistic neuroses. Earlier (1914), Freud used the word paraphrenia as a synonym for psychosis. He postulated that the narcissistic neuroses consisted of paraphrenia (or schizophrenia) and depression. By contrast, the transference neuroses consist of the obsessional neuroses and hysterias, which included the continuum of conversion hysteria and anxiety hysteria but not anxiety neuroses. In summary, there are three main categories—the transference neuroses (obsessional neurosis and hysteria), the narcissistic neuroses (schizophrenia and depression), and the actual neuroses (anxiety neurosis and neurasthenia).

In what ways are the narcissistic neuroses sufficiently unique as to merit a separate category? The primary factor, according to Freud, is that libido has become detached from the object. In the transference neuroses, it remains attached and, if the patient needs to withdraw, both libido and object are introjected. In the narcissistic neuroses, the libido lacks an object, and what Freud called the primitive objectless state of narcissism results. This is primary narcissism, because in secondary narcissism the libido is attached to the internalized object, an object that becomes part of the self. Freud understood, without actually using the term, that secondary narcissistic object relations consist of self-objects. Freud asserted that objectless narcissism makes the patient incapable of forming a transference. For transference to occur, libido must become attached to an external object. In the narcissistic neuroses, because of the adhesiveness of the libido and its withdrawn objectless state, this does not happen. Inasmuch as there is no transference, the patient can not be treated psychoanalytically.

These points are not accepted by the entire psychoanalytic community. That the narcissistic neuroses cannot be treated psychoanalytically is still asserted by some analysts. Transference, however, does occur in narcissistic patients. This is not debatable; it is an empirical fact. Freud himself treated a paranoid psychotic patient in 1894 (Freud 1894).

Some seminar participants had been taught that transference refers to that which is transferred across the repression barrier. The psychotic patient does not have a well-formed repression barrier, and supposedly does not present transference. Freud did *not* say transference was dependent upon the repression barrier, but that repressed infantile feelings and impulses are transferred onto the therapist. Nowhere did he assert that if they were not repressed this would not constitute transference. The essence of transference is viewing current object relationships in terms of the infantile past. Whether or not they are repressed is not the decisive issue. In the neuroses, primitive infantile feelings are usually repressed. Infantile feelings toward archaic objects of the past are projected onto the analyst. From this viewpoint, the psychotic transference would form more readily, because there is less repression and thus these feelings can be transferred more readily. They can be easily displaced, since they follow the rules of the primary process, and cathexis is freely mobile from one object to another. There are many clinical data to support this. In treatment, if a transference develops rapidly, the analyst should suspect a psychosis.

Freud recognized that the beginning phases of schizophrenia are characterized by speech peculiarities. For example, a schizophrenic patient expressed an abstract saying literally—often by a somatic symptom—The patient believed that her lover had deceived and betrayed her. In German, such a person is called *Augendreher* (eye twister). This patient had eye symptoms; she believed she had twisted eyes and saw the world through her lover's eyes. Freud distinguished this schizophrenic response from hysterical symptoms. A hysteric would not have spoken freely about twisted eyes and related them to her lover, would not have been able to explain the origin of her symptoms, would have no knowledge about lovers who betray. That would all be repressed. The hysteric would have eye spasms but would know nothing about their origin. She would look for, or cling to, an organic etiology.

It may seem that the psychotic would be easier to treat. At least, such a patient could view situations and somatic symptoms in terms of a relationship, even if there were distortions, while the hysteric could not. Indeed, some hysterics are very difficult to treat, and the differences between them and schizophrenia are becoming increasingly blurred.

Psychoanalytic treatment depends upon how the transference is handled. The fact that psychotics have transference is no longer argued. Still, can the therapist work with the psychotic transference? Is such transference amenable to reality corrections? Should transference distortions be corrected?

Perhaps the most important factor is how the analyst reacts to these distortions. Let us take the situation of a patient who begins with an ordinary enough transference, a transference that can, to a large measure, be worked with because the patient is capable of recognizing its infantile origins. Then the analyst unwittingly reacts directly to something the patient has done by disapproving of it, thereby ignoring the transference. The patient unconsciously reacts to this disapproval, usually with anger, but is not aware of the cause of the reaction. The anger appears irrational and infantile, but as transference, it cannot be corrected. Actually, it was provoked by the analyst's intrusive behavior, although neither the patient nor the analyst was aware of it. The analyst usually convinces himself that he is dealing with an intractable transference, perhaps a psychotic transference.

As an example, at a recent conference an analyst reported telling a patient that he was selfish. The patient was divorcing his wife. Initially, she had not wanted a divorce but he had. When she agreed, she wanted to disengage herself from her husband in order to form other object relationships. He continued to see her and have sexual intercourse with her; he monopolized her time. According to the therapist, he was selfish. The therapist called this "confrontation" and "facing the patient with reality" rather than interpretation. The patient agreed that he was being selfish and did, in fact, change his behavior. However, shortly after this interchange, the patient began talking about his mother who, he believed, was never really interested in him as a person. She was always involved with someone else, and whenever there was an altercation, she always took the other person's side. During treatment he felt isolated, depressed, bitter, and resentful, and he soon began directing these feelings toward the analyst. The patient criticized the analyst, who interpreted this material as an aspect of the maternal transference. Instead of the patient "correcting this reality distortion," the feelings persisted. Actually, the patient was reacting to the analyst in a "correct" fashion. The analyst had, indeed, intruded into the patient's life in favor of his wife and not in his best interest. Unfortunately, many similar situations have been evaluated as transference psychoses, making the patient responsible for being untreatable. In actuality, the analyst has transgressed the treatment situation and the patient is reacting by protesting such non-analytic behavior.

Freud continued to give examples of how schizophrenics react to words as if they were concrete objects. He stated that words are treated in the same way as latent dream thoughts. He discussed a patient who would squeeze pimples and emit fluid. Though Freud did not believe the squeezing of pimples, by itself, signified anything, the words to describe this activity were indeed significant. The squeezing led to an emission, and the word emission can be equated with masturbation.

Here, he modified his assumption that object cathexis is abandoned in schizophrenia. Object cathexis consists of two components, the thing-cathexis and the word-cathexis. The thing-cathexis is abandoned in schizophrenia. Freud developed his thesis by stating that the preconscious, not the unconscious, contains the word-cathexis. This makes sense, since the word, which is a concept of a concrete thing, requires some degree of organization to be formed. The unconscious contains the thing-cathexis. In schizophrenia, according to Freud, the word-cathexis is retained and the thing-cathexis is abandoned.

Ordinarily, we think of schizophrenia as the outcome of a regressed state. In the abandoning of the thing-cathexis, there is a progression from the unconscious to the preconscious rather than a regression in the opposite direction. Still, this does not represent a progression.

Freud postulated while studying the Schreber case (Freud 1911) that schizophrenic phenomena were the result of an attempt at restitution, an attempt to recathect the external world from which libido had been withdrawn. This is not a progression, because the passage from one system to another carries defective libido—defective because it has abandoned the thing-cathexis as it proceeds to the word. This process is parallel to Freud's (1911a) formulation of first libido being withdrawn from external objects, which is followed by trying to fill the void that has been created in the external world with objectless libido.

Freud ended this article by discussing thought processes. Thoughts are remote from the perceptual residues from which they are derived. Consequently, they no longer contain the qualities that are required for becoming conscious. He conceptualizes thoughts as being without word and thing representations, as if they were free-floating energy. They can become conscious only by being re-linked with words, and this gives them a quality that is capable of becoming conscious. These now-conscious thoughts represent relationships between presentations of objects. Freud is careful to emphasize that this word cathexis only leads to the *capacity* for reaching consciousness, not to the acquisition of consciousness. The word-cathexis achieves preconscious—not conscious—status. It follows that the act of becoming conscious involves a hypercathexis. This means that we have to have both a word and a thing cathexis. The word cathexis is especially important because it leads to the organization required for perception.

Finally, Freud once again postulated a pathway from the unconscious to the preconscious to consciousness, which is punctuated with censors and repressive barriers, whereas the reverse path remains open. If one stops to think about this reverse direction from the consciousness to preconscious to unconscious, it becomes obvious that it is impossible. Perception does not directly enter consciousness, but proceeds from the retina to the optic nerves, then to the optic radiation, occipital cortex (via many intermediate pathways) until it finally reaches consciousness.

2

Studies on Hysteria

SYNOPSIS
This chapter will concentrate upon what I consider to be the essence of the *Studies on Hysteria*. The following are discussed in this chapter: "On the Psychical Mechanisms of Hysterical Phenomena," by Breuer and Freud; "Anna O.," by Breuer; "Hypnoid States," also by Breuer; and "The Psychotherapy of Hysteria" by Freud.

ON THE PSYCHICAL MECHANISMS OF
HYSTERICAL PHENOMENA

Although "On the Psychical Mechanisms of Hysterical Phenomena" was a joint venture of Breuer and Freud, Freud appears to have been the work's dominant creative force. It is amazing how many ideas that are today taken for granted are found in this section, which was the first psychoanalytic treatise. Both authors seemed to be exerting considerable effort to remain in a psychological frame of reference. They began by emphasizing that hysteria is not a degenerative disease and the outcome of constitutional weakness, as the French (Charcot and Janet) had postulated. Breuer and Freud preferred explanations that stressed environmental vicissitudes, and they postulated the etiological significance of psychic trauma. However, Breuer viewed the effects of trauma in a fashion that did not necessarily exclude organic factors. Breuer believed that a traumatic event caused the formation of a

29

hypnoid state; that is, the trauma becomes encapsulated in a part of the ego (the hypnoid state) that then becomes dissociated from the main psychic stream. This is strikingly familiar to the splitting mechanisms we frequently employ in our current clinical formulations.

Freud gradually abandoned Breuer's hypothesis because it was static and nondynamic and in some respects not that far removed from the ideas about constitutional degeneracy expounded by the French. It was implied that a weak ego eventually succumbs to dissociative forces and that a hypnoid state develops to contain the traumatic experience. Freud preferred to think of hysteria in relation to repression, a term which he first employed in this section of *Studies on Hysteria*, in two senses: first, as we do today, as an exclusion of unacceptable impulses and thoughts from consciousness into the unconscious—they cannot be recalled just by conscious volition; and secondly, as synonymous with suppression. In any case he was trying to establish a psychodynamic approach.

Freud for the first time described the interplay between nature and nurture as variables in the production of emotional illness. A decade later, in the "Three Essays on The Theory of Sexuality" (Freud 1905), he formalized this hypothesis by naming it *complemental series*. Freud always believed that there are constitutional predispositions; in fact, psychoanalysis has been attacked as being too biologically oriented.

The concepts of abreaction and catharsis appear for the first time in this essay. These concepts represented a departure from Charcot's hypnotic approach, which, in essence, consisted of suggesting symptoms away. Breuer was attempting to deal with etiological factors rather than just surface manifestations. Freud extended the hypnotic approach to evolve our present technical psychoanalytic procedure.

THE CASE OF ANNA O.

Freud was extremely impressed with Breuer's treatment of Anna O., especially since he had recently watched both Charcot and Bernheim use hypnosis with hysterical patients. Breuer's approach consisted of having his patient recover traumatic memories during a hypnotic trance and then relive the threatening experience while experiencing its proper affect. The treatment painstakingly pursued each symptom as it was attached to a traumatic experience. This is the essence of the theory of abreaction and catharsis.

Anna O. had some interesting and bizarre symptoms. Similar to patients with conversion symptoms (apparently common at that time), Anna O. had various somatic symptoms, a particularly prominent one being a cough, *tussis nervosa*, which Breuer interpreted as a punishment for her unconscious wish to abandon her sick father. She also had amnesia, fugue states, hallucinations, and on occasion destructive acting-out. Breuer related all these phenomena to memories of past and current traumas. He abruptly ended Anna O.'s treatment when she had a relapse and fantasized that he had made her pregnant. Apparently, he had been frightened and never again pursued psychoanalytic explorations, although Freud encouraged him to do so and tried to reassure him by explaining transference, which he had recently discovered.

Hypnoid States

This chapter contains Breuer's original formulations about hypnoid states which in some ways are conceptually similar to dissociative phenomena or splitting mechanisms. He postulated that hysteria occurs when a trauma cannot be disposed of as soon as it occurs. He meant that because of inhibiting and prohibiting circumstances, the psyche was unable to make the proper appropriate affective response to the trauma. Rather, the ego splits off a part of itself, what Breuer called a hypnoid state—to encapsulate the trauma. Presumably the affect, which should have been discharged, instead becomes strangulated in this dissociated hypnoid state. The aim of treatment is to release this affect, thereby bringing the memory and experience of the traumatic event into consciousness, where it can be subjected to reality testing. Once brought to the light of day, the experience becomes something from the past; similar dangers have already been mastered and the experience is no longer threatening enough to cause feelings of vulnerability and helplessness. Breuer had stumbled upon the value of making the unconscious conscious, a technical maneuver around which Freud constructed the psychoanalytic treatment procedure.

The Psychotherapy of Hysteria

In the final section of *Studies on Hysteria*, Freud developed an amazing number of ideas that have become important cornerstones for the development of psychoanalysis as a treatment method. He almost openly disavowed the concept of hypnoid states, stating that he personally had never seen a case of hypnoid hysteria. Freud had by now separated the actual neuroses, neurasthenia and the anxiety neurosis, from the obsessional neurosis and hysteria. Earlier he had separated retention hysteria from dispositional and acquired hysteria. Retention hysteria corresponded to Breuer's hypnoid state, dispositional hysteria was the result of constitutional weakness, and acquired hysteria was explained by intrapsychic factors. He wanted to understand neuroses as more than just phenomenological clusters. He explored neuroses in terms of basic causes, and once again emphasized multiple factors. Nevertheless, he stressed that whatever other factors are involved, a sexual component must always be in the forefront. This hypothesis eventually caused Breuer to break with Freud and to leave psychoanalysis altogether.

Freud had always been dissatisfied with hypnosis. He had encountered some patients who could not be hypnotized and thus he questioned the therapeutic efficacy of hypnosis. Perhaps in deference to Breuer, Freud conceded that is was sometimes useful, but pursued his explorations of other techniques.

Freud described in this section his discovery of free association. He had visited his patient, Emmy von N. while she was being massaged, and was astonished to find that, just listening to her, he learned as much about her as he might have if she had been in a hypnotic trance. This was the beginning of free association.

Freud then described the pressure technique, which consisted of having the patient lie down, touching his head, and asking him to say what came to mind regarding the onset of his symptoms. From these experiences Freud learned about resistance, which is a dominant theme in all of his writings about techniques. He also developed his ideas about transference in the context of resistance.

Although *Studies on Hysteria* is only a beginning, it is a phenomenal beginning.

On the Psychical Mechanisms of Hysterical Phenomena

In this first chapter of *Studies on Hysteria* (Breuer and Freud 1895), originally written in 1893, Freud was just beginning to formulate psychological explanations, but his approach was not particularly psychodynamic, in that he did not yet have an instinct theory. The medical community must have been shocked when Freud reported his ideas, since hysteria was considered to be a degenerative disease. Freud was very disappointed by the way the medical community responded; he never attended another meeting of the Vienna Medical Society after presenting an account of his experiences in Paris with Charcot and his psychological theories of hysteria. His narcissism had been wounded. Ellenberger (1970), however, stated that Freud's medical colleagues, although somewhat critical, were not hostile, and excerpts from some of the discussions seem to confirm this.

Freud did not present this chapter to the society, just some of the ideas contained in it. He asserted that hysteria was not confined to women. This was hard for the medical community to accept, after all, "hysteria" means wandering uterus, and men do not have uteruses. Freud also tried to explain hysteria as artificial hypnosis. However, he did not deny the place of organic factors, especially syphilis, in hysteria. He also believed in an hereditary predisposition to hysteria.

Breuer and Freud concentrated on the precipitating causes of hysterical symptoms. They discovered that events of many years before are often instrumental in the production of the illness. For the most part patients are unable to recollect these events or are unable to make a connection between the events and the symptoms of the illness. Hypnotizing the patient, however, can sometimes establish these connections. There are many different types of hysterical symptoms. Among those that can be considered neurological are neuralgias, anesthesias, contractures, tics, paralyses, and various forms of epilepsy, as well as vomiting, anorexia, visual disturbances, and hallucinations. The severity of the symptoms may not correspond to the severity of the single precipitating event. Sometimes the precipatory event is traumatic, yet the deleterious effects of the trauma are the result of psychic rather than physical injury.

Breuer and Freud here formulated the existence of the hypnoid state—a part of the psyche that incorporates the trauma and becomes split from the rest of the mind. The cause may not be a single large trauma but rather a series of slight traumas working under the principle of summation. Sometimes the trauma seems trivial. Such a patient may have been particularly susceptible to that trauma at the time it occurred, or the trivial trauma may be covering up another, more significant, trauma.

Freud introduced a very important concept here, which he explicitly formulated in 1905—the concept of *complemental series*. This is another way of stating the nature–nurture synergy that the greater the trauma, the less the predisposition, and vice versa.

Breuer and Freud concluded this theoretical section with the intriguing comment that psychic trauma does not simply lead to a symptom that discharges it. Instead, the memory of the trauma acts like a foreign body, unintegrated within the ego, and persists as an active agent. Freud went along with Breuer in postulating that the trauma is isolated from the rest of the psyche by being split off in a hypnoidal state. Soon, however, he began to evidence dissatisfaction with this concept. Integration and assimilation fit better with his viewpoint.

Clinically, it is interesting that making the memory of the traumatic experience conscious by putting the affect into words causes the symptoms to disappear. This is conceptualized as a discharge which the authors called *abreaction*.

Breuer and Freud's success with their patients may have been due to suggestion rather than abreaction. Freud was often quite authoritative, even omnipotent. He actually ordered his patient Emmy von N. not to have symptoms, but this probably occurred in a benevolent atmosphere. Many of these patients had what might be called affective explosions, which led to amelioration of symptoms. The expression of feelings is important for any treatment. The term "blowing off steam" was part of our language long before Freud. There is something physiologically relieving about it, and it should be therapeutically effective. Perhaps there is something inherent in the organism that lends itself to this discharge hypothesis. One gets relief from abreaction, from catharsis, from raging oneself out.

Freud, in a sense, demanded that his patients express their thoughts and feelings. He later formulated the fundamental rule as the modus operandi of psychoanalytic treatment. He instructed his patients to tell him everything that came to mind without selecting or suppressing thoughts or feelings, as otherwise they would be resisting, and resistance has to be overcome. Sometimes treatment was actually terminated because the patient would not talk. One of the seminar participants was seeing a patient who did not want to talk but who had a conflict about remaining silent because she believed that she could say something useful. Perhaps, it is important that she may have some feelings about saying useful things. The therapist, following the fundamental rule, expected the patient to talk. However, I believe it is the patient's choice as to whether he free associates or remains silent. Silence can be adaptive, and it may be necessary to experience it in analysis. Indeed, a patient of mine, a professional man raised in the standard tradition of the fundamental rule, said that I did not know how wonderful it was to lie down and say nothing and not be expected to say anything. What a marvelous feeling it was not to be intruded upon.

Breuer and Freud questioned the relationship between traumatic neurosis and traumatic hysteria. In the traumatic neurosis, the trauma, usually an injury or accident, is obvious, whereas in traumatic hysteria, it is subtle and often can only be revealed through hypnosis. This distinction is not precise, as even patients with traumatic neuroses do not necessarily have the affect generated during the experience at their conscious disposal. According to Breuer and Freud, if both the event and the affect are made conscious, the symptoms will disappear. The converse of this proposition is also essentially true: if a patient recollects a phenomenon without the accompanying affect, then there is no curative effect. Breuer and Freud emphasized that the original events must be vividly experienced and verbalized and that the symptoms may intensify momentarily but then disappear.

The terms *catharsis* and *abreaction* appeared for the first time in this chapter. A completely cathartic effect is possible only if the affect is experienced, i.e., verbalized, and discharged. If there is no reaction to the trauma, the affect and the event remain pent up and continue causing symptoms. As the authors stated, "Hysterics suffer mainly from reminiscences."

A normal person brings the memory of the trauma in conjunction with "the great complex of associations." These other experiences may contradict the traumatic memory in the sense that they set things straight again. For example, after an accident, the danger is remembered along with what happened afterward, such as being safe or being rescued. In this way, the trauma is worked out. We might say it has been subjected to reality testing, and this does not involve abreaction. Other, minimally traumatic memories may simply fade away and be forgotten.

As psychic elements approach consciousness, they are subjected to logical operations and, in a sense, are corrected; if they remain unconscious, they cannot be corrected. The distortions give in to reality testing when they are made conscious. In essence, this is the process of working-through, a process that modifies the structure of the original memory.

To repeat, *The only adequate reaction to a trauma is an action that causes complete catharsis, as there is no pent up tension remaining which will lead to symptoms.* Think about the appeal of revenge as a reaction to the trauma of being exploited and unjustly treated. At one time, *The Count of Monte Cristo* was considered one of the ten best novels of the world for just this reason, in spite of its questionable literary merit.

Patients traumatized by their parents may have vengeful fantasies; they may want retribution and even have death wishes. Acting out these fantasies would be of no benefit; as they would be conflicted by other feelings such as dependence on and affection for the parents. According to Breuer and Freud, the patient cannot discharge anger, that is the desire for revenge. It remains pent up and leads to symptoms. This vengeful attitude toward parents is not the same as the traumatic incidents described here. The child's reaction to parents is based upon a relationship rather than an incident, whereas Breuer and Freud were describing a single etiology theory. They also placed the trauma later in life rather than in infancy. Freud soon thereafter postulated that the etiology of hysteria is early infantile trauma (Freud 1896). He does not, as yet, connect these later incidents with similar ones which may have occurred in childhood.

Memories that can lead to hysterical symptoms are not accessible to consciousness. Memory is dissociated from the rest of the psyche and can emerge only under hypnosis. Since memories are not available to the higher levels of the personality, they cannot be abreacted. There are two sets of conditions responsible for insufficient abreaction. First, the patient does not react to a traumatic event because the trauma (such as the death of a loved one) may be so severe that the behavior or feelings that would dispose of the trauma are not permitted.

This article contains the word "repression" for the first time in the psychoanalytic literature. Repression is the outcome of the wish to forget. Freud also referred to an "intentional" repression. By this he did not mean that repression is consciously willed, as in the case of suppression. He wished to suggest that the patient represses with motivation, that there is a reason for the repression. Here, the authors use the concept of repression correctly. Later in *Studies on Hysteria*, Freud equated suppression and repression, and used the terms interchangeably until he specifically defined repression in 1915. He also used the word ego loosely until 1923, when he formulated the structural hypothesis (Freud 1923). In 1894 and 1896 Freud formulated the concept of defense. He was able to view psychopathology in terms of a conflict between conscious and unconscious parts of the personality.

The second set of conditions causing insufficient abreaction is related to the psychic state of the patient at the time of the trauma rather than to the trauma itself. The trauma may be indifferent, but inasmuch as it occurred during an abnormal psychic state, its effects can be paralyzing. As long as the patient suffers from an abnormal psychic state which is characterized by a looseness of organization or, as Breuer and Freud called it, a dissociated state, the patient is susceptible to trauma. How did he arrive at such a state? The implication is that the trauma had nothing to do with the patient's lowered threshold of susceptibility, but was responsible for the patient's subsequent weakened psychic state, as would be true in acquired hysteria.

Breuer and Freud again emphasized that the trauma occurred while the ego was in a state of dissociation, a hypnoid state. They agreed with Janet and Charcot, although Freud was already beginning to doubt that the splitting of consciousness leads to the formation of a second consciousness, the *double conscience*, as named by the French school. Breuer and Freud replaced Charcot's aphorism "Hypnosis is artificial hysteria" with the hypothesis that the conditions and causes of hysteria are the outcome of hypnoid states. The elements that are contained within the hypnoid state may achieve a high degree of organization and be well integrated with each other. Their degree of isolation from the main conscious stream varies, as does the depth of hypnosis which ranges from very light trances to deep somnambulism. Regardless of the degree of dissociation, in hypnosis the dissociated material can emerge in a highly explosive fashion. Breuer and Freud stated that once the dissociated material becomes associated again with the mainstream of the psyche, a higher degree of organization is achieved.

Breuer and Freud then distinguished between dispositional and acquired hysteria. Dispositional hysterics have personalities with an innate weakness, which makes them more susceptible to splitting, regressing, and dissociative states. Breuer and Freud did not question that this innate weakness might have a history in itself, but saw the weakness as a constitutional instability similar to Janet's view of hysteria as a structural inferiority; however, their view did not necessarily involve moral judgments. By contrast, the concept of acquired hysteria does not assume any innate defects or looseness of associations. Patients suffering from acquired hysteria have experienced a significant trauma which has been repressed, that is, defended against. This theory constituted the beginning of a dynamic approach rather than the static formulation of hypnoid states. (I conjecture that Freud slipped this in this very early paper, perhaps surreptitiously.) Dispositional and acquired hysteria bring to mind the concept of complemental series I discussed earlier, dispositional hysteria emphasizing constitutional factors and acquired hysteria environmental ones.

In the final section, Breuer and Freud highlighted some paradoxes. In hysterical patients, there are islands of extreme psychopathology and rational states of normalcy. They compared this discrepancy with dreams of normal people, the dream being similar to an isolated psychosis; normal people are, in a way insane when they dream. It is interesting that the authors emphasized that hysterics are not psychotic, although this is not always accepted today, and the case of Anna O. casts doubt on Freud's reasoning. The equation of the hypnoidal state with the dream is also quite interesting. In hysteria, the hypnoidal state breaks into the waking state and is characteristic of hysteria. The dream, on the other hand, occurs during the sleeping state. In 1906, Jung said that a schizophrenic is a person who is awake and dreaming. These two statements— Freud's that the hypnoidal state breaking into the waking state is characteristic of hysteria, and Jung's that the dream breaking into the waking state is characteristic of schizophrenia—could be interpreted to mean that schizophrenia equals hysteria. This may sound fanciful, but it is true that many patients initially diagnosed as hysterics turned out to be florid schizophrenics.

In the next section Breuer and Freud referred to Charcot's four phases of the hysterical attack: (1) the epileptoid phase, (2) the phase of gross movements, (3) the hallucinatory phase (attitudes passionelles) and (4) the final delirium phase. The hallucinatory phase is a reproduction of a traumatic situation or a series of partial traumas during which the patient experienced very strong feelings responsible for the formation of the hypnoidal state. Breuer and Freud explained motor attacks without hallucinations in a similar fashion, as symbolic of the traumatic constellation. However, they thought of motor attacks as also having universal significance. They referred to tantrums, for example, as being manifestations of an undifferentiated, motoric outburst and gave clinical examples, such as a little girl who had convulsions that were reactions to an attack by a dog. In this connection they tried to establish some general principles as well as discussing specific elements of traumatic reactions. At the beginning of psychic life, affective states are experienced globally. Each affect has some motoric element, inasmuch as it is expressed as well as felt. In regressed states it is this motor element that is reproduced. If justifiable anger occurs in a well-coordinated, mature ego state and then undergoes regression to a more infantile state, it will be converted to purposeless screaming and kicking, perhaps even incontinence. What might have been rational, intellectual argument and discourse is now expressed in a somatic and visceral fashion. The hysteric patient reproduces the more archaic, the more primary process aspects of that affective state. Ordinarily, the ego has control over somatic expression, but in the hysterical attack, this is no longer the case.

The memories of traumatic experiences that lead to hysterical attacks can also be responsible for chronic symptoms. As long as such memories are excluded from the mainstream of consciousness they cannot be worked through either by the integrative elements of thought processes or through abreaction. The motoric phenomena accompanying hysterical attacks are, in part, reaction formations (overcompensations) of the memories accompanying affective states and represent the modes of expression of these memories. Inasmuch as traumatic elements remain in the hypnoid state and achieve a high degree of organization and integration with each other, Breuer and Freud once again referred to Charcot's concept of *condition seconde*—second consciousness.

An hysterical and a normal process can coexist without influencing each other. In this situation, an hysterical attack can be provoked by a new experience similar to the pathogenic one. Breuer and Freud then mentioned the stimulation of hysterogenic zones but did not elaborate.

Charcot discovered certain spots on the bodies of his hypnotic subjects which, if touched, stroked or pressed, could cause a hysterical attack, primarily manifested by such phenomena as convulsions or opisthotonus, although it might take many forms. The phenomenon of hysterogenic zones is linked to that of hysterical stigmata. The latter are signs and symptoms that might be considered pathognomonic of hysteria, and that could not occur in any organic disorder, such as hemianesthesias that end at the hairline, or stocking-and-glove anesthesias. Hysterical stigmata include tunnel vision, peculiar contractions of the peripheral visual field, and Janet's sign. The last involves telling the patient to say "yes" whenever he feels a pin prick and "no" when he does not. I treated a young lady who had a rectangular area of anaesthesia on the thigh, which I was able to outline using this method. She was not aware of the contradiction of saying "no" when she did not feel anything. In such cases unconscious forces drive the patient to this type of response, although some element of conscious design or secondary process may be at work.

Breuer and Freud explained that the psychic equilibrium of the hysteric is very unstable and attacks occur when the normal personality is exhausted or debilitated. They raised the possibility that a meaningless attack—a simple motor response—may also occur, indicating a susceptibility to a general weakening of the psychic organization.

Breuer and Freud emphasized that there may be symptoms that are no longer needed. This is similar to Hartmann's concept of secondary autonomy. A symptom, such as compulsive hand-washing, may symbolically resolve certain internal conflicts. It is possible that after the resolution of the underlying conflict, as might occur in analytic treatment, the patient may still wash his hands frequently. This habit may not possess the driving character of a compulsion, and may even be useful if for example, the patient is a dentist. One might say that a symptom that had previously been a defensive manifestation of intrapsychic conflict has become an adaptation in tune with reality.

While a resident, I was taught that the aim of supportive psychotherapy is to achieve secondary autonomy. Although not stated in exactly that fashion, this seems to have been Breuer and Freud's point. One of my teachers believed that many patients have resolved intrapsychic conflicts, either spontaneously or because of changed favorable life circumstances. Once resolved, the symptom is not too difficult to deal with; freed from its compulsive urgency, it is not clung to as tenaciously and is easily modified. On the other hand, if the symptom is painful, it is the therapist's task to get rid of it, which is again not difficult because the symptom is not needed in any fundamental sense. The therapist can use such maneuvers as persuasion, suggestion, and even hypnosis to make the symptom disappear. It will not recur or be substituted for by another symptom, because the personality has already achieved equilibrium. This formulation sounds very good but very seldom, if ever, works out this neatly.

Breuer and Freud believed that further research was required to determine the factors that lead to hysterical attacks and those that cause chronic symptoms. This was the beginning of a question that is still of great concern—the question of choice of neurosis.

In the last section of this paper Breuer and Freud described therapeutic procedures and their rationale. Basically, the strangulated affect is discharged through abreaction, which occurs during hypnosis as the patient relives the traumatic events of the past. Once the affect has been abreacted, it can then connect with the general associative stream. That is, from our viewpoint, primary process has converted to secondary process by subjecting primary process elements to the rules of consciousness. When primary process products are consciously experienced, they gain considerable organization consonant with external reality and become integrated into the psyche. This is what Freud meant when he stated that they join the associational stream.

Breuer and Freud were somewhat pessimistic regarding the prognosis of dispositional hysteria. They felt that although a particular symptom complex can be cured through abreaction and suggestion, another hypnoidal state or hysterical symptom will inevitably develop with future traumas because the psyche is constitutionally weak and susceptible.

Perhaps neither Charcot nor Freud recognized that the therapist's intense interest may keep the pathological process, or at least the expression of symptoms, alive. The patient may create new symptoms in order to maintain the therapist's interest; the patient feels he has to be picturesque, unique, and maybe even amusing. There is, for example, a very interesting picture of Charcot hypnotizing a woman during one of his Tuesday lectures. He apparently had her in a trance, manifested by her extreme opisthotonus. At the back of the room is a picture hanging on the wall of a woman in a similar position, a picture that the subject could not have failed to see from the stage. It is almost a dead giveaway. She knew what interested these people and she was there to please, to put on a good show. Still, these phenomena are not necessarily just malingering or simulation. Certainly there is always an element of this in hysteria, but we also know that there are many other, more serious, internal factors operating simultaneously. What is going on in patients is still dictated by the unconscious and, to a large measure, is outside of their control. As Freud stated later in this book, it is almost as if the symptoms joined in the conversation. The illness and the patient's relationship with the analyst have a certain style.

Case Histories: Anna O.

Freud spoke extensively about Anna O. in the first of his Clark lectures (Freud 1909a). At that time he gave Breuer credit for being the discoverer of psychoanalysis, although later, in his autobiographical paper, he corrected himself (Freud 1915a). In his first Clark lecture, Freud outlined the clinical course and history of Anna O. and then gave Breuer enormous credit for having persisted with her treatment. In 1880, and even in 1910, the diagnosis of hysteria had a perjorative connotation, and respectable physicians did not work with such patients. Breuer had allowed himself to become deeply involved in this case.

Anna O. remembered very little about her treatment with Breuer. This phenomenon is particularly striking. I recall a six-year-old boy whom I treated for two years. At the end of that time, I told his mother that even though he had made considerable symptomatic improvement, it would be judicious to reassess the situation when he entered adolescence. I believed that the stress of adolescence might upset his equilibrium and perhaps further therapy might be indicated at that time. The mother, being a conscientious social worker, suggested to her son when he reached adolescence that he might like to see a psychiatrist. She reminded him that he had had a period of treatment when he was a child, but the patient had absolutely no recall of it. She handed him a list of names, my name being somewhere in the middle of the list. The young man selected my name and came to see me. He did not recognize me and did not remember our previous therapy. Still, we both felt very comfortable with each other and we worked together for about a year. He never recalled our previous relationship. Still, his feelings toward me seemed old and familiar. As I look back upon it, I feel this amnesia was a good sign. I concluded that he was so well able to integrate his previous therapeutic experience into ego-adaptive systems that it lost the concrete and discrete qualities of a memory. Our experience had been, in my mind, more thoroughly assimilated.

It is hard to say how Anna O. would have reacted if her amnesia had been directly confronted. She was a very rigid, controlling woman who kept her attention focused upon what she wanted it to be focused upon and did not allow herself to be distracted.

Anna O. is now known to be Bertha Pappenheim, the founder of the social work movement. There has been some recent controversy as to the identity of Anna O., although evidence supporting conflicting theories is not very convincing. (It is interesting to note that the initials A. and O. are each one letter ahead of B. and P. in the alphabet.) Bertha Pappenheim disappeared for six years shortly after her treatment. Jones (1955) asserted that she was in an institution and was rather troublesome in that she formed an intense erotic transference toward the director of that institution, which eventually made it impossible for her to continue there. It is not certain where she went afterward, but she reappeared in Frankfort in 1888. She began doing social work and eventually took over the directorship of an orphanage.

Shortly before her intended interrogation by the gestapo, Bertha Pappenheim died of an illness associated with old age, perhaps respiratory failure. Shortly after her death it was rumored that the Nazis were going to take over her orphanage and turn it into a brothel. The ninety-three residents, having heard the rumor, dressed in their finest clothes and committed suicide by taking poison.

Breuer describes the young Anna O. as willful and obstinate; her obstinacy gave way only to her willingness to help other people. This description seems to fit the Bertha Pappenheim of later years. Anna O. may have suffered from a paranoid psychosis during those years. There is no absolute proof, but the possibility is consistent with her later personality—angry, rigid, opinionated, and suspicious. Was Bertha Pappenheim ever hospitalized for mental ilness? It is rumored that she had been institutionalized for paranoid schizophrenia. There are six years of her life that have never been explained.

What happened immediately after her treatment with Breuer, however, was revealed by Freud in his autobiography (Freud, 1915a). Freud alluded to the fact that something personal had gone on between Breuer and Anna O. Jones (1955) wrote about what he calls Breuer's countertransference—the story of Breuer's treatment of Anna O.—having been told to him by Freud. Apparently Breuer was becoming so engrossed with Anna O. that his wife became bored listening to him talk about his interesting patient and grew to feel jealous, unhappy, and morose. When Breuer realized what was happening, he decided to bring the treatment to an end. However, Anna O. herself set the date for the termination of her treatment—June 7, 1882, the anniversary of the date she was sent to the country because of suicidal preoccupation. This ironic choice must have represented a low point in the treatment relationship, and therefore an unlikely termination date, according to Jones. Jones emphasized that Breuer set another termination date later that summer and told his patient about it during one of his morning visits. When he returned to see her that evening, much to his shock, Anna O. seemed to be going through the pains of childbirth. This young lady, who had never discussed sex throughout the entire course of her treatment, seemed to have been harboring an invisible pregnancy, which was now expressing itself in pseudocyesis (phantom birth). Breuer quickly hypnotized her, calmed her down, probably suggested the pregnancy away, and the next day took his wife on a second honeymoon in Venice, where she supposedly became pregnant. This child, a daughter, was said to have committed suicide in New York City many years later. Neither point has ever been proven; Mrs. Breuer was already pregnant before the trip to Venice, and her daughter did not commit suicide.

Clearly, Breuer was frightened especially since his patient accused him of being the father. It was months before he could get himself to tell Freud about Anna O's reactions, and it took a number of years before Freud could convince him to publish the case. Freud explained to Breuer that the phantom pregnancy was a transference phenomenon and that he had no reason to blame himself. Freud emphasized that this was an inevitable consequence of the therapeutic process. This helped Breuer a little, but not enough to keep him engaged in psychoanalytic work.

This raises the question of what would have happened if Anna O. had been Freud's first patient. Perhaps he too would have been frightened and not able to reach fundamental insights about psychoanalysis, such as the formulation of the transference phenomenon. The fact that she was not his patient and he was not acquainted with her might have given him sufficient distance to be objective about what was happening to Breuer, an esteemed and revered older colleague.

There are several ways of approaching this case, knowing what we know now about transference–countertransference phenomena. We could be critical of the way Breuer handled this case; sending a suicidal patient away, as Breuer did, is a tremendous technical error. But of course, this is an unfair judgment, and what Breuer did accomplish is quite noteworthy. Freud remarked in Breuer's obituary that spending hundreds of hours with one particular patient, as he did, represented a novel and bold approach. He praised him for such interest and innovation.

These details are important because, inasmuch as Freud based his theory of the neuroses upon cases considered to be examples of the transference neuroses, we may question the foundations of his conceptual system. If it turns out that the data he used were more characteristic of the narcissistic neuroses, as he called them, or the character disorders and psychoses, as we refer to them today, our attitudes about indications and contraindications for analysis have to be reevaluated. If the theory was formulated on the basis of an erroneous diagnosis, then what Freud said about the types of patients that can be treated psychoanalytically must be questioned. If the cases he treated were indeed examples of characterological problems rather than of intrapsychic conflicts stemming from oedipal problems, his indications for analysis would apply to patients with characterological problems.

Susan Reichard (1956) reevaluated the cases Freud wrote about in *Studies on Hysteria*. She viewed them as examples of characterological problems rather than classical psychoneuroses. Freud's other cases can also be examined further. We cannot say much about the Rat Man (Freud 1909b) since he died in World War I, but certainly Little Hans (Freud 1909) and the Wolf Man (Freud 1918) could be formulated differently, that is, in terms other than psychosexual fixations and regressions. One can think of them as structural defects. Perhaps Freud's patients tended to erotize more than patients today, since sex is more freely expressed in our culture. However, underneath this erotization, there may have been ego defects much like those we see today.

One wonders how many of Freud's cases demonstrated a supraordinate type of sexuality in which the erotic factor is transposed upon the structural defect. Perhaps, to some extent, Freud's patients did this to please him, as might have occurred with Little Hans. Hans' father, who attended Freud's Wednesday afternoon seminars, was very enthusiastic about Freud's newly discovered sexual theories and they may have figured prominently in the way he related to his son. Hans, too, may have learned to respond in the same fashion. I do not mean to imply that children do not have sexual curiosity or are not fascinated with sexual matters. Certainly I am not denying the existence of infantile sexuality. However, prohibiting its expression and at the same time tantalizing the child by showing immense interest in it must have created highly sexualized expressive modalities. Today, this is less likely to happen because most children are not forbidden or tantalized in the sexual area as much as they used to be. Current sexual permissiveness and freedom make it easier to integrate sexuality into the personality. It is therefore taken in stride and does not become a bone of contention; or receive so much attention.

We could look at this case from either of two viewpoints: first, in terms of how well Breuer did with his limited knowledge and sophistication: or second, critically, using concepts not available to Breuer, such as transference and concepts from ego psychology.

Many people find it difficult to remember all the details of this case. The material is not hard to follow, but it is not easily retained. I may have read ten or fifteen pages of the case history, and then put the book aside for a week or so. When I begin reading again, I find that I have to start all over because the point at which I left off does not bring to mind what preceded it. I find it almost impossible to preserve a sense of continuity. I read and re-read and find it elusive. I can not keep in mind when the cough began or the somnambulism entered into the clinical phenomena or even delineate the various phases of the illness and treatment.

One of the difficulties is that Breuer did not describe events in a chronological fashion, but jumped back and forth in time. Furthermore, he did not provide us with a conceptual framework, in which to organize the material. He felt his way along, not knowing what to highlight; everything was given equal weight. He had only one general idea—that of the hypnoidal state, which he wanted to use to justify his therapeutic technique. He was not trying to construct a theory that would be generally helpful for our understanding of psychopathological phenomena. Many of Freud's case histories are not chronologically ordered, either; and instead read like novels, but Freud had a conceptual plan in mind; he did not give everything equal weight, and was not simply reporting clinical data. Rather, he used clinical material to broaden and expand his metapsychology. The reader is thus less likely to become confused and is more apt to be able to retain the material.

To help understand this patient, a brief chronology of the case is provided here. Anna O.'s father fell ill in July of 1880; she began to nurse him, apparently quite energetically. This is in itself somewhat strange; what was her mother doing? By December of 1880, Anna O. must have been completely worn out. When her mother took a trip, leaving her alone with her father, she had an hallucination of snakes, and saw death-heads at the end of her fingers. She also developed a cough; which was associated with hearing music. Although she was not consciously aware of her feelings, Anna O., apparently would have preferred going dancing to taking care of her father. Most of her bizarre symptoms seem to have occurred after she began nursing her father, which led to exhaustion, probably both physical and psychic. Anna O. was not just nursing her father; she was *alone* nursing her father; this is a highly significant fact.

Later in this book, in his discussion of the psychotherapy of hysteria, Freud discussed defense hysteria and retention hysteria; the second of which includes the hypnoidal state. Freud stated that most cases of hysteria are defense hysterias, and most cases of hysterias which are diagnosed as retention hysterias are also defense hysterias. He said that he has never actually seen a case of the hypnoidal variety of hysteria, but acknowledged that perhaps Anna O. was an exception.

Breuer was in a way considering the idea of defenses. Anna O's cough developed in reaction to an unacceptable idea. As stated, she would rather have been out dancing than alone taking care of her father. This implies that the cough was the expression of an internal conflict, but not necessarily the solution (as a defense might be). Under the sway of the conflict between her devotion to her father and her wishes to be elsewhere, she developed a variety of paralyses and parasthesias. By December, 1880 she had become completely nonfunctional and bedridden. At this point, Breuer began visiting her daily and she started to improve.

The fact that she wanted to go dancing instead of taking care of her father might indicate health. It would seem natural for a high-spirited girl such as Anna O., to want to do something like that, but developing a cought would not indicate health. Anna O. was not aware of wanting to go dancing, or of wanting to leave her father. That was unconscious and had to be worked out, which did not occur until much later.

There are cases in which a patient has a conscious wish but, because the family forbids the realization, of the wish, the patient learns not to express it. Anna O., however, was not *forced* to take care of her father. Indeed, she threw herself into it with tremendous, compulsive energy. So, why the cough? If Anna O. had simply suppressed the expression of a feeling or a wish, she would not have had to somatize it. However, her father was suffering from a lung abscess and coughed profusely. She could well have identified with her father. To punish herself for a disloyal or perhaps unfaithful wish (to do dancing), she took over his symptoms. She suffered as he did, and in her suffering remained near him instead of being out with someone else.

In December 1880 she fell into two states: one in which she was melancholy and anxious but her frame of mind was relatively normal, and the other in which she was actively hallucinating, frequently playing the part of a naughty girl. During her psychotic period, she had an extraordinary range of symptoms; thought disorder, deterioration of language, and once, with Dr. Breuer, total muteness. Although she made tremendous efforts to speak, she was unable to do so.

Breuer spent a long time every evening with Anna O., allowing her to drain off the excitations of the day under hypnosis. She had to talk twice as long if he missed a session. Breuer's attentions were beneficial, and by the first of April 1881, Anna O. was able to get out of bed. Ironically, her father died five days later. Anna O. then went into a period that Breuer called "persistent somnambulism," which lasted for nine months. Breuer limited himself to reviewing the events of the day with his patient; he did not look at things from a deeper point of view. Perhaps he was frightened to do so. On the other hand, he might have been quite perceptive and able to persist with a particular procedure because he felt it was doing some good. Remember that this was 1880, thirteen years before Freud had written his share of the preliminary communication, and remember also that Breuer was not a psychiatrist. He was what might today be called an internist. How many internists would you find today that would devote this kind of attention to psychologically determined symptoms? Breuer did not have a psychodynamic orientation and he knew nothing about unconscious motivation.

Perhaps Breuer accepted this type of treatment as a lifelong procedure. He could get rid of excitations and tensions, but then new excitations and tensions would continually occur. He was aware of the fact that, at the time, the prognosis for hysteria was extremely poor.

After her father died in April, Anna O. developed new kinds of symptoms, and became more profoundly regressed. For example, she could only see one flower in a group of flowers. She also experienced difficulty recognizing familiar people, and did so only in a very primitive way. She first had to identify the nose, then the hair, and then other parts of the body as having specific characteristics. This process seems to support the theory of part objects. For a time, Breuer was the only person she recognized, and he was her only contact. She stopped eating, and Breuer started feeding her. After a while, she allowed nurses to feed her. Perhaps, figuratively speaking, Breuer was the one flower Anna O. could see—her sole basis for an integrative relationship. Sometime between December 1880 and April 1881, Anna O. had a period of two weeks in which she was completely mute; afterwards, she started speaking in English. Breuer believed that something had offended her and that she did not want to talk about it. This formulation was, in essence, psychodynamic.

Then Breuer took a vacation. I suspect this was not a recreational vacation, but that Breuer was called off on some kind of emergency or consultation. Viennese doctors did not go on vacations for just a few days; Freud, for example, took months at a time when he vacationed. Breuer's trip may have been part of a developing pattern: Breuer got close to his patient, allowed her to become extremely dependent on him, and then drew back.

While Breuer was gone, he brought in a consultant to look after Anna O. This consultant treated Anna O. rudely, (blowing smoke into her face, for example). When Breuer returned at the end of three days, he found Anna O.'s condition had deteriorated. She had eaten nothing while he was away. Anna became suicidal, and throughout the month of May her tendency toward self-destruction intensified. Breuer arranged for her transfer to an institution in the countryside, where she got even worse. She threw things, hallucinated, and had what Breuer called prolonged periods of absences in which she was apparently out of contact with everyone except Breuer, who still saw her, although much less frequently —probably two or three times a week rather than the five to seven times a week he had seen her before her institutionalization. When he was present, he fed her, but when he was away, she stopped eating entirely. She especially could not tolerate bread. Perhaps bread represented to Anna O., the staff of life. We could speculate about phallic elements, but there is no data to support such speculation.

She continued on a downhill course, but improved at times. During the summer, she became much worse and developed the symptom of being unable to drink water. Breuer provided the first example of abreaction when he learned that this symptom was connected to feelings of disgust Anna O. experienced when she observed a lady visitor's dog drinking water out of a bowl.

In the fall Anna O. returned to a new house in Vienna. Her family had moved. She had improved, Breuer now saw her on a more frequent schedule, and she seemed to be integrating. In November 1881, however, she deteriorated suddenly. Why she got worse at this point, just a year after her earlier deterioration, brings up questions about etiology that we do not have sufficient data to answer. We do not have free associations, fantasy material, or relevant dream material. We do not know why Anna deteriorated one year earlier, and it may be that the factors operating then were also operating a year later. Thus, it is not an anniversary reaction as such but rather a reaction to the same psychic forces and events that were responsible for Anna O.'s first decompensation. Anna O.'s deterioration occurred approximately nine months after her father's death which, of course, causes us to speculate about pregnancy fantasies. Again, it is difficult to be conclusive from these data, which are mainly phenomenological descriptions.

After Anna O.'s second deterioration, Breuer started using abreaction, which consists of reliving traumatic experiences with the appropriate affect attached to the experience. Anna O. complicated the issue by dealing with events that occurred not only that day but a year before, which seems to support speculations about anniversary reactions. Anna O. succeeded in getting Breuer to see her twice a day. During her periods of disorientation, she lived in the previous year, and when she realized that she was not in the same house as she was in the year before, she panicked. Breuer handled this situation by putting her to bed at night and giving her the suggestion that she was not to open her eyes until he came back the next morning. One might say he opened her eyes for her.

Using this method, Breuer connected all the symptoms to specific situations. He found 108, 57, and 28 situations associated with particular symptoms, and all of them had to be relived. This made the treatment very tedious. The transference and Anna O.'s need to maintain Breuer's interest intruded into this case. Nevertheless, he continued using this method progressively and painstakingly until April 1882, when Anna O. had another anniversary reaction to the actual anniversary of her father's death. She took a distinct upturn. She re-experienced the trauma that caused her to have the hallucinations of the snakes, the trauma that could be considered the source for all the later traumas and symptoms. It had not been sufficiently abreacted until this final phase of her treatment. (Breuer concluded that her monotonous family life and her habit of daydreaming were contributing factors in the production of hypnoid states, which made her especially vulnerable to life experiences.)

The central dramatic scene of Anna O.'s trauma was as follows: After Anna O.'s mother had left for Vienna, Anna O. was left sitting beside her father's bedside. Her arm, which was hanging over the back of the chair, had gone to sleep. (This is the "Saturday night syndrome," in which a person gets drunk and falls asleep with an arm hanging over a chair, causing pressure on the brachial nerve. On awakening, the arm is paralyzed.) Something similar, had happened to Anna O. When she looked at her hand each finger had turned into little snakes, or the ends of which were death-heads instead of nails. At the same time, she saw a black snake coming out of the wall.

According to Breuer, it was possible that Anna O. had tried to use her paralyzed arm to ward off the snake coming out of the wall. Consequently, anesthesia and paralysis became associated with the hallucination of the snake. Different phenomena occurring at the same time thus became associated to each other. Failing in her attempt to move her arm, Anna O. tried to pray, but language failed her until she was able to find some child's verses in English, and then she was able to think and pray in that language. The whistle of the train bringing the doctor broke the spell. The next day, on a stroll, she saw a bent branch, which revived the hallucination of the snake.

Was this a hallucination or a dream? This distinction would not make any difference in terms of intrapsychic conflicts being symbolized in the manifest material, but it would be significant in terms of character structure. If Anna O. had a hallucination, it is more likely that she had a psychotic organization, whereas if she were dreaming, this would not necessarily be so. On the other hand, why would the sound of a whistle interrupt a delusion? It would more likely interrupt a dream. Indeed, if Anna O.'s arm were actually paralyzed, and there was some evidence to indicate that it was, then she would have had to have been asleep. She would not have put such pressure on the arm if she were awake.

We do not have sufficient data on hand to make a psychodynamic formulation but let us try to do so anyway. Since we are not hampered by the accumulation of facts, we can become somewhat inventive. I believe that we can reach some conclusions regarding Anna O.'s character structure. Remember the strong erotic component (not in the oedipal sense but rather as a pregenital superimposition) in her character, perhaps manifested in the snake hallucinations, her pseudocyesis, and her later behavior toward the directors of institutions.

How would we approach such a patient today? She is a 21-year-old woman who became severely incapacitated after seven months of giving nursing care to her father who fell ill in the spring. She was totally functionless and had to be put to bed in the fall. What would we have done if we were called at that time to take care of her?

I do not believe that there is any question that she would have been hospitalized long before she had reached total helplessness, unless there were some factors pertaining to the sociocultural milieu that we either do not know about or have ignored. In those days, there was a propensity to treat patients at home, just as most babies were delivered at home. Of course, there were private institutions for patients such as Anna O., but hospitals were more dangerous then than they are today, and well-to-do families were able to support their sick and take care of them better at home. Anna O. also had an extremely strong sensitivity to separation. When people left the room, she became quite agitated. Today the bizarre character and severity of her symptoms would probably have led to institutionalization rather than treatment in an out-patient setting. I can recall several patients whose methods of thinking, behavioral aberrations, and somatic symptoms were just as bizarre, if not more so, than those of Anna O., not merely in terms of systematized delusions, although I have seen that too. However, they were able to remain sufficiently rational to come regularly to their appointments. All of these severely disturbed patients saw analysis as an essential part of their lives, and no matter how chaotic their behavior might have been in other areas, their attitude toward analysis was always one of constant dedication (Giovacchini, 1968).

As a general principle, some of the difficulties we as analysts encounter in treating patients on an outpatient basis are related to our anxiety. If we are not anxious but instead confident that an analytic relationship can be established, the simple anticipation of that relationship will give patients sufficient organization to be maintained as outpatients. There are, of course, many other factors, including whether the environment can tolerate them outside of the hospital. Once analysis is firmly offered, the patient also makes himself sufficiently adaptable to the external world.

Tarachow (1963) made the statement that psychoanalysis succeeds because the therapist makes mistakes, that is, demonstrates that he is human to the patient. Tarachow seemed to be paraphrasing Winnicott, who stated he made mistakes that signified to the patient that he, the therapist, was not omnipotent, that he was human. This does not mean, however, that the psychotherapeutic procedure *depends* upon making mistakes. All Winnicott says is that when errors occur, the analyst exploits them to their fullest advantage, rather than remaining austere and attempting to preserve self-esteem by acting omnipotent; Winnicott was not encouraging mistakes.

For the sake of organization, we can divide Anna O.'s symptoms into two categories (1) somatic symptoms: coughing, dysphagia, anesthesias, paralyses, among others; (2) symptoms associated with behavioral or psychic states: hallucinations, absences, dissociated states, and violent behavior. There is some homogeneity between these two groups, which might tell us something about characterological adaptations and defenses.

Within the somatic sphere, symptoms such as anorexia, coughing, and hydrophobia all emphasize the oral modality. Also the incorporative aspects of orality might be emphasized, and this would include the eye symptoms. Anesthesia and paralysis point to Anna O.'s generalized inhibitions and vulnerability and helplessness. She could not control her limbs, and thus lost mastery over her own body. Of course, there is more striking evidence of her helplessness, as when she was bedridden and completely immobilized. Her symptoms also included violent behavior, such as breaking things. The snakes coming out of the wall were potentially threatening and destructive.

Anna O. also exhibited considerable eroticism and rapid changes from one ego state to another. This general lability of ego organization indicates a capacity to regress, but Anna O. also reintegrated rather easily whenever Breuer was present. That she had the capacity to respond to people was undoubtedly a favorable prognostic factor regarding her therapeutic accessibility. After her father's death, Anna O. had a deep and total regression, but she was able to sustain a relationship with Breuer. At that time she developed tunnel vision and language deterioration.

Anna O. was capable of another, better organized type of regression characterized by dissociative states. The regression following her father's death might be considered a global disintegration, whereas the regression associated with hypnoid states contains certain defensive adaptations, i.e., splitting mechanisms. In addition to these qualities Anna O. was capable of considerable erotization, which we have considered to be another defensive manifestation. None of us has chosen to formulate the sexual factor in terms of an oedipal conflict based on a strong incestuous component, as Freud so often did in his formulations.

It could be stated that Anna O. was revealing an oedipal orientation when she rescued wayward girls from being sold to Turkey to be prostitutes. However, they were not wayward girls but orphans. One reason men seek out prostitutes is to defend themselves against incestuous feelings, which is of significance here.

In some quarters, the case of Anna O. would probably be considered an example of a psychoneurosis based upon oedipal factors. Breuer and Freud called her hysteric, but they also spoke of psychotic features. In fact, they used the expression "hysterical psychosis" in this monograph. Perhaps all of these symptoms could be explained as melodramatic expressions of oedipal problems. Anna O. might even be accused of having simulated: being a naughty girl meant being naughty sexually. Certainly her relationship with Breuer could be seen as incestuous, and the pseudocyesis that occurred during the end of treatment supports such a conjecture. The hallucinations could be formulated as reverie states, orgasmic states, in which the snakes represented large phalluses coming at her. If one were intent upon making an oedipal interpretation, it could be argued that these were not psychotic hallucinations, but instead extremely intense, visual, erotic fantasies, although I do not agree with this.

Diagnostic formulations such as the oedipal one described above were much more common twenty years ago. Since then, the equation of hysteria with schizophrenia has been frequently established, and I believe most clinicians would tend to think of Anna O. as being much more seriously disturbed than one would expect to find in a well-organized psychoneurosis.

Anna O.'s somatic symptoms point to conflict and indicate states of helplessness and inhibition. How did she feel about herself? This would give us some information about the organization of her self-representation. How did she adapt to the external world in terms of her ego defects or deficiencies? We know after her illness she adapted very well but we do not know how that fits into the context of her psychopathology. Regarding her later adaptations, could she have created a special world for herself in order to maintain a cohesion of character? If she did not have orphan girls to care for, if she did not have the talent to originate and organize the social work movement, if she did not have these outlets in which her adaptive techniques were operative and could satisfy some of her needs, what would she have been like? Would she have had a psychotic breakdown? I am postulating that she might have externalized her psychopathology and created a segment of the external world that was in harmony with it.

It is remarkably curious that throughout the detailed course of this illness, there was never once any reference to feelings of guilt, common remorse, or self-recrimination. She never showed any signs of sensitivity to the feelings of others; she was completely self-centered, although there were some feelings of sensitivity involved in her *tussis nervosa*. When she heard the music and wanted to be out dancing, she developed the cough. Still, did she ever consciously experience a self-critical feeling or believe that she had done something wrong? Did she ever blame herself for anything? Possibly she did not have to because she somatized these feelings. Still, there is always some feeling left that does not succumb to somatization. Even conversion hysterics with *la belle indifference* never completely succeed, they often feel inadequate or tend to blame themselves.

Breuer said that Anna O. actually looked melancholic, but he never talked about any affect of depression. Her cough could be explained on a different basis, as a reaction to fellatio fantasies or an identification with her father. Still, Anna O.'s identification with her father can be thought of in terms of guilt. She identified with his symptoms, took them over as a punishment for her forbidden feelings of wanting to go out dancing. This requires a higher level of ego organization, compatible with an hysterical or psychoneurotic state. It could also be compatible with a characterological disorder in which this identification is not founded on guilt, but rather on other factors.

If Anna O. had been a member of a lower-class, economically deprived family, would she have received the same kind of considerations? Would she not have been considered wicked or misguided, and might not her treatment have consisted of punishment and ostracism? Breuer never mentioned if Anna O. had been overindulged. On the contrary, her family was somewhat aloof, and her life was monotonous and unexciting, which could mean there was very little contact with external objects. Perhaps her parents related to their children in terms of their own narcissistic needs and not in terms of their children's needs. The parents might have had unrealistic expectations of them or used their children to enhance themselves.

Oral preoccupation, as exemplified by some of the somatic symptoms and rage and as evidenced by other aspects of Anna O.'s behavior, indicate that pathology occurred at early developmental stages. Her fixation would have to have been relatively primitive although not at a very early point. True indifference on the part of the parents, in which they do not relate at all to their child or relate only on an intellectual level, as occurs with some autistic children, would lead to a fixation at an extremely primitive level, a stage of amorphous ego organization. With

Anna O., there was a relationship; it may have been conflictual, but it did lead to structure. In this light, Anna O.'s ability to maintain a relationship with Breuer when she was decompensating in all other respects, is indicative of a fairly good adaptive ability. She was able to sustain herself by creating some kind of symbiotic relationship with him.

Thus her ego organization could not have been all that primitive. She had the capacity to see that one flower. She had the capacity to reach out, pray and recite nursery rhymes. In other words, she was able to turn to memories of gratifying experiences which indicates that, at one time, she had been gratified, even though she experienced considerable frustration. Anna O. knew the meaning of gratification, which would not have been the case if she had suffered only absolute indifference in her neonatal months. Her talents and creativity also indicate a certain degree of psychic organization. In many ways, she was precocious.

Perhaps Breuer found her fascinating because of her talents. Perhaps this was characteristic of Victorian era Viennese doctors. Freud frequently described his patients as being people of unusual caliber; he constantly referred to "this gifted young man," "this beautiful lady," "this talented and sensitive person." He was dealing with character structures that, in spite of ego defects, had islands of precocious organization that could lead to creative expression.

Patients who were attracted to early psychoanalysis probably had two qualities: they were very needy, and they were gifted. They could probably appreciate psychoanalysis as a fascinating philosophy, a fascinating conceptual scheme. A narcissistic element was also involved. To spend an hour five times a week as the exclusive object of attention from a person who is respected and authoritative, must have been a fulfilling experience.

Breuer did not discuss Anna O.'s family at length. It might have been difficult for him to make observations about family relationships because his comments could have been construed as negative or critical, and Viennese middle-class society was family-oriented and highly conservative. Perhaps he wanted to protect the integrity and dignity of the family and not discuss their relationships and behavior from a clinical perspective.

Neither Breuer nor Freud was able to formulate, especially in those days, in terms of developmental factors. True, Freud shortly afterwards postulated a psychosexual scheme of development, but he never correlated exact vicissitudes occurring during various stages with specific psychopathology. He did, of course, equate specific psychosexual fixations with the different psychoneuroses, but he did not go into any detail about the actual disturbances and the object relationships that would have been characteristic of particular phases.

Anna O. was narcissistic, as indicated by her extreme need for her father and the way she clung to Breuer and demanded his attention and time. She could also be called borderline. Narcissism and borderline are not mutually exclusive. I would call the extreme need for someone else to sustain a person narcissistic. Narcissism might even be defined as the extreme need to be admired. In both instances, we are dealing with extreme needfulness, and the narcissistic character is needy. We are struck by the enormous amount of time that Breuer gave Anna O. Could she somehow have had a hand in this? Had she been successful in manipulating him to devote all of this attention to her? This must have been a reflection of her neediness. Breuer might have found her fascinating, but she was not so irresistable that he had to spend all of those hours with her. Somehow she made him do it. These are pretty good grounds for thinking of her in terms of some kind of narcissistic fixation. Still, how this fits into her psychic economy has to be elaborated.

In terms of the transference, Anna O. wanted to return to a state in which one person would in essence take over responsibility for her life. She might have felt that there were bad things inside of her, call them what you wish, negative introjects, destructive forces, something of that sort. Breuer, somehow, had omnipotently to protect her from these internalized bad objects. She managed to obtain this kind of protection from him for a period of time. Presumably there was a period in her life when she was not able to work out a comfortable symbiotic tie with some significant figure and later needed to return to that phase. She was left with some elements of the bad self which she managed to dissociate from the rest of her ego. Now she had to defend herself against this bad self, and she sought aid from Breuer, a powerful, idealized, external object. We need not be concerned about whether this is an idealized mother or father, simply some power able to counteract the badness and see that it did not get wildly out of control.

This is a very plausible formulation and there is much in the case to support it. Although there may not be any overt manifestations of guilt, many of Anna O.'s symptoms can be understood in terms of intrapsychic conflict. Her feelings about her father, her erotic wishes, her paralysis, and her inability to pursue the dictates of her instincts could lead to a psychodynamic viewpoint. For example, her hallucinations of snakes and deathheads represent destructive wishes directed at her father. However, Anna O. can be understood most effectively in terms of structural problems.

Let us think in terms of early object relationships and the development of the self-representation. I believe that Anna O.'s parents related to her in terms of their own needs. These must have been experienced as impingements, perhaps even as assaults. During these early symbiotic stages, when Anna O. was experiencing her parents as both gratifying and impinging, a concept of polarized objects emerges—the dichotomy of good and bad objects. The defense mechanisms typical of this phase are splitting mechanisms, in which the bad and the good are dissociated from each other. Perhaps catharsis would be most effective for patients suffering from such fixations, inasmuch as a bad object can be expelled. In the next phase, objects would be seen neither in terms of total good or total bad but as combinations of both. This is the stage of ambivalence, a much more advanced phase and one in which superego elements become effectively operative. There are several possible outcomes of these fixations, especially in terms of how a patient views himself. I do not believe Anna O.'s ego had effectively reached this level. In the stage of ambivalence, patients may feel helpless, as Anna O. did, but unlike her, they are very self-critical. They see themselves as unworthy, inadequate, and vulnerable. Anna O. did not revile herself in this fashion; she had built a series of defenses against her vulnerable feelings. Such defenses help maintain self-esteem and perhaps the patient may view himself in a grandiose fashion. Today, we refer to such patients as suffering from narcissistic character disorders. They have overcompensatory defensive adaptations which, as in the case of Anna O., may lead to the formation of precocious psychic areas constructed on the basis of innate talent. These so-called narcissistic defenses make up for the basic inner core of inadequacy.

It is possible that Anna O.'s father was viewed as a savior. Then he became ill and left her helpless, as he was no longer able to support her narcissistic defenses. On the contrary, she had to save and protect him. She tried, but her rage must have been immense. She felt abandoned, cast adrift, and experienced basic helplessness. The symptom of coughing might have been a reaction to hearing music and wanting to go out dancing, but it could also have represented a projective–introjective mechanism. On the projective side, it could mean expelling the hateful, bad, vulnerable self, and on the introjective axis, it could represent incorporating the father, inasmuch as coughing must have been one of his symptoms. Then she would effect a fusion with him and be magically rescued, but this time she would have to do the rescuing. However she could not accomplish this because her neediness was too great. Then she made a total identification with her father and became bedridden. Someone else had to be brought into the picture as the savior, at which point Breuer entered the scene.

She was successful in creating a totally dependent relationship with Breuer. She fused with him and viewed him as a rescuer. He supported her narcissistic defenses in the same way her father had earlier. When her father died she regressed to earlier stages of development in which her helplessness was not defended against, allowing her to reach out directly. Again Breuer was there to save her. Apparently, through her relationship with Breuer, Anna O. was able to restore her narcissistic defenses and bring them into the sphere of her own talent, at which point she could move into the external world.

After Breuer terminated her treatment, she once again became enraged and was not able to maintain her narcissistic equilibrium. She spent six years in various institutions. Still, she was able to pursue external objects to give her the kind of enhancement she needed to maintain her self-esteem. She eroticized her relationships with the directors of sanitoriums. These erotic relationships, although short-lived because the directors became too uncomfortable, served to restore her sufficiently in that she was again able to direct her attentions to the external world, taking care of orphan girls and forming the social work movement. These activities must have received sufficient positive reinforcement from the external world and became incorporated into her defensive system.

This suggests that erotism is the fuel, the vehicle, by which Anna O. reconstituted her narcissistic defenses. Erotism was part of her narcissistic defenses. Sexually, she was reassuring herself: "I am not inadequate. I am not horrible or ugly. I am beautiful." She was not, however, flirtatious or engaging.

Anna O.'s pseudocyesis represented symbiosis. Either she or Breuer could have been the fetus; it really does not matter. Pregnancy would have been the outcome of their union or fusion. If she were the mother and Breuer the fetus, she would be taking care of him. If she had been the fetus, he would be looking after her. The details do not matter because in these stages individuation had not yet taken place. The important factor is that two have become one. Here, however, we are elaborating beyond our rights. Breuer undoubtedly withheld much information that could have given us a more exact picture of what was going on between Anna O. and himself; all the embarrassments he suffered might have made him reluctant to emphasize such material.

Perhaps Anna O.'s pseudocyesis was an attempt on her part to drive Breuer away. This often happens with patients who, on the one hand, want a symbiotic fusion and, on the other hand, fear it because they feel that whatever vestige of autonomy they have will be destroyed. Anna O.'s basic integration probably did not really change because of treatment, but she was able to make an adaptation and function quite effectively even after her father was dead by the reconstruction of a very adequate functioning personality based on narcissistic defenses. We all know many people operating on a similar basis today. We can see how Anna O. used infantile character traits in the service of adaptation. For example, during her social work career, the board of trustees often opposed her decisions. She responded to this opposition by having temper tantrums and resigning. The board would then have to coax her to come back and, in so doing, let her have her way. Apparently this occurred many times.

It seems that the father was more central to Anna O. than her mother. The father's dominance in the emotional life of children may have been more significant during mid-Victorian times, and fathers in those days could be quite maternal, even though they may not have spent much time with their children. Perhaps this is one of the reasons that the Oedipus complex seemed to be so important. Possibly it was an artifact. Little Hans, for example, certainly had ambivalent feelings toward his father, but the maternal elements in that relationship, although expressed in erotic overtones, were quite evident. If the father's role was so maternal, what was the mother's role? The typical Viennese middle-class family had maids and nannies to look after the children. Helene Deutsch, for example, had nine nurses. Mothers were really administrators of the household; it was quite beneath them to do any actual work. In terms of the emotional life of the family, the mother seemed to be pretty much in the background. The situation with Sigmund and Anna Freud was interesting in this respect. Recent books emphasize that Martha Freud (Freud's wife) did not impose herself or have a prominent part in the family affairs.

Some years ago, one of the members of a postgraduate seminar was assigned the task of writing up the case of Anna O. as he would have any patient he might have seen in the outpatient clinic (Case History, see pp. 60–62).

Hypnoid States

Breuer, who wrote this section, stated that there are two ways in which ideas can be excluded from consciousness. One we can call the "Freud hypothesis,"—the defense or psychodynamic hypothesis—in which ideas are deliberately repressed from consciousness. The "Breuer hypothesis" proposes that an idea arises in a hypnoid state and cannot be

Case History

Patient

Anna O., a 21-year-old white female.

Presenting Symptoms

Dissociative states with hallucinations and assaultive behavior; loss of consciousness and confusion; dysphagia; multiple motor and sensory symptoms, including paralysis, pareses, and anesthesias.

Present Illness

Apparently precipitated by father's illness (lung abscess), which began in July 1880 and terminated in his death nine months later. When he first became ill, the patient and her mother devoted themselves to nursing him. At some time during the first few months of father's illness the patient began to exhibit dissociative symptoms, at first resembling petit mal seizures but gradually becoming more marked and extensive and characterized by a transient rigid extension of the right arm and visual hallucinations of snakes. The dissociations appeared to date from an occasion when the patient was at the father's bedside and experienced a "waking dream" in which snakes attacked her father; her arm (which in fact had gone to sleep) was paralyzed, her fingers became snakes with death's heads, and she was unable to speak until she thought of some children's verses in English. The whistle of a train (bearing her father's physician) dispelled this state.

On subsequent occasions this dissociative state, re-evoked by objects resembling snakes, became more and more extensive.

The patient, during the initial phase of her father's illness and while the dissociations remained relatively mild, developed many neurasthenic symptoms, and a psychogenic cough, which eventuated in the family's decision to prevent her from caring for her father. This interception of her nursing duties, which occurred about five months after father's illness began, apparently initiated a sharp worsening in the patient's condition. The dissociations became more intense and frequent, making a regular appearance each evening, and multiple motor and somatic symptoms appeared. The patient became bedridden, and regular psychiatric care was initiated.

Family History

Sparse. Some psychosis in distant relatives. The immediate family is cultured and in good economic circumstances but is said to be "puritanical." This suggests a rigorous, strict, and even harsh morality, and may be extended to imply an authoritarian father and compliant mother.

Developmental History

Patient is said to have been consistently healthy as a child, giving evidence of extreme intelligence. No other details.

Educational and Occupational History

No details except for the implication that patient did well in school.

Social and Sexual Development

Patient lives at home, and is said to have never been in love. Her close friends appear to be professional men with whom she has an intellectual relationship. She impressed her therapist as being sexually undeveloped to an astonishing degree. (*Author's note*: The implications of all this for a transference in which the sexual element must be urgently concealed are striking.)

Premorbid Personality

Intellectuality coupled with energy and determination, appear to be salient characteristics. Along with a mention of mood swings, suggest cyclothymic or hypomanic character components. (*Author's note*: it is of interest that manics frequently display histories in which the *wunderkind* "my son, the doctor" theme of achievement is prominent and helps maintain a pattern of oral overindulgence. The patient is also said to have been imaginative and to have engaged in systematic and extensive daydreaming which, while coextensive with, did not interrupt her daily activities and social contacts. (*Author's note*: These elements have, of course, a schizoid or autistic ring.)

Therapeutic Plan and Course of Illness

At the time psychotherapy was initiated, the patient's day consisted of several distinct phases: a day period marked by episodic, seizure-like dissociations, followed by an afternoon phase of increasing drowsiness that gradually shaded into a comatose, trance-like state during the evening. If during the evening trance, the patient could be stimulated—by repeating to her the broken phrases she uttered during the day—to relate the fantasies she was believed to have constructed during the day, she would awaken from her trance calm and lucid, and spend the early night period in tranquil, rational activities.

This generalized cathartic activity was coupled with a more specific attack on her speech difficulties, an attack which was necessitated by her becoming mute. Her muteness was interpreted as a manifestation of her having taken offense at some incident and determining not to speak of it. With this interpretation (in March of 1881, about three months after psychiatric care was initiated and about one month before the father's death) and with the patient's venting of her "repressed" feeling, speech returned, and there was a reduction in the severity of her motor symptoms. Improvement continued until the death of her father about one month later (April 1881). A burst of violent activity was succeeded by a stuporous depression of two days. The stupor then gave way to symptoms of depersonalization and withdrawal characterized by negative hallucinations.

A direct assault on the primitive denial (which might be equally well described as sponsoring a recital) coupled with an interruption of several days duration in treatment, led to an exacerbation of the illness characterized by manifest delusions and suicidal attempts during the day. Increasing deterioration, and danger of suicide necessitated moving the patient to the country, which after a three-day outburst of violence and hallucinations, appeared to favor a more quiet adjustment.

The therapeutic regime of verbal catharsis in the evening hypnoid state continued, and there was a gradual slow improvement in the patient's condition, which, however, seemed to depend upon continuous therapeutic contacts. In the autumn of 1881, about six months after the father's death and about nine months after the regular psychiatric care began, the patient was sufficiently improved to return to the city. However, as the December anniversary of her original confinement approached, her condition worsened

again, but now, the hallucinoid experiences of the day that had to be talked out in the evening hypnoid state consisted of a re-experiencing of the events at the time of father's initial illness. It was during this phase of treatment that the origin of each separate hysterical conversion was traced (eye blurring—tears; coughing—music; hydrophobia—puppy; death's head of father—mirror; arm paralysis —sleeping). This uncovering phase culminated in the patient's re-experiencing the original bedside hallucination and her cure.

Dynamics

"Spoiled" eldest child with a pre-oedipal attachment to father. Wished to "produce" for him, but intellectually (anally) rather than genitally, necessitated by his rejection of sexuality and seductive interest.

The equation of ideas and babies, and her need to (and her rage about having to do so) display to win father's love is uncovered in treatment but not worked through.

Dx Impression

Schizoaffective psychosis.

remembered. The notion of motivation recedes into the background. Splitting and dissociation are based upon the failure of the ego's synthetic and integrative functions.

Breuer made the broad claim that the genesis of hysteria is based upon the formation of hypnoid states. There are two ways in which the hypnoid state and actual hypnosis are similar: (1) amnesia accompanies both states, and (2) both ultimately result in a splitting of the mind.

The hypnoid state is the basic etiological factor of hysteria for Breuer. He compared the hypnoid state with autohypnosis and remarked that a hypnoid state is, in fact, a state of autohypnosis and that autohypnosis always occurs in hysteria. The amnesia that is the result of this dissociative activity prevents the ideas arising in the hypnoid state from being scrutinized by waking thought and being subjected to examination and criticism. Amnesia protects ideas from being eroded away and leads to an increase in psychical splitting.

Breuer spoke of susceptibility but did not specifically mention a constitutional factor. He discussed how certain types of experiences affect psychic structure and cause it to lose its integration. In a way he had evolved a type of ego psychology, a position that we have returned to today. Breuer then postulated that another state, "absence of mind," can lead to the formation of hypnoid states. (I am not entirely clear as to what he means by absence of mind, but it may be suspension of self-awareness.) Absence of mind may be pathogenic or not. Pathogenic absence of mind is associated with intense affect and inhibition of ideas. Two particular circumstances are responsible for its development: attending the sick, as was the case with Anna O., and being in love. Nonpathogenic absence of mind would include intense creative or intellectual work or unemotional twilight states. Creative absorption is nonpathogenic because the process of working out the problem or constructing the product results in a diminution of excitation so there are no deleterious consequences. The difference between creativity and psychopathology depends upon one small step; in creativity the excitation is discharged, and in psychopathology—in hysteria—it is not. According to Breuer, the lack of discharge accounts for the formation of neurosis.

It would be fair to say that Breuer was talking about sublimation, in that affect gets discharged in some useful kind of work. Freud would have elaborated upon this and insisted that these affects had to somehow be connected with sexual elements because that is the way sublimation is defined. Sublimation is a process in which libido is discharged, but in being discharged, it is also desexualized or delibidinized. Sublimation is a controversial concept. Because it supposedly leads to discharge, it is not considered a defense. It is amazing how many concepts found in the *Studies on Hysteria*, such as overdetermination, displacement, projection, and transference, later became elaborated into the psychoanalytic system.

Once more Breuer raised the issue of predisposition. He speculated that some persons may have an increased susceptibility to hypnosis and to the production of hypnoid states, but that such states can occur spontaneously, indicating perhaps that the constitutional factor is minimal. While in the unconscious, hypnoidal states remain pathogenically operative (Freud's concept of the dynamic unconscious). At the end of the section, Breuer stressed that these states are not immutable, that they can be brought up to consciousness and discharged, leading to therapeutic resolution. This is a fundamental psychoanalytic principle.

Breuer stated repeatedly that the symptoms reside in the hypnoidal state, whereas Freud's psychodynamically oriented theory would not require dissociation. However, it seems clear that hysterical symptoms occur in both hypnoidal and nonhypnoidal states. Perhaps both theories can be used. Breuer formulated in terms of structure, while Freud depended heavily upon an energic hypothesis. Breuer, however, also considered energic factors to be important in that he relied heavily on the processes of catharsis and abreaction. Still, one could say that Breuer's theory is fundamentally structural and requires energic factors, whereas Freud's deals primarily within the psychodynamic context. Freud rejected the structural aspects of Breuer's theory and retained the psychoeconomic ones. Freud first took one part of Breuer's hypothesis, the part pertaining to catharsis and abreaction, and developed it into a theory of conflicting instincts and defenses. Today, we are returning to the other part of Breuer's hypothesis when we formulate psychopathology on the basis of various parts of the self being dissociated from each other, in splitting and projective defenses.

Still, present-day, modern ego psychology did not stem directly from Breuer. Freud began by developing the psychodynamic hypothesis, and only much later formulated the structural hypothesis, having moved toward concepts of psychic structure and splitting mechanisms after working out innumerable clinical and theoretical concepts.

Schlessinger (1967) compared Freud's and Breuer's writing style and concluded that Freud was hypotheticodeductive, whereas Breuer made wide impressionistic leaps. After reading this book and knowing something about the background of these two men, we would be inclined to agree with these descriptions of differences in their scientific approach. Breuer was an older man and had been established in the practice of internal medicine for many years. He dealt with clinical phenomena every day and his thinking must have been primarily that of the clinician, not that of the scientist who examines every step in the process leading to his conclusions. Freud, on the other hand, was young, enthusiastic, and dedicated to establishing a new system of thought. Unlike Breuer, he did not have an extensive background of clinical practice. He had spent many years in a laboratory working in a more formal scientific tradition.

The Psychotherapy of Hysteria

Freud began this section by stating that an hysterical symptom is removed when the memory of the pathogenic recollection is recalled and accompanied by affect. By putting the affect into words, the idea is abreacted, and thus an associative correction is achieved. Freud then agreed with what he had written in the preliminary communication with Breuer but also had some new ideas. These new viewpoints arose from two particular points: (1) the fact that not all hysterics can be hypnotized, and (2) the factors that distinguish hysteria from other neuroses. Regarding the second point, Freud observed that not all hysterics improved when Breuer's method was used but that other nonhysteric neurotics may have benefited from abreaction and catharsis. Freud wondered, inasmuch as the Breuer method worked on some of these patients, whether they had been misdiagnosed and were really hysterics. He rejected this conjecture.

Freud had not had a great deal of clinical experience with patients other than hysterics. He had written about obsessive-compulsives and a case of paranoia whom he was treating at this time. In *Studies on Hysteria*, he reported four cases: Emmy von N., Lucy R., Katherina, and Elisabeth von R. He classified these women as hysterics, and it is possible that he used Breuer's method with all except Katherina. He tried to get them to recall the events associated with the onset of the trauma, but whether or not they experienced catharsis and abreaction is not particularly clear. In some instances he used hypnosis, but in others he did not.

In "A Case of Successful Treatment by Hypnotism" (1893), Freud wrote about a case in which he successfully used hypnosis, but it had very little resemblance, if any, to abreaction. He used suggestion to counter the patient's thoughts (counter-will) that were working against her wishes and aims. This method was not even remotely related to catharsis, but, in fact, constituted a battle of wits.

Freud often seemed dictatorial in his treatment approaches. Emmy von N., for example, seemed to have the capacity to infuriate him. He once got very angry at her, insisting that she accept his explanation that anxiety was the basis of her symptoms. He threatened to break off treatment if she did not agree, so during the next session, she accepted his explanation but then went on to add that she accepted it only because he had told her to.

Freud never described in detail regressions to traumatic events and explosive affective reactions, although he alluded to them. He did, however, describe a patient's gradual series of recollections. One might consider them a mini-series in which there is no single dramatic, intense, traumatic moment but rather a slow unfolding of memories that, in essence, represent various facets of the infantile environment.

It seems clear that by the time *Studies on Hysteria* was written, Freud had given up the view of a single traumatic etiology and had a very different approach than the one he shared with Breuer at the beginning. Freud analyzed patients provisionally as hysterics. However, only the outcome of the analysis would indicate whether the original diagnosis was correct. He added that etiologies are invariably sexual, but that there are different sexual factors involved in each neurosis, although he did not say what these factors are.

Freud now continued exploring the differences between hysteria and other neuroses by constructing a nosology in outline form. He had first attempted diagnostic distinctions a year earlier (Freud 1894). Here he juxtaposed hysteria with three other conditions: neurasthenia, obsessional neurosis, and anxiety neurosis. This was the first mention of neurasthenia. Freud concluded that no psychical mechanisms are involved in neurasthenia, whereas in the obsessional neuroses there are complex psychological factors operating. He believes that neurasthenia must be distinguished from the anxiety neurosis, which also lacks psychical elements. He elaborated on this distinction in a paper that we will soon read (Freud 1895a).

It is confusing to conceive of a neurosis without psychological or mentational factors. Even more confusing is Freud's observation that most neuroses are mixed neuroses.

The actual neuroses are described in "The Unconscious" (Freud 1915c). Here, he was not as clear-cut in his distinctions, but in essence he was describing dammed-up sexual tension that cannot be satisfied by sexual activity and is instead deflected into physiological channels and discharged as anxiety. This is the anxiety neurosis, and it differs from hysteria in that no psychological systems are activated. Later Freud postulated the existence of anxiety hysteria, which is a phobic state, and combines elements of anxiety neurosis and hysteria (Freud 1909).

We have discussed a continuum from anxiety neurosis to conversion hysteria and finally to anxiety hysteria in the paper "The Unconscious." Freud first postulated the existence of anxiety hysteria when discussing Little Hans (Freud 1909). In *Studies on Hysteria* he had not yet established the psychodynamic features that enabled him to postulate that the actual neuroses are, in a manner of speaking, core neuroses, which become elaborated into the psychoneuroses as they acquire defensive superstructures. Here, he was impressed with the ubiquity of sexual factors in all psychopathology—anxiety neurosis, neurasthenia, hysteria, and anxiety hysteria. Neurasthenia is a depletion state in which sexual energy, instead of being accumulated, is drained off through constant masturbation, and the symptoms these patients suffer from are manifestations of this depleted state: fatigue, headaches, lack of energy and initiative, and perhaps despondency.

Freud proceeded to diagnose the patients discussed in this book. Anna O., he believed, was a rare example of pure hysteria. I find this opinion difficult to understand in view of the wide variety of symptoms she suffered from, ranging from somatic disturbances to complex dissociative and hallucinatory states. Since we have not discussed Freud's patients we need not enumerate the diagnoses he made. Freud conjectured that all of his patients had mixed neuroses with hysterical elements and sexual disturbances. At this point, he still believed that syphilis was a predisposing factor in the production of hysteria. Somehow he linked this illness with constitutional weakness, although I am not certain whether he thought that syphilis created such a weakness or whether congenitally weak persons were especially prone to syphilis. Perhaps he was having some difficulty in breaking away from the prejudice of the medical community against hysterics.

The formulation of the actual neurosis may be an intermediate step between hereditary weakness and the psychoneuroses. Instead of dwelling on an organically based inferiority, Freud postulated that patients suffering from the actual neuroses have a lowered threshold for developing psychoneuroses. What leads to the acquisition is not specifically discussed, and Freud left room for the possibility that hereditary and constitutional factors may be important. Regarding the anxiety neurosis, Freud was quite explicit in pointing out its situational etiology, which we will soon discuss in detail.

Freud now returned to the fact that not all hysterics can be hypnotized. The cathartic method of treatment has drawbacks and limitations; e.g., it has no influence on casual factors. Freud, however, here defended the cathartic method, stating that some of the difficulties of this method are not inherent in the method itself and may be due to accidental complications possibly related to the patient's personal circumstances. Freud compared this to surgical complications unrelated to the technical procedure.

What about complications that are related to the doctor's personal circumstances rather than the patient's? This question introduces countertransference factors, which can never be ignored. Still, it must be remembered that the cathartic method obscures the transference–countertransference interaction because of the therapist's active use of suggestion and directing the patient's attention to traumatic events.

Symptomatic therapies, according to Freud, are not to be scoffed at. A treatment that deals with etiological factors would not be able to undo the harmful effects of symptoms, although it could arrest their development. Psychoanalysis is, of course, a treatment method that attempts to resolve basic conflicts; in other words, it is designed to unearth causal sequences. Freud was evidently involved here with concrete medical sequences of pathogenicity and degeneration. He had not considered the psyche's plasticity or its tendency to achieve higher states of integration once constriction and inhibiting forces are overcome.

In cases of acute hysteria, Freud felt that the cathartic method is completely successful. Apparently, he believed that some patients with sexual problems have acute hysterical neuroses, and he referred to fluctuations in sexual tension.

Freud did not always explain how he arrived at his conclusions. Obviously he was struggling to organize his clinical concepts. The chief theme of his clinical formulations is that traumatic factors are important determinants in the production of hysteria. He had already recognized, as had Breuer, that there is no single etiology. He, as did Breuer earlier in the book, postulated the principle of overdetermination, that many variables are involved in the causation of a neurosis. An acute hysterical neurosis is principally due to trauma. Inasmuch as the traumatic element is in the foreground, such a neurosis is amenable to catharsis and abreaction. Freud was impressed with the ubiquity of sexuality, so it would logically follow that the traumas involved are sexual. Soon after he postulated an etiological theory of neuroses based upon the infantile occurrence of sexually traumatic events.

Freud again compared hysteria with organic illnesses. He referred to "spontaneous" cures and acknowledged an objection to the cathartic method: the symptoms it clears up would be resolved during the natural course of the malady. However, he asserted that treatment leads to a strengthening of the ego, which gives it greater capacity to deal with pathogenic influences. In this regard, the cathartic method accomplishes more than alleviation of symptoms.

Each hysterical symptom represents a weak point in the ego. In what essentially began as a monosymptomatic hysteria, further symptoms will develop similar in nature to the initial symptom. This would indicate that the aberrant symptomatic producing impulses break the same weak spot of the psychic apparatus. This weakness is a *locus minoris resistentia*.

When I was a medical student, one of my supervisors scolded me because I asked whether it would be necessary to do a physical examination on a patient who had clearly described a hysterical paralysis of the left arm, including glove anaesthesia, as well as other typical hysterical symptoms such as tunnel vision. My supervisor became harsh with me because he recognized that the likelihood of an organic illness was greater with this patient than in another without hysterical symptoms. He reasoned that a hysterical symptom will choose a part of the body that is or has been damaged. For instance, if the muscles of one arm were atrophied and weakened because of poliomyelitis, hysterical paralysis would focus on that arm rather than the other, healthy one.

However, such dramatic somatic symptoms as hysterical paralysis and tunnel vision are seldom encountered. In my experience, patients who do have them often belong to minority groups. I have also encountered such symptoms in groups that are relatively unsophisticated: I saw a fair number of conversion reactions in the army among a rural population; In Brazil, clinicians frequently find classical hysterics among practitioners of voodoo; I also have seen some in the clinics of a city hospital but never in my private practice.

Freud pointed out that the cathartic method is exhausting and time consuming. The physician must be dedicated to the patient, and must also have respect and fondness for him. With other types of treatment, such as those of ordinary medicine, it does not matter so much whether the doctor has personal sympathy for patients. In the treatment of the neuroses, however, some kind of good feeling is essential. The patient also has to be sensitive, intelligent, and singularly motivated.

Perhaps Freud asked too much both of his patients and of himself. Still, once a patient is in analysis or being treated by the cathartic treatment, the sharing of intimacies creates some kind of emotional bond. Freud was in essence discussing the role of transference in the therapeutic process. Although I realize I may be giving Freud more credit than he deserves, his statements are suggestive and need only slight extending to bring them in perspective with modern technical considerations.

I believe Freud was referring here to both transference and suggestion. In all patient–doctor relationships the patient attributes some degree of authority to the therapist but Freud went further. He postulated that built into the neurotic condition is a propensity to give the doctor certain powers. In today's language, we would say that transference becomes manifest in regressed states. The analyst's influence can be viewed as the result of the patient's need to be rescued by an omnipotent protector, clearly an infantile wish.

Now Freud returned to technique and reminded us of his assertion that not all hysterical patients can be hypnotized: some patients refuse to submit themselves to hypnosis, and others seem quite willing to be put in a trance but the hypnotist is unable to accomplish anything significant. According to Freud, both types of patients have a resistance to being hypnotized. This resistance must have its own origins. Nothing about hypnosis itself warrants resistance. Obviously, it is what is associated with hypnosis that is threatening. To patients with certain personality types, having someone else in control and being passive may be threatening. For instance, some masochistic subjects enjoy hypnosis, but others may have considerable conflict and fear of exposing the helpless and vulnerable parts of their self-representations.

How hypnosis operates is far from clear. When I was a resident I tried to hypnotize a middle-aged woman patient suffering from hysterical aphonia. I believed this was a good opportunity to demonstrate the dramatic curative effects of hypnosis, although I was not contemplating the emergence of traumatic experiences. My intention was simply to use suggestion and persuasion to get the patient to regain her normal voice. I tried very hard to hypnotize her, but as far as I could discern my efforts were completely thwarted. I felt especially frustrated, perhaps chagrined, when the patient, in a soft whisper, tried to console me. I felt as if she had been in complete control and that I had been manipulated. She seemed quite pleased, in a patronizing fashion. I asked her to come back the next day so we could try again. She smiled pleasantly, indicating, I thought, that she knew better. I did not expect her to return, but she did. However, she was no longer aphonic. She told me that she had felt an uncontrollable drowsiness the previous afternoon. She took a nap and awakened with her normal voice! Since then I have never again used hypnosis. Perhaps she felt that the second attempt at hypnosis would break through her defense of condescending manipulative superiority so she decided to give me a present by giving up her symptom, thus sparing herself what might become a threatening ordeal.

Freud did not like hypnosis. He had to devise a technique of treatment that did not require expanding the patient's sphere of consciousness by putting him in a trance. Perhaps this could be accomplished in another way. Freud described a memorable episode that occurred during his treatment of Emmy von N., (p. 56). While the patient was being massaged he observed that her conversation was not rambling and without meaning. He found that it led to the same pathogenic complexes he had encountered during hypnosis. This is the first description of free association.

Freud here illustrated what, to my mind, is the most fascinating feature of psychoanalysis—how theory and technique are so completely intertwined. Because Freud found hypnosis ineffective, he had to seek a method that gave him access to the patient's unconscious while the patient was awake. In his search, he made observations about the patient's behavior which could be translated into psychic processes that gave him clinical understanding from a psychodynamic viewpoint. He opened new vistas that have become the foundation of modern concepts of psycho-pathology. He began by recalling a hypnotic experiment conducted by Bernheim. Bernheim told the subject, who was in a trance, that she would not be able to see him. He was trying to create a negative hallucination. Then he hovered over her and made all sorts of bizarre gestures, but she took absolutely no notice of him. Then he awakened her and asked her to describe his actions. She replied that she was unable to describe anything, apparently because she had seen nothing. Bernheim insisted that she could and as he kept pressing her to remember, she finally was able to recall everything. As discussed earlier, Freud's observance of posthypnotic suggestion by Bernheim led him to formulate the theory of the dynamic unconscious. And in our present context, Freud was able to use Bern-heim's results in order to devise a treatment approach that does not require hypnosis.

Freud also relied heavily on insistence, asking his patients about the circumstances surrounding the onset of symptoms. It is hard to imagine that a patient today would be able to supply that type of information. This is due to several factors, perhaps the most important being that we seldom encounter clear-cut symptoms with a definitive beginning. Freud also found it difficult to collect such data, but he was able to explain the difficulties. He noted that as he kept insisting that they reproduce the events associated with the onset of symptoms, some patients were able to bring some bits to the surface. The more he insisted, the more they were able to recall. This was a laborious and tiresome procedure, and Freud felt that the harder he insisted, the more the patient fought him. He viewed the procedure as a struggle, as a battle of wills. The patient's efforts to not bring various experiences to conscious awareness is part of resistance.

Freud was quite perceptive when he recognized that the resistance that was directed against his exploration is the same force that is responsible for the initial formation of symptoms. This is what I meant above about the intertwining of theory and technique. Freud's need to devise a psychotherapeutic procedure led him to conclusions about the psychopathological process. He began to understand hysteria as the outcome of conflicting forces, and he used such words as defense to indicate that one part of the personality had to institute defensive measures to protect it from unconscious forces that were perceived as dangerous. These same defenses, now known as resistance, are directed against the therapist who tries to uncover the unconscious pathogenic complexes.

Freud's procedure for eliciting information from his patients was simple. He pressed his hand against the patient's forehead and assured him that some picture or thought would appear, usually in connection with the traumatic event. Apparently he first used the technique on Elisabeth von R., the last of the case histories reported in the *Studies on Hysteria*. There is a slight contradiction as to the method he used; in one section of the book Freud stated that something will occur to the patient as he applies pressure, but elsewhere he stated that this happens only after the pressure is released. Anyway, by 1904 or perhaps earlier, Freud had abandoned this technique.

The resistance took many forms. Often patients reported that nothing occurred the first time Freud applied pressure, in spite of Freud's insistence that something would emerge and not to withhold anything for any reason whatsoever. Some time later they would admit they had had thoughts, which were there even the first time Freud asked, but they had thought they were too trivial to mention, or on other occasions, acknowledged that the thoughts were too painful. Freud wondered whether the unconscious had an intelligence of its own because of the varied rationalizations behind the patient's deliberate withholding, but he rejected this idea.

Freud was describing suppression rather than repression, inasmuch as the patient had thoughts or memories but consciously refused to express them. This is confusing because it seems to imply that resistance is a conscious phenomenon. Yet, according to Freud, the essence of the therapeutic process is to make resistance conscious and then to do away with it.

Of course, the analytic process is much more complicated than that, but the question as to whether resistance is conscious or unconscious is important. Freud pointed out here that the manifestations of resistance are conscious; because of the pressure technique, the patient suppresses, but is unaware that he is resisting the process and does not understand his motives for resisting. The therapist, however, cannot proceed directly to the unconscious core of the patient's conflicts.

When the patient finally acknowledges that something has occurred to him as a result of the stimulus of the pressure technique, he may speak of familiar memories in a new context or thoughts that serve as intermediary links to the pathogenic complex. Being a clinician, Freud supplied a series of vignettes to support his belief that the pressure technique will produce significant results. He also discussed various elements of the therapeutic relationship, such as the physician's personal influence and the fostering of what today we would consider a therapeutic alliance. He emphasized that the motive for resistance must be weakened and replaced by another motive, which he does not explicitly define but which could easily be considered to be the fostering of the self-observing function.

It is remarkable how much detail Freud provides in describing the various characteristics of the pressure technique, considering that psychoanalysis was only just beginning. Because of clinical demands, it may have been necessary for Freud to formulate technical innovations long before he had a complex and sophisticated underlying theoretical system. His therapeutic principles were consistent with his conceptual foundation, but the former were much further advanced than the latter. In fact, some of his ideas about treatment are strikingly modern, such as the development of the self-observing function through establishment of an analytic setting. Freud did not exactly state it in this fashion, but he did write about his respect for his patient and the workings of the patient's mind. He advocated an attitude which is noncritical of the content of the patient's associations, but he condemned resistance. Freud's attitude was considerably mitigated when he gave up the pressure technique for free association. Then he did not have to insist overtly about anything. The patient could pursue the course of his thoughts or feelings without being commanded to explore a specific area.

The reader of Freud's writings can discern that Freud's conviction about the importance of conflicts and defenses—psychodynamic considerations—kept intensifying and gradually replaced formulations that apparently were made in collaboration with Breuer. Freud postulated three types of hysteria: (1) defense hysteria, (2) hypnoid hysteria and (3) retention hysteria in this chapter. Obviously he preferred to think of his patients in terms of defense hysteria. His theory that unacceptable impulses emanating from the unconscious seek access to consciousness is still useful today. This unacceptable impulse, which Freud soon after identified as sexual, is barred from consciousness by the censor through the defense mechanism of repression. The impulse is weakened in that it is divested of its affect, which is converted into somatic excitation. The mechanism that leads to the formation of somatic hysterical symptoms is conversion, and the exploration of these processes creates resistances that are the outcome of repressive forces.

Hypnoid and retention hysteria, on the other hand, do not involve resistance. However, the only case of hypnoid hysteria that Freud felt any certitude about is that of Anna O.. This may be a subtle rejection of Breuer's ideas: Freud may have paid lipservice to the concepts of hypnoid states, but then he remarked that the only such case in existence was Breuer's patient.

Retention hysteria is very difficult to understand. Freud's explanation is far from satisfactory, but then it is likely that Freud was not particularly satisfied with this diagnosis. The most we can say about it is that the traumatic situation cannot be discharged, for one of the reasons mentioned earlier, but since there is no resistance it is easily disposed of by abreaction. Freud wryly remarked that one of these "easy to treat" patients turned out to be a very difficult patient.

Throughout the remaining few pages of *Studies on Hysteria*, Freud used a psychodynamic frame of reference. In essence, he constructed a psychological model, the first ever created in psychoanalysis. He had models in the *Project for a Scientific Psychology* (Freud 1895), but they were neurological models. In discussing his psychodynamic model, Freud first described a central nucleus around which similar types of memories arranged in a linear fashion are concentrically stratified. These various strata represent the resistance and become stronger as they get nearer to the central core. He then postulated a third type of organization, a dynamic one, in which psychic elements are organized according to thought content. A logical thread takes an irregular and twisting path toward the nucleus, moving back and forth between strata and forming a zigzag broken line. Freud aptly compared this movement to that of a knight on a chessboard, but the psychodynamic situation is even more complex than this. The zigzag line has nodal points. Two or more similar threads will converge upon one another and then pursue their course together. Freud, here, is describing the multidetermined or overdetermined etiology of hysterical symptoms. Figure 1 is a diagrammatic interpretation of Freud's model.

Freud conceded that this model became further complicated when he considered the possibility of a second pathological nucleus, resulting in the outbreak of a second hysterical attack that has its own etiology but which is, in some way, related to an earlier acute hysteria.

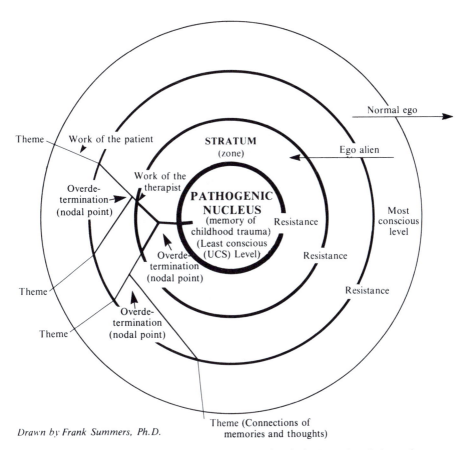

Drawn by Frank Summers, Ph.D.

Figure 1. Freud's early model of the pathogenesis of single-outbreak hysteria (*Studies on Hysteria* pp. 288–295). Each circle layer represents a given level of consciousness ("modification of consciousness"). The increasing thickness of the lines between layers represents increasing resistance at the more unconscious levels.

Freud's talent for constructing metaphors that foreshadow much later theoretical developments, was once again exercised here. He compared these pathological nuclei to foreign bodies. A foreign body within the psyche today would be considered a destructive introject that cannot be assimilated and has to be encapsulated. Freud was always the first to acknowledge the limitations of his metaphors, and he questioned the clear-cut separation of the foreign body from the surrounding inflamed tissue. So he then modified his idea about a foreign body and called it instead an infiltration, indicating that it is difficult to differentiate the pathological from nonpathological, especially as we probe into deeper layers of the psyche. This also has its therapeutic implications. The therapist does not extirpate the pathological nucleus; he merely removes the resistance and by so doing re-establishes the circulation, which leads to healing.

This formulation defines the essence of psychoanalytic treatment. Some hindrance, an obstacle to development, is removed by projection, and what can be considered an innate developmental drive is once again set in motion. The analyst helps create a situation in which self-healing can occur. This treatment procedure has a psychodynamic foundation.

Freud relentlessly pursued memories through various layers. However, only one memory can pass through the narrow straits of consciousness at a time. This point was made repeatedly by Freud in his later writings, especially in *The Interpretation of Dreams* (Freud 1900).

This model is mechanistic and has detective-like qualities, both in terms of solving riddles and pursuing the culprit (the traumatic sexual incidents). Still, Freud learned a good deal from this approach, and today many of the observations he made are part of our clinical experience.

At this point in the text, Freud again de-emphasized the role of suggestion and asserted that we can not influence the patient by making a bad guess or wrong interpretation; it will do no harm, and the patient will eventually set the analyst back on the right track.

This seems to be an invulnerable position: an analyst can do no harm; he can make correct or incorrect interpretations, and it does not matter. If that is the case, anyone with an imagination can practice analysis. Of course, the problem is not that simple. Analytic skill resides in the therapist's ability to hear the patient, to learn from him, and to accept his corrections gratefully. That is not as easy as it sounds. Many analysts would rather blame the patient for resisting than recognize that they themselves might have been wrong. To protect themselves from acknowledging errors, analysts make further interpretations, not to help the patient gain understanding but to maintain their self-esteem and to attack the patient. To me, this is using professionalism as a defense for the analyst.

The analytic interaction has many subtle aspects. Somatic symptoms can participate in the "dialogue"; and Freud mentioned that they join in the conversation; when a particular area that had something to do with the production of the symptoms becomes activated in treatment, the symptom may intensify. In therapy, the patient may have to get worse in order to feel better, an aphorism we have all heard and which dates back to this book.

Sometimes after an important piece of analytic work has been done, the patient remarks that he had always known what has been uncovered; he may recognize this as the self-deception it is. Memories at the peripheral layers of the psyche always had access to consciousness, but their relationship to deeper layers was unknown. Their intermediary links with other thoughts enabled them to achieve conscious representation as material emanated from the unconscious nucleus. Just as frequently, however, a patient whose treatment has been successful will still not be able to remember, although convinced of the validity of what has been reconstructed. This fact caused Freud to wonder if the anlaysis has actually *created* memories or thoughts that previously were only potentials. This leads, in my mind, to two interesting questions: First, does the therapeutic interaction create psychic structures that produce memories and fantasies that were not operative in the production of the initial psychopathology? Our experiences with patients fixated on early stages of development indicate that this does, in fact, occur. Second, do all of the psychic elements associated with the patient's disturbance have to come to light? Freud believed that the essence of psychoanalytic resolution is the lifting of infantile amnesia. Still, this seems to happen rarely in current analyses. Perhaps when patients regress to primitive mental states, the content is preverbal. When this content is expressed in terms of fantasies, they are not actual memories or occurrences. The analysis has made it possible to communicate what had previously been incapable of being communicated. Early symbiotic and presymbiotic ego states gain secondary process accretions. When they emerge in analysis, they do not represent an actual replication of the past; they are more refined, so to speak, and are a product of the analytic interaction.

Freud now returned to technical issues. He considered the possibility that the pressure technique may fail, in which case the patient may not have any further associations because he has run out of them, so to speak. This would mean that the patient has resolved his problems and there is nothing more to be said. The patient's tranquility and "calmness of facial expression" confirm this viewpoint. But do patients, even if they are ready to terminate analysis, ever run out of associations? This would be hardly conceivable if we accept the concept of a timeless and continuously active unconscious. So Freud then considered that the cessation of associations may be the outcome of resistance, a reluctance to enter into deeper levels of the psyche. He had already discussed resistance, but he extended it here by placing it in the context of the patient–therapist relationship.

Freud considered disturbances of this relationship to be the greatest therapeutic obstacle that can be encountered. He was describing transference; he emphasized the resistive elements of the transference relationship in a later paper (Freud 1912). This was Freud's first use of transference in its psychoanalytic sense. There are several ways in which transference may manifest itself. First, the patient may denigrate the psychoanalytic procedure or the physician because she* feels insulted or not sufficiently appreciated. She may also have heard negative comments about the analyst or his method. These difficulties, according to Freud, can be easily resolved through discussion and explanation. In a sense, Freud was ignoring his most important postulate, that of psychic determinism, in which the patient's attitudes have an unconscious component. The psychoanalytic viewpoint always focuses on the contribution of intrapsychic processes. Instead he here considered their exclusive source to be the external world. Next, Freud dealt with the transference reaction that is commonly encountered today in the treatment of patients suffering from structural defects, especially patients with a poorly structured identity sense, who are afraid of becoming too attached or too dependent upon the analyst. Freud believed that they were concerned about losing their independence or of becoming sexually attracted to the analyst. (Today, we would refer to this as the patient's dread of losing autonomy.) Finally, Freud wrote about the content of transference feelings being determined by displacement, which he called "false connections." In order to ensure the success of treatment, these obstacles have to be overcome by making them conscious.

The depth of Freud's insights about the therapeutic process in this earliest of psychoanalytic communications is truly astounding. He recognized that what is transferred onto the therapist has genetic antecedents. Moreover, he reached the interesting conclusion that the patient's resistance to recognizing transference feelings is equally as great as the resistance to acknowledging conflictful feelings toward the external object of the infantile environment.

Studies on Hysteria ends with a laconic and, in my mind, somewhat pessimistic statement about therapeutic outcome: "Much will be gained if we succeed in transforming . . . hysterical misery into common unhappiness."

*For some unknown reason, Freud always referred to patients with transference resistance as female.

3

"Further Remarks on the Defence Neuro-Psychoses" (1896)

SYNOPSIS

This article represents a natural extension of *Studies on Hysteria,* as Freud here scientifically departed from Breuer and pursued his clinical investigations in the context of his developing psycho-dynamic concepts. This frame of reference became the mainstay of psychoanalysis, understandably so since it developed from the hypothesis of the dynamic unconscious and psychic determinism. It gave breadth to a deterministic unconscious and became the foundation of psychoanalysis. This paper is where the word psychoanalysis first appeared.

Freud here emphasized basic etiological factors. He retained the belief that trauma is a significant causative agent but emphasized that all traumas are sexual. This pronouncement stimulated negative reactions (and still does to some extent today) and caused many clinicians to reject psychoanalysis. In some quarters psychoanalysis and sex were synonymous, as Freud continued to postulate that a sexually traumatic incident could be discovered to be the basis of every neurosis. We know that not much later he revised this viewpoint so that a fantasy of a trauma, rather than an actual trauma, would suffice to cause neurosis.

Freud distinguished separate etiological bases of hysteria and the obsessional neurosis. In hysteria, the trauma occurs around age 3 or 4 and was passively experienced, whereas the obsessive neurotic usually actively seduces a younger child and suffers from unconscious self-reproach. Freud did not write about the unconscious sense of guilt until many years later (Freud 1923), but unconscious self-reproach could easily be viewed as being similar.

Freud was beginning to understand psychopathology in terms of conflict and defense. He identified the various neuroses on the basis of characteristic defensive processes. He had not yet postulated specific conflicts and fixation points, but he had already described the different defenses that distinguished hysterics from the obsessive neuroses.

In the final section of this paper, Freud gave a fairly detailed account of his treatment of a paranoid woman, demonstrating how she used projective mechanisms, and he was able to understand her delusions and hallucinations as being the outcome of the defense of projection and regression.

This paper is an extension of Freud's earlier paper "The Neuro-Psychoses of Defence" (Freud 1894). These are among the first of his clinical studies in which he presented his ideas without Breuer's contributions and moved further in the direction of psychological and away from neurological explanations. It is not surprising that the term *psychoanalysis* first appeared in this paper. Psychoanalysis was immediately identified with theories about sex. Freud postulated that the etiology of the neuroses can be traced back to sexual trauma in childhood. A year later Freud began to doubt whether these traumas actually occurred or whether they were the products of fantasy. He revealed his doubts in a letter to Fliess (Freud 1950, letter 69), but he did not publicly announce his repudiation of these ideas until ten years later (Freud 1906). It appears that Freud was extremely disturbed about having been "deceived" by his patients, but I doubt that he ever considered giving up psychoanalysis (as I have heard some analysts who had known Freud personally state, such as Franz Alexander). Freud was in the midst of his self-analysis and had just discovered the Oedipus complex. I would say he was in the vortex of ideas coming from various areas such as his patients, self-analysis, and his studies of the dream process. He had to sort things out.

In the first section of this paper, Freud discussed the specific etiology of hysteria. Still adhering to Breuer's formulations about undischarged affects caused by early trauma, he focused upon the qualities of trauma, which must be sexual and which occurs very early in life, usually around 3 or 4 years of age. The trauma may go back to the limits of memory (age 1½ to 2) but not after ages 8 to 10. The trauma has to be passively experienced and must consist of an "actual irritation of the genitals (of processes resembling copulation)." Usually an adult—a relative, sometimes the father in the cases of female hysterics, who seem to be more numerous than males—is the instigator. For boys, nursemaids, governesses, and domestic servants were frequently implicated.

Modern family structure, which is so different from that of mid-Victorian times, and the current paucity of live-in domestic help, could be partially responsible for the infrequency of hysteria today. This seems to be somewhat of an oversimplification, although it may be true that the type of seductions Freud discussed may not be as frequent today. We know that incest still occurs quite often, but it seems to result in severe personality disturbances rather than conversion hysteria.

Freud noted from his observations of patients that older children, for example, male siblings, were often responsible for the seduction. Both parties fell ill of what Freud now refers to as a defense neurosis, the older child of an obsessional neurosis, and the younger of hysteria. Again, the actual incident of sexual trauma is no longer considered to be the crucial determining factor.

Freud did not consider masturbation in itself to be a trauma, but rather the consequence of trauma. This conclusion makes considerable sense in a clinical context. Early traumas, which we often think of as being assaultive in a terrifying sense—rather than simply frightening or seductive and thus to some extent pleasurable—lead to states of disruption. Because of an intrusive environment, the child does not achieve efficient adaptive techniques to master inner tension and unbearable feelings of annihilation. Masturbation could represent an attempt at self-soothing and organizing inner chaos.

Freud made an important distinction between traumas occurring early in childhood and those later in life. After puberty the memory trace of the early traumas is aroused and is responsible for the outbreak of hysteria. Infantile traumas have greater effects than those of adulthood because they are inflicted upon a child in a state of sexual immaturity. Freud made the interesting point that the revival of the memory of the trauma during sexual maturity will have a greater effect than the actual traumatic event did when it happened; the trauma will provoke strong excitations because the sexual apparatus is capable of reacting, whereas previously this was not the case. This Freud called the deferred effect of a childhood trauma.

I do not believe that Freud was one-sided in explaining the genesis of neuroses simply on the basis of when traumas occur and how they are experienced. He added that there are persons who have experienced traumas but have not developed a neurosis. He believed that other factors are also involved in the formation of neuroses, particularly constitutional factors. Freud was heading toward a theory of neuroses and was grappling with the problem of the choice of neurosis by concentrating on several variables: The nature of the trauma is important, as stressed here, but specific defenses are characteristic of particular neuroses. Freud also formulated later that these defenses are associated with certain kinds of conflicts and levels of psychosexual development. Here he was just beginning to delineate the role of defenses in determining how psychopathology is formed.

In section 2 of this article, Freud turned his attention to the conditions that underlie the obsessional neuroses. The future obsessional patient has aggressively indulged in pleasurable sexual acts. This accounts, according to Freud, for the prevalence of obsessional males. This sexual aggression, inasmuch as it occurs in childhood (after the age of 8), is precocious, and it always implies a previous experience of being seduced, which explains why obsessional patients have an underlying layer of hysterical symptoms.

Obsessional thoughts are transformed self-reproaches, which in turn are reactions to aggressive sexual acts. As in hysteria, repression is a dominant defense mechanism; during childhood these self-reproaches are repressed, but later they break through the repressive barrier and cause the formation of the obsessional neurosis.

Freud outlined the development of the obsessional neurosis as follows: the earliest period, in which seductions occur, is called childhood immorality. Seduction makes later repression possible. If the child was a passive participant in the sexual encounter, the groundwork has been laid for later hysteria. Childhood immorality is followed by acts of sexual aggression against the other sex that cause acts involving self-reproach during the outbreak of the obsessional illness.

It is not clear from the above description how far this immorality extends. Although Freud would not formulate the existence of a superego for many years (Freud 1923) he was writing here about a childhood span where there is very little superego operation. However, the self-reproaches that follow indicate that there must have been a superego, one which may have been unusually harsh. Indeed, Freud later emphasized the obsessional patient's strict conscience (Freud 1909b). Furthermore, he believed the superego is heir to the Oedipus complex (Freud 1923), which occurs around age 4. The period preceding the development of the Oedipus complex contains the seeds of later hysteria, whereas the post-oedipal period, characterized by the influence of the superego, leads to obsessional neurosis.

Modern views about superego formation differ from Freud's in that the superego's beginning has been pushed further back on the developmental timetable. This is in accord with our observations of obsessional patients, who seem to be fixated at relatively primitive levels of emotional development. The obsessional patient attaches self-reproaches to memories of pleasurable childhood sexual actions. However, the initial experience of sexual passivity leads to repression, which is maintained by what Freud called primary symptoms of defense: conscientiousness, shame, and self-distrust. The latter two are part of the self-reproaches, but conscientiousness is the outcome of reaction formation, a formulation that Freud arrived at later (Freud 1909b).

Freud believed that the sexual maturation of the obsessional patient occurs prematurely. Sexual precocity is usually the outcome of a stimulating environment, which is often experienced as intrusive and assaultive. Precociousness becomes a character defense to protect the self against disruptive excitement. Freud described traumatic incidents that could easily lead to the construction of such a defense.

Freud then continued explaining the development of the obsessional neurosis. After the formation of defenses, such as reaction formation, a period of apparent health or successful defenses, there is another phase, which is characterized by the return of the repressed, that is, a failure of defense. The self-reproaches emerge from repression but they appear in consciousness as compromises between the repressed ideas and the repressing forces. Freud had already described these compromises as occurring in the production of conversion symptoms. The participation of conflicting forces regularly occurs in the production of all symptoms and is not limited to any particular neurosis. The return of the repressed in these patients, however, is experienced as obsessional ideas and affects.

It is remarkable how much Freud understood about the obsessional patient in this early paper. He wrote of two types of obsessional neurosis, depending upon whether what enters consciousness represents the *content* of the act or the *affect* connected with the self-reproach. Much later, while discussing the famous case of the Rat Man (Freud 1909b), he elaborated on this distinction, emphasizing that the symptoms of the obsessional neurosis are dominated either by the id impulse or the superego prohibition. In his 1896 paper, he did not use the term superego but he was clearly referring to it.

Because of repressing forces, symptoms are the products of disguise. Regarding symptoms chiefly determined by instinctual forces, something contemporary replaces events or feelings belonging to the infantile past and something sexual is replaced by analogous but nonsexual elements.

Self-reproach can emerge as shame or hypochondriacal anxiety. The latter is manifested by fear of physical injury, which signifies punishment for the sexual misdeed, and may lead to delusions of being noticed. Although Freud was here describing projection of the superego, he did not discuss projection per se until the next and final section of this paper.

At this point in the paper, Freud discussed what today we would call characterological defenses. He stated that the ego creates secondary defenses to protect itself against the derivatives of the initially repressed memories. These defenses consist of protective measures against obsessional actions and affects, and often consist of very complicated rituals. They never contain aggression, although they are defenses against aggression. Later (Freud 1909b) these protective measures were called compulsions. Compulsions emanate from the superego and use the defense mechanism of undoing; that is, they are designed to undo the destructive intent inherent in the obsessional preoccupation. Many of the symptoms of the obsessional (or as we are more prone to say, the obsessive-compulsive patient) may be explained on this basis.

In the final section of this paper, Freud presented material from the treatment of a 32-year-old, married, paranoid patient, who Breuer had referred to him. Freud treated her with what he called the "Breuer method," and referred to the therapy as psychoanalysis.

Freud had definitely stated that psychoanalysis was contraindicated for patients suffering from narcissistic neurosis, and he included the psychoses in this category. This was based upon his conclusion that these patients would not be able to form transferences. However, clinical experience has amply demonstrated that this conclusion is not true, although some clinicians question whether such transferences are manageable.

Freud, at this early point in his career, did not consider contraindications to treatment, but he was not really using Breuer's method. Breuer had hypnotized Anna O. and then attempted to get his patient to discharge pent-up affects, that is to abreact. Freud, however, did not use hypnosis, but instead applied the pressure technique. His concept of the therapeutic process, however, was the same as Breuer's; he fought through the resistance in order to bring unconscious memories and their corresponding affects to the surface.

Freud compared paranoia with hysteria and obsessional neurosis which he treated in a similar fashion. He concluded that paranoia is also based upon defense, "a psychosis of defence" but that it has a special mechanism of defense—projection—that distinguishes it from the two psychoneuroses, which also have their unique defensive mechanisms. Hysterics adapt through conversion mechanisms, and obsessional neurotics rely upon displacement.

Had Freud considered the role of transference in the therapeutic process? Freud later divided emotional illness into three categories; actual neuroses, transference neuroses, and narcissistic neuroses, and he concluded that only the transference neuroses could be treated by psychoanalysis. It might be understandable that in 1895 Freud would treat a case of paranoia, because he had not yet made such distinctions. Certainly, Freud knew about transference as a phenomenon, but I doubt whether he knew anything beyond that. I do not believe he viewed it then as a therapeutic vehicle. He wrote about transference in *Studies on Hysteria*, and mentioned it again in *The Interpretation of Dreams* (Freud 1900) as a theoretical rather than clinical concept, as a transference of cathexis from the unconscious to the preconscious. He first emphasized transference in the framework of a treatment relationship in his report on Dora (Freud 1905). He treated Dora several years before he wrote up her case. He acknowledged that the analysis was prematurely terminated because he failed to recognize and to analyze the erotic transference. Freud later returned to the subject of transference in an extensive fashion in his technical papers (Freud 1911-1915). In this paper, however, no mention whatsoever is made of transference.

The first signs of illness in the patient referred by Breuer occurred six months after the birth of her child. She became noncommunicative, and distrustful of her husband's siblings. She also perceived that her neighbors in the small town she lived in had become rude and inconsiderate. She felt as if she were being watched. (This is a fairly typical beginning paranoid picture.) One day, while home alone with her maid, she felt some sensation in her lower abdomen, which she believed was caused by an improper thought the maid had at that very moment. (This is an example of the omnipotence of thoughts, but we might consider it to be a reverse omnipotence: The maid's thoughts were omnipotent in that they could affect and produce somatic changes in the patient.) The patient's symptoms intensified to the degree that she had to be hospitalized. In the sanatorium, she began to have visual hallucinations consisting of images of the lower part of a woman's abdomen with pubic hair. Sometimes she would see male genitals as well. These hallucinations vanished after several months.

Visual hallucinations are often found in patients with organic and toxic psychoses. Such patients should be carefully evaluated medically and neurologically. However, Freud's patient did not seem to have any physical ailment. After the visual hallucinations disappeared, she developed auditory hallucinations, which are more typical of paranoid patients. She heard voices that critically commented about her movements and actions. Freud did not say whether these voices were male or female, but they reproached her and made threats. In a much later paper, Freud (1914) compared this type of hallucination to the acquisition of conscience, which even later became known as superego (Freud 1923); the child feels observed and criticized until he incorporates these moral judgments as his own. The paranoid patient undergoes a regressive degeneration of conscience, in that what has been internalized is again externalized.

Freud's patient concealed her hallucinations from him. The only unusual thing she revealed was that she had made appointments with her brother in order to confide something important to him but that she never did tell him anything.

Freud stated that this patient's behavior in treatment was similar to that of hysterical patients, meaning that the therapeutic process contained the same elements. Both types of patients resist the memories of past events that will explain symptoms. In this case, Freud placed the situations responsible for the illness in infancy. He did not link the symptoms in this patient with a trauma that occurred later in life, as he did with most of the other cases in *Studies on Hysteria*. What was responsible for the outbreak of symptoms at the age of 32? Freud provided no information except that six months earlier she had a child, whose sex is not given. Perhaps the sex of the child might have been significant in determining the symbiotic fusion, which the 6-month-old infant might be emerging from. It is now known that psychosis sometimes occurs after the birth of a child, (postpartum psychosis), and the mother "loses" part of herself. The loss of the child through birth may be experienced as a catastrophic narcissistic injury. What part of the self the mother projects into the infant varies. Some mothers view the baby as a hated, destructive part of the self. Separation may hinder the use of the child as a narcissistic extension or signify loss of control. The hated parts have once again become part of the self, which can lead to loss of psychic equilibrium. At 6 months of age, an infant is beginning to explore the external world as a separate entity and no longer completely molds himself with his mother. To a highly ambivalent mother, this can be intensely traumatic.

Seen in this context, some of Freud's patient's symptoms are understandable. Her feeling that others were looking at her critically might have been based on the fear that others would become aware, might detect her violent hatred. Not being able to trust others could signify not being able to trust herself, a feeling based upon her anxiety about losing control. Freud tried to understand and treat her in the same way he dealt with hysterical patients. Whatever we might think of his formulations, his observations are interesting. For example, he noted that the hallucinations of the lower part of the women's abdomens were accompanied by physical sensations in the patient's abdomen. This phenomenon reminds us of Tausk (1919), who wrote a very important paper, "On the Origin of the Influencing Machine in Schizophrenia," in which he stated that some paranoid patients hallucinate a machine that controls their bodies. A particular movement of part of the machine will cause a similar movement in the patient. The machine represents projections of the somatic aspects of the ego.

According to Freud, this patient revealed a series of memories in which she had felt ashamed of being naked in her bath in front of her mother, sister, and doctor. She also reproduced a memory dating back to the age of 6 in which she was undressing in front of her brother without feeling any shame. Freud was very clever in fitting these past memories with recent events and then using these connections to understand her symptoms. He learned that the patient's husband and brother quarreled. The patient stopped seeing her brother, and became depressed. Then she misinterpreted some remarks made by her sister-in-law as being snide allusions to her conduct with her brother. Freud made the very interesting point that the patient was concentrating on the sister-in-law's tone of voice more than on the content of what she said. This is typical of paranoid patients and makes their delusions impervious to correction by logic and facts. A truly paranoid delusion can not be confronted directly; the patient can manipulate reality in a way that will support his beliefs, and can turn something completely around to suit his needs.

I remember a story told to me of a resident who had a patient in his office, a paranoid young man, who claimed that someone was standing outside the door listening. The resident got up and opened the door to show the patient that no one was there. No one was there, but this had no effect on the patient. On the contrary, the resident's behavior merely strengthened his conviction. Of course, someone was listening, but he became invisible. The resident must have been concerned as to the truth of the patient's assertions if he had to get up and find out for himself. The paranoid patient is a master at making ad hoc assumptions to support his thesis, and within his unique framework he can be infuriatingly logical.

Freud also must have understood the rigidity of his patient's delusions. He did not try to correct them, but instead wanted to explore them and trace them back to their origins. Apparently the patient was somewhat cooperative and reproduced erotic early memories to which Freud could attach etiological significance.

If we are correct in surmising that the patient had structural defects accentuated by her child's evolving maturation, why would the patient's symptoms "join in the conversation," as Freud also describes for this treatment? This is not exactly deception, anymore than any defense is. The patient may have been focusing on the area of childhood sexual experiences because she sensed Freud's interest. She may have wanted to please him, and this may have been related to certain archaic needs of her own—to divert the treatment from painful, vulnerable areas. What Freud might have considered relevant material that would lead to synthesis may have been in itself a resistance. I agree that Freud's sessions helped his patient maintain synthesis, but not as the outcome of progressive structuralization. Rather, the setting may not have been conducive to regression. The patient may have experienced some erotic satisfaction from the treatment that enabled her to split off the rageful, destructive parts of herself.

Such patients often have a subtle understanding of the analytic process and can cleverly manipulate their therapist into not conducting analysis. True, there are not many therapists who wish to treat such patients analytically, but sometimes it happens that a therapist wants to attempt an analysis and meets with resistances that indicate that the patient is fundamentally quite sophisticated as to the essential elements of the analytic process. For instance, a patient, in his twenties was typically paranoid: He had ideas of reference and felt constantly observed. He believed that there was a pipeline between my office and that of his father so that everything said in our session could be heard and recorded. He also heard voices. In spite of his florid psychosis, he was eager to continue his sessions but did not want to be analyzed. In contrast to his other material, he had no esoteric notions about analysis. He simply did not want to lie down or free-associate. He knew that I felt uncomfortable in a face-to-face relationship and was aware of my negative feelings about engaging in a non-analytic relationship, but he was not concerned about my discomfort. He wanted things his way. For some reason, I decided not to insist upon his being on the couch and let matters develop as they would. My patient was especially astute in sensing other person's unconscious motivations. He would talk at great length as to how members of his family related to each other and to himself. He was quite psychologically oriented and described all of these interactions at the id level, making extensive use of symbols. He even listened to my contributions and felt very much at ease. Occasionally he would tease me, stating that what we were doing was not analysis. Still, if I tried to steer these discussions of unconscious motivation to myself, that is, if I attempted a transference interpretation, he would angrily retort, "Don't give me that psychoanalytic bullshit." This patient had gross defects in the reality sense, but his self-observing process was sufficiently operative that he could distinguish between a psychoanalytic and a nonpsychoanalytic exchange. He could use his awareness of the psychoanalytic process as a resistance.

Freud referred to his patient's wish to make appointments with her brother although she would have nothing to tell him during the appointment. We might think of this odd behavior in terms of fusion: if two persons are fused, words are superfluous. Freud preferred the patient's belief that she only had to look at her brother in order for him to understand her suffering; he was, in fact, the only person that could understand, since he was part of its etiology. After she had reproduced the various scenes of her sexual relationship with her brother, which lasted from age 6 to 10, her symptoms for the most part disappeared. However, in a footnote (pp. 180–181), Freud explained that he wrote up the case while the patient was still in treatment. In fact, her condition subsequently deteriorated and she had to be institutionalized. She continued on a downhill course, and eventually died of pneumonia during another hospitalization.

Freud's lack of therapeutic success with this patient, does not mean that all his formulations about her were invalid. He consistently stressed that her hallucinations represented parts of the content of repressed childhood experiences, the return of the repressed. He did not believe that the voices she heard were memories of past events, but rather were thoughts being spoken aloud. Another clinical vignette will substantiate this point. The patient, a brilliant scientist in his early thirties, could literally hear himself think. Whenever he was working on a problem, he would hear clear and distinct voices that would tell him the direction he should follow. These were benign, helpful voices, and I believe they were intrinsic to his talent and creative imagination. The range of his sensory spectrum was wider than usual. (This is similar to the expansion of the visual modality that is characterized by eidetic imagery.) It is interesting to note that, as this patient regressed, the voices degenerated into ordinary persecutory auditory hallucinations.

Freud observed that his patient's voices often made remarks about trivial items, but these remarks, which often had a "diplomatic indefiniteness," contained allusions to intimacies in her married life and family secrets. The voices were basically self-reproaches attached to her childhood trauma.

Freud made a similar formulation about the obsessional neurosis earlier in this paper. In the obsessional neurosis, however, the patient experiences self-reproach as self-distrust. By contrast, in paranoia, self-reproach is handled by projection, which results in distrust of others. This is the first time the defense mechanism of projection appears in the analytic literature. Freud (1911a) later described projection as involving the externalization of homosexual impulses, whereas here he limits himself to the patient's negative self-appraisal.

This last section of the paper is amazingly rich in its description of the paranoid's delusions. Freud added here that the content of visual hallucinations often consists of contemporary elements being substituted for infantile scenes. In this instance, the abdomen hallucinated was that of an adult rather than of a child. I am reminded of the trend in the theater of presenting plays in modern dress and contemporary settings. Many of the classics of the Greek theater have been produced in such a fashion.

There are many similarities between paranoia and obsessional neuroses. Many obsessionals regress to paranoid states. Freud believed that an essential difference between the two is that the paranoid patient does not construct secondary defenses against his symptoms, but instead incorporates the symptoms into the ego, causing an "alteration of the ego." I believe that Freud was writing about a structural change, an ego defect, which affects reality testing. Ideas that would correct the reality distortion are repressed. Today we would view this as a manifestation of impaired reality testing. Once again, very early in Freud's career, we can see the nucleus of concepts that are very much in the forefront today, in this instance the formulation of characterological psychopathology.

4

"On the Justification for Detaching a Particular Syndrome from Neurasthenia under the Description 'Anxiety Neurosis'" (1895)

SYNOPSIS

In this article Freud began to formulate a nosological scheme based upon his understanding of psychic mechanisms. He tried to place anxiety in a central position that helped him explain both symptoms and psychic operations that characterize specific psychopathological entities. First he postulated that anxiety was a physiological response, and he then stressed that the phobias of obsessional neuroses are psychologically motivated. This latter point seems self-evident, but Freud's view of anxiety as purely physiological and without psychic meaning is difficult for us to accept and seems almost non-analytic. Still, Freud was able to construct his clinical formulations in such a manner that he could fit them into a consistent and harmonious theoretical edifice. He postulated the existence of two neuroses, neurasthenia and the anxiety neurosis, which he called the actual neuroses and which were basically a manifestation of the discharge of libido without any mental content. However, as defenses are further formed, perhaps as superstructures to the actual neuroses, we find ourselves in the realm of the psychoneuroses. Anxiety is a driving force in the formation of psychopathology.

Freud was by now certain that sexuality was the primary etiological factor of the neuroses, whereas anxiety was the result of undischarged sexual tension, a formulation that is the essence of the first anxiety theory. A good portion of this article is concerned with examples to support this thesis, such as abstinence, coitus interruptus, and other acts that prevent final sexual consummation. However, contrary to what some of his opponents believed, Freud did not ignore the proposition that other factors beside sex may also be significant contributing causes to the production of emotional illness. He believed in the principle of multiple causality and wrote that the sexual component may be reenforced if the psyche's resistance is lowered by debilitating experiences, such as overwork.

Freud's emphasis throughout this paper was on inner forces striving for discharge, indicating that his formulations about anxiety were closely linked to his development of instinct theory.

━━━━━━━━━━
━━━━━━━━━━

As the title of this paper implies, Freud was attempting to make nosological distinctions. However, he also wanted to separate various entities in terms of inner forces and at the same time construct a comprehensive theory of anxiety. What Freud described here has been called the *conversion theory* or the *first anxiety theory*. Later, Freud (1926a) postulated what is now known as the *second anxiety theory* or the *signal theory of anxiety*, a theory that is somewhat different from and more ego psychologically oriented than the theory in this paper. Whether these two theories are really that different has been questioned. In my opinion, Freud was able to construct a continuum between the two theories and retained the belief that the first theory was applicable to primitive developmental periods, in which an imperfectly developed ego is very much at the mercy of the id, whereas the second theory applied to relatively well-structured ego states that have the capacity to respond to internal dangers with an alerting signal affect, which sets defensive processes in motion.

Neurasthenia, a term coined by the American psychiatrist and neurologist, G. M. Beard (1839–1883), apparently encompassed a large variety of symptoms. Freud felt it would be advantageous to distinguish from neurasthenia proper certain symptoms that seemed to be connected with each other. He believed by so doing he would demonstrate different etiologies. He concentrated on a particular syndrome whose components could be grouped around the main symptom of anxiety. He labeled this syndrome *anxiety neurosis* and went on to enumerate its symptoms. Alongside his descriptions, Freud made some interesting observations and conjectures, and he reached conclusions that became basic to later fundamental formulations. For example, the first quality that he found in patients suffering from anxiety neurosis was general irritability, a particular manifestation of which is auditory hyperesthesia (oversensitivity to noise).

Freud did not restrict this symptom to anxiety neurosis. He stated that it belongs to many different emotional states and attributed it to a general accumulation of psychic energy which is poorly tolerated. He related auditory hyperacuity to an innate relationship between sounds and fright, implying that the earliest frightening experiences are auditory; this is supported by observing the disruptive effect of noise upon the infant. I have seen this same type of hypersensitivity in patients suffering from structural defects. Some patients are extremely sensitive to any extraneous sounds and are remarkably adept at hearing noises that would, for the most part, go unnoticed. These patients are constantly on guard; they are vigilant because the outer world is perceived as intrusive and assaultive. Freud was really describing character traits here.

He next referred to anxious expectations, which "shades off imperceptibly into normal anxiety." Anxiousness, also manifested by a generally pessimistic attitude, pervades the patient's ego and determines how the world is viewed and how situations are assessed. Hypochondria, according to Freud, is a particular form of this anxious character trait, what we might also consider to be a constant state of vulnerability. Anxious expectations may also take the form of moral anxiety, which is evidenced by scrupulousness and pedantry. He described this anxiety as Gewissenangst, which literally means "conscience anxiety." Freud was again writing about obsessional traits, but the role of the later-formulated superego has to be considered.

Freud then enumerated various forms of anxiety attacks, specifying the organ system usually involved, cardiac respiratory or gastrointestinal. His brief remarks about anxiety attacks interrupting sleep are especially interesting and perhaps prophetic. This condition pavor nocturnis, is characterized by extreme fright accompanied by dypsnea and sweating. Children with pavor nocturnis also have an intense fear of the dark and a phobia about going to bed; they have what seem to be nightmares, but as a rule the content is not recalled. In adults, Charles Fisher described states of extreme terror, as evidenced by powerful disruptive affects and accelerated pulse rates that sometimes reach 160 beats per minute. The dream state accompanying this phenomenon is a concrete representation of a threatening situation. What I find to be truly remarkable is that in both children and adults, these states occur in stage IV sleep rather than REM sleep, which could indicate that these so-called dream states are founded upon different principles than ordinary dreams. They are apparently not products of organized drives but rather seem to be failures to synthesize perceptions and maintain equilibrium. By equating these states with the anxiety neurosis, Freud was clearly asserting that he believed they were without mentational content, since the anxiety neurosis is purely a somatic phenomenon, a disruption brought about by the accumulation of internal tension. This tension is not associated with psychological structures. Although many have been quick to criticize Freud for his ideas about the actual neuroses, it seems to me that the more we learn about primitive emotional states, the more applicable are his formulations—with modifications, of course.

Freud also concluded that vertigo and giddiness are found in some anxiety neuroses. Some years ago, I reported some clinical data on sudden losses of psychic equilibrium, that had more to do with the overwhelming nature of internal or external stimuli than with their content (Giovacchini 1958). These patients experienced dizziness, a manifestation of the patient's inability to maintain a steady state of integration, and they also had auditory hyperacuity as part of their defensive vigilant status. When something penetrated these vigilant adaptations, disruption followed which was experienced as vertigo.

Freud next explored the mechanism of phobias, classifying them into two groups: one relating to general psychological danger, and the other associated with locomotion. He included such common phobias as fear of snakes, thunderstorms, darkness, and mice, in the first group. Freud considered these phobias to be "instinctively implanted." A person who is generally anxious, that is, beset with anxious expectation, will employ anxiety to reinforce these natural aversions. Again, Freud was not attributing any psychological meaning to them. This may seem strange when one thinks of the obvious symbolism involved in some of these phobias, such as the fear of snakes. However, Freud believed that some symbols have a kind of universality. Remember that in *The Interpretation of Dreams* (Freud 1900), he concluded that when symbols appear in dreams, they are not further reducible; that is, the patient cannot free-associate to them. This is consistent with what he wrote about this type of phobia. However, analysts find that patients *can* free-associate to symbols.

An example of the second type of phobia is agoraphobia, the fear of open spaces. These phobias are related to locomotion. Walking, for example, may be accompanied by a sensation of vertigo, which may cause the patient to be afraid to venture out in the open. The same thing could be said of claustrophobia, only here the patient is wary of falling in narrow or closed spaces.

Freud compared phobias of the anxiety neuroses with those of the obsessional neuroses, which have a psychogenic etiology. An idea becomes obsessional when it is attached to available affect. One might say the idea becomes hypercathected. In the phobias of the anxiety neuroses, however, the affect is always anxiety, and, as has been repeatedly discussed in this paper, this anxiety is a physiological response rather than the outcome of intrapsychic conflict. Freud concluded that such phobias cannot be treated by psychotherapy, which is consistent with his attitude that the actual neuroses are not psychological phenomena.

The phobias of the obsessional neuroses are psychologically determined. The content of the simple phobias of the obsessional neuroses, however, can be changed by substitute ideas occurring subsequent to the phobia. The substitutes are what can be referred to as compulsive protective measures, such as brooding manias designed to reassure the patient that he is not insane. *Folie du doute* (doubting mania) arises from a person's doubt about the intactness of his train of thought, which is constantly being interrupted by the obsessional ideas.

Freud concluded this section by discussing the symptoms of the anxiety neurosis and related them to specific organ systems, such as the gastrointestinal and the musculoskeletal. The descriptions he gave are consistent with the hypothesis that anxiety is the outcome of accumulated excitation.

Freud divided anxiety neuroses into two types, hereditary and acquired. Sexual excitation, or what Freud called *sexual noxae*, is always involved in acquired neurosis sometimes alongside banal (I assume he means nonsexual) noxae, which are contributory to the production of the neurosis. He described various situations responsible for the outbreak of the anxiety neurosis in women, including cases of "virginal anxiety," anxiety in newlyweds, in women whose husbands suffer from premature ejaculation or who practice coitus interruptus, in widows, in women who are intentionally abstinent, and in menopausal women. Freud was stressing that anxiety is the outcome of accumulated, undischarged sexual tension.

The same circumstances apply to men; situations in which complete discharge of sexual feelings is not attained will create anxiety. Men who are abstinent for whatever reasons, situational or neurotic, men who practice coitus interruptus, and older men whose potency is decreased while libido is increased (or perhaps relatively increased) may all fall prey to the anxiety neurosis. (Incidentally, the word libido first appears in the literature in this passage.)

Freud was really distinguishing here between drive tension and the adequacy of the ego's executive techniques. In truly anesthetic women and impotent men, there is little disposition for the formation of an anxiety neurosis since there is a low level of libido. Freud did not, however, explain this low level. Later, he wrote of repression, but we would expect that repressed libido would lead to emotional disturbances, which Freud did not go into. Still, he stressed again that the etiology of the anxiety neurosis has to be considered in terms of multiple variables.

Freud anticipated arguments to discredit his formulation of sexual etiology by examining situations in which no sexual factor is obvious: the patient may succumb to an anxiety neurosis after a death or overwork, or may develop symptoms while studying for an important examination. Freud discovered that some sexual element was always present: the person may have been practicing coitus interruptus; a student studying for an examination may have suffered from undischarged sexual tension because of abstaining from sexual relations with his fiancee due to fear of making her pregnant. These are examples of multiple causality and summation; the sexual factor alone would not have been enough to produce an anxiety neurosis, but when set alongside other "stock" noxae, as Freud called them, an anxiety neurosis results.

In developing a theoretical basis for the anxiety neurosis, Freud made comparisons with hysteria, which may be the outcome of a single fright or trauma. This is not true of the anxiety neurosis. This again emphasizes that psychical elements do not have a role in the anxiety neurosis although they are prominent in hysteria. Consistent with this theory, patients suffering from anxiety neuroses often complain that sexuality (that is, lack of sexual satisfaction) cannot have much to do with their condition, since they have no desire. Freud emphasized that this lack of desire can be explained by the "deflection of somatic sexual excitation from the psychical sphere, and in a consequent abnormal employment of that excitation."

Freud described the process of sexual excitation beautifully, and it could be easily extended into instinct theory, as will be discussed in Chapter 5. The development of sexual feelings first involves a somatic excitation, a buildup of pressure on the walls of the seminal vesicles, which excites nerve endings, which in turn create a continuous visceral excitation that seeks conscious expression and energizes sexual ideas. In modern terminology, the visceral sexual need cathects memory traces of gratifying sexual experience, which set in motion adaptive techniques that will lead to the gratification of the sexual impulse. However, in the anxiety neuroses, the visceral sexual impulse never reaches the levels where these memory traces and adaptive techniques reside. Consequently, there is no psychical discharge. Instead it is deflected into the soma and is discharged somatically without mentational representation. What is felt is only anxiety rather than sexual excitation, and discharge is experienced as painful rather than pleasurable. We can raise the question of how much satisfaction (if we view it as Freud did, in terms of discharge) depends upon the contribution of a mental representation.

Freud recognized that there are optimal adaptations, and if these are replaced by less adequate modes of gratification, the outcome is psychopathology. For example, the replacement of normal coitus by masturbation or spontaneous emission results in neurasthenia. To remain consistent, we have to add that Freud must be referring to masturbation and spontaneous emission as being associated with sexual fantasies, because without such a psychic element we would have anxiety.

For some reason, Freud believed that "alienation between the somatic and the psychical sphere" occurs more readily in women than in men, and that it is harder to effect a reconciliation between these spheres in women. However, anxiety has many physical similarities to sexual excitement, such as accelerated breathing, palpitations, venous congestion, and perspiration, although in an anxiety attack these activities are more intense.

Freud finished this section with some very interesting provocative thoughts. He first asked why deflected sexual tension is experienced specifically as anxiety. He had already alluded to physiological similarities between anxiety and sexual excitation. Now he added that inner sexual stimuli are projected outward and that what is perceived as coming from the external world is experienced as dangerous. The reaction to danger is fear, which is the essence of anxiety. The difference is that the anxiety due to an external danger is momentary, whereas that emanating from an internal danger is chronic, and chronic anxiety is characteristic of neurosis. Exogenous excitation operates with a single impact; endogenous excitation operates as a constant force. Freud used practically the same words twenty years later (Freud 1915), when he wrote about how the neonate distinguishes between an inner drive and an external percept.

Finally, Freud acknowledged that most clinically encountered neuroses are of a mixed type. He believed that fortuitous factors may be responsible for the formation of hysteria. For example, a patient who is suffering from an anxiety neurosis because of her husband's sexual inadequacy, may fall in love with another man, which then creates intra-psychic conflict (hysteria). We may take issue with the thought that such events occur fortuitously, and Freud himself later recognized the inevitability of such sequences (1920), when he postulated the existence of the repetition compulsion, in which neurotic patients repeat sequences of infantile constellations and traumas.

The interrelationship between neuroses is an interesting element of clinical experience, and in this paper Freud began stressing reciprocal relationships. He stated that the anxiety neurosis is the somatic counterpart of hysteria; in other words, when psychic defenses are introduced as superstructures to protect the psyche from the painful anxiety discharge, hysterical symptoms are formed. These symptoms may also be deflected to the somatic sphere as occurs in conversion, but the conversion phenomenon is based upon intrapsychic conflict. In 1911, Freud developed a similar theme about schizophrenia, what he referred to as a narcissistic neurosis. Hypochondriasis, the damming-up of libido withdrawn from the external world, has the same relationship to schizophrenia as the anxiety neurosis does to psychoneurosis. The delusional system of the schizophrenic patient is, according to Freud, a defensive restitution to reestablish contact with the external world, that is, a reaction to hypochondriasis which is the result of the withdrawal of libido and turning it toward the self. Freud, in working out a psychodynamic viewpoint, began to develop a theory of instincts which we will discuss in Chapter 6.

5

"Instincts and Their Vicissitudes" (1915)

SYNOPSIS

This article is Freud's definitive exposition on instinct. In previous papers, he focused upon various facets of instincts but here he pulled together various issues. There is an advantage to reading this fundamental paper before some of the previous ones such as the *Three Essays on the Theory of Sexuality* (Freud 1905) since it provides a general orientation, whereas earlier papers deal with specific topics—subcategories of what is discussed in "Instincts and Their Vicissitudes." As previously stated reading Freud's works chronologically is not the best approach.

Freud distinguished between inner (instinctual) and outer stimuli. Inner stimuli are continuous, in contrast to the momentary impact of an outer stimulus. One can escape outer stimuli by action or flight, whereas inner stimuli cannot be avoided. Freud defined instinct operationally, as a borderland concept between the soma and the psyche characterized by its impetus, and having a source (a somatic origin), an aim (satisfaction), and an object (the person or situation that achieves satisfaction).

Freud postulated four vicissitudes of instincts: (1) reversal of content, (2) turning toward the self, (3) repression, and (4) sublimation, but in this paper he confined himself to the first two. The first reversal of content involves love turning into hate, and may also involve a change from activity to passivity. The second vicissitude, instinct turning toward the self, is another example

99

of active being transformed into passive. These formulations have specific implications about the process of psychic structuralization, in which early activity is followed by passivity. However, early orientations, affects, and attitudes continue to exist along with later acquisitions. Such coexistence calls attention to the phenomenon of ambivalence, first described by Bleuler, in which antithetical psychic elements exist side by side. There are three types of ambivalence: (1) emotional, as occurs when a person is simultaneously loved and hated, (2) voluntary, in which a decision regarding an action has to be made but in which the alternatives seem equally desirable and, (3) intellectual, in which antithetical ideas are preserved. The phenomenon of ambivalence stresses polarities.

The final section of this essay focuses upon the polarities of love and hate, which can be conceptualized as three dichotomies: *love-indifference*, which typifies the distinction between the ego and the outer world; *love-hate*, which corresponds to pleasure and pain; and *loving-being loved*, which exemplifies both active and passive orientations.

These polarities and the various sequences that characterize instinctual vicissitudes are fundamental elements of the developmental process. Freud was very much concerned here with determining orientations and affects that are characteristic of primitive stages and with identifying the changes they undergo as the psyche continues to structuralize. He traced the development of sexual and self-preservative instincts, a dual-instinct theory that replaced his earlier distinction between ego and sexual instincts.

Freud's metapsychology is based upon a dualistic instinct theory. This paper, I believe, is Freud's definitive essay on instincts; here he pulled together many ideas from a number of other papers. This is a very sophisticated treatise, and Freud opened it with more than a page of fundamental methodological principles, in which he stressed that observations always contain some concepts not directly related to the data on hand. The very act of observing is dependent upon some abstract ideas, that is, we introduce concepts as well as a conceptual framework to the clinical material we are trying to understand. Freud viewed these abstractions as conventions (perhaps definitions) that can be discarded as our knowledge advances, since science does not tolerate any rigidity, even in definitions. In fact, Freud wrote a considerable amount of material on methodology, but it is scattered among various papers and is hard to locate. I have collected these passages in a paper I wrote on methodology (Giovacchini 1967).

In any case, Freud felt that instinct is one of these indefinite abstract concepts. He approached instinct from a physiological perspective, and examined it alongside stimuli as they activated the reflex arc. Clearly, the essence of Freud's psychoeconomic tension-discharge hypothesis is that an external stimulus applied to a living organism is discharged by action toward the outside world.

Freud distinguished between external, and inner (instinctual) stimuli. An external stimulus has a momentary impact on the psyche, whereas an instinctual stimulus has continuous impact. We discussed the same point in Chapter 4.

Now we come to a controversial point that will merit discussion. Freud goes on to state that the "almost entirely helpless living organism as yet unoriented in the world" (I assume that he is discussing the neonate) would soon (he did not specify how soon) be able to distinguish between inner and outer stimuli through muscular action. If the neonate can abolish the stimulus through muscular action, that is by flight, the stimulus is external; if not, it is internal and instinctual. Freud was again describing, without directly saying so, the principle of constancy, which he had formulated in neurological terms in his *Project for a Scientific Psychology* (Freud 1895) as well as in *The Interpretation of Dreams* (Freud 1900) and later in *Beyond the Pleasure Principle* (Freud 1920).

Although this material seems familiar since it has often been discussed and is taken for granted by analysts, there are nevertheless many subtle and perhaps distressing questions we can raise as we look at it more closely. Let us begin by asking what "inside" and "outside," mean to a newborn. The earliest phases of psychic life supposedly are characterized by a lack of distinction between the psyche and external objects; presumably there are no boundaries as yet. Therefore, the distinction between drives and external percepts could not apply to such early states.

Could not the infant, even at these early neonatal stages, somehow acquire the capacity to make connections between certain feelings and reactions that bring relief? If a flashing light causes pain, he may very soon "learn" that shutting his eyes will soothe him, even though he may not yet be able to understand the source of the disruption. A protective action such as shutting the eyes is practically at the reflex level. If the infant is hungry, such a simple muscular maneuver will not work. The child may very early be able to discriminate between different types of sensations without locating their sources since, as yet, he knows nothing about source.

Freud's theories were often based upon two principles: the principle of constancy, and the pleasure principle. The function of the nervous system and the psychic apparatus, according to the constancy principle is to keep excitation at its lowest point. However, recent evidence from neurophysiology indicates just the opposite. The organism seems to be stimulus-seeking rather than stimulus-avoiding. Sensory deprivation is an unpleasant state in which internal percepts become disruptive. Many analysts have felt that the psychoeconomic hypothesis, a hydrodynamic, tension-discharge hypothesis, is not particularly useful. It is historically interesting in that it fits in the context of mid-Victorian science. I believe that we might restate the principle of constancy by asserting that the organism seeks a state of equilibrium, as Bernard (1865) formulated in his principle of internal constancy and Cannon stated (1932) in his concept of homeostasis.

The pleasure principle, in which increased tension creates pain, and lowered tension (which connotes release and relief) is experienced as pleasurable can also be challenged. Excitement is often pleasurable, sometimes ecstatically so, whereas low energy levels often accompany apathy and withdrawal. Pleasure and pain cannot be reduced to such simple quantitative fluctuations.

Freud characterized the pleasure principle as consisting of a tendency of living organisms to avoid unpleasure. In *Beyond the Pleasure Principle* (1920), Freud indicated that the rhythm of changes of excitation is responsible for the generation of pleasure, and he concluded that the principles of pleasure and constancy are identical. In the same paper, he referred to the principle of constancy as the "Nirvana principle," in which the organism attempts to reproduce the intrauterine state. His final writings attributed the Nirvana principle to the death instinct, and its modification into the pleasure principle as the outcome of the life instinct.

Returning to Freud's development of instinct theory in "Instincts and Their Vicissitudes," he defined instinct as a borderland concept, on the frontier between the somatic and the psychic—a psychic representation of stimuli originating from inner organic sources. The word instinct has caused some difficulty for English readers. Freud used the word *Trieb*, which could be better translated as drive and stresses mentational elements, whereas instinct or its German correspondent *Instinkt* refers to a biologically oriented innate behavioral pattern. Freud stressed here that the instinct is the psychic representative of inner organically derived stimuli. In other papers such as "The Unconscious" (Freud 1915c) which we discussed earlier, Freud wrote about instinctual representation, that is, the psychical representation of an instinct; the instinct itself could never become conscious. I do not believe these distinctions to be important; they are a matter of semantics. Freud then enumerated the characteristics of instinct. An instinct has impetus, an aim, an object, and a source. The impetus (the impelling force) represents what Freud called the motoric element of the instinct, and can be understood as requiring energy, or an expenditure of work. We can view this inpetus as a forward-pushing pressure, which would cause us to consider all instincts as essentially active. Freud pointed out that a passive instinct is one with a passive aim.

The aim of the instinct is simply its satisfaction. According to the principle of constancy, the organism has to discharge the tension the instinct creates and lower the energy level. This process is perceived as satisfying. However, there are many paths that lead to the same end, so Freud postulated that there may be intermediary aims, which may be inhibited. Freud acknowledged that there may also be aim-inhibited drives which have recently been viewed as belonging to secondary process activities and higher ego functions.

The object of instincts is the vehicle that achieves satisfaction. It represents the person or situation by which satisfaction is obtained, and can even be part of one's own body. Object relationship theory is a psychological system that involves early developmental phases and has many clinical implications. Thus the role of both internal and external objects is of central importance in the achievement of instinctual satisfaction. Freud acknowledged the importance of objects, but his chief interest was the development of libido and changes within the psyche rather than interactions with the external world. He added, however, that of all the attributes of instincts the object is the most variable. Sources and aims are not exchangeable, but the object, that is the method of obtaining satisfaction, can often be exchanged for another one. This is especially true for sexual instincts, but the self-preservative instincts require the constancy of the object, which initially is food and which can be generalized to nurture. Freud also pointed out that the same object may be able to satisfy several instincts. Adler referred to this phenomenon as a "confluence of instincts."

The source of an instinct is hypothesized to be its organic origin: The sexual instinct would presumably begin with certain cyclical sensory stimulation in the seminal vesicles, or the ovaries and the instinct of hunger with stomach contractions. Freud knew that the situation was much more complicated, and guessed that these questions would eventually be answered in terms of biochemistry. This aspect of instincts interested him the least. Still he had some notions about the source of instincts and their qualitative characteristics. In my opinion, he became confusing regarding the question of the qualitative differences of instincts. He believed, first, that all instincts are qualitatively alike and that their differences are due only to their energic cathexis, to the intensity of excitation. Then he added that the differences in the mental effects of instincts can be traced to their sources. To me, however, differences in mental effects means qualitative differences, although perhaps Freud thought otherwise.

In view of Freud's operational definition of instincts, one could ask how many instincts can be distinguished, since there are so many different organic sources. In addition, there are numerous behavioral patterns characteristic of the human species, so one might wonder if these are the manifestations of special instincts, such as play, gregariousness, and destruction. Freud considered this question and concluded that all of these activities could be reduced to two fundamental instincts—the sexual and the self-preservative. Previously he had formulated sexual and ego instincts (Freud 1910). He had difficulty maintaining dualism when he introduced the concept of narcissism (Freud 1914); the discovery of ego-libido obliterates absolute distinctions between ego and sexual instincts, but we will discuss this later. For the moment, Freud was less concerned with the evolution and development of instinct theory than with the nature of instincts and their vicissitudes.

In a general vein, Freud believed that the tenents of biology supported his division of self-preservative and sexual instincts. The sexual instinct, for example, has two purposes: the sexual enjoyment of the individual and the preservation of the species. This belief conforms to Freud's separation of sexuality and self-preservation. Concerning the latter, Freud felt that the individual is simply a transitory appendage to an immortal germ plasm.

The knowledge that has been obtained about instincts is derived from the study of psychopathology. Freud's investigation of the transference neuroses—hysteria and the obsessional neuroses—permitted him to make many formulations about the sexual instincts. He acknowledged, however, that very little is known about the ego instincts but with his usual foresight predicted that more would be learned about them through the study of the narcissistic neuroses. We need not think in terms of discrete instincts, but the study of patients suffering from character defects (who Freud would have considered examples of narcissistic neuroses) has caused us to focus our attention on ego processes and developmental factors.

Nevertheless, Freud constantly emphasized developmental factors. For example, he postulated that at the beginning of psychic life there are many independently operating sexual instincts, which spring from various organic sources and are satisfied by autoerotic activities. This is the autoerotic phase of component instincts, which presumably occurs before there is any definitive ego. Of necessity, such a phase would be characterized by an amorphous, unstructured psyche. Freud postulated that development proceeds from the global to the discrete. He called the satisfaction of these primitive instincts "organ pleasure." Only later, when they became synthesized with each other under the dominance of the genital instinct, could they be used in the service of reproduction.

Freud has been accused of sexualizing everything. Even though many of the arguments used against him are naive and tendentious, this is perhaps an example in which he emphasizes erotism to an absurd degree. He described the phase of autoerotism as existing before there is any organized ego, so it must be a beginning neonatal stage. Still, he described "erotic" component instincts and "pleasure," reactions that would be beyond a newborn infant's sensory capacities. Apparently, he was describing needs that have to be met so that the organism can survive and develop. Meeting a need is not initially associated with satisfaction, pleasure, or erotic gratification, as these are highly structured reactions which develop later.

One of the difficulties in formulating psychoanalytic concepts is that there is a tendency to understand another person's mind in terms of our own frame of reference—we are compelled to adultomorphosize. This may be why Freud extended sexuality into early life phases; if we think in terms of developmental drives and a biological impetus to move from the global and amorphous to the discrete and structured, and if we exclude erotism, much of what Freud postulated is still applicable.

Freud seemed to need to retain sexuality as an inherent elemental force, but his introduction of ego instincts represented, to my mind, an attempt to introduce a nonsexual developmental factor. He still wanted to unify ego and sexuality; but he must have recognized the necessity of stressing the biological striving to survive and achieve homeostasis. For example, he stated that at first the sexual and self-preservative instincts are combined. Some sexual instincts remain attached to the ego instincts and represent their libidinal components. Only during illness do they become detached from the self-preservative instincts, but they may still seek the same object for gratification. Freud had already discussed this a year earlier in his paper "On Narcissism" (1914), and there he called this type of object choice "anaclitic"—that is, the sexual instincts lean on the ego instincts. All of these formulations are extremely pertinent to our understanding of psychic development in general.

In "Instincts and Their Vicissitudes," Freud focused upon fundamental changes that occur to the elemental instinctual forces. Freud called these changes "vicissitudes," which is how the editors of this work translated the German word *Schicksal* (literally meaning fate). Freud also believed that instinctual vicissitudes also constitute defenses against the direct expression of the instinct. He enumerated the following fates that instincts may undergo: (1) reversal of content, (2) turning toward the self, (3) repression, and (4) sublimation. In this paper he dealt with the first two, having considered repression in a separate contemporary article (Freud 1915a). He may also have written a paper in which he specifically discussed sublimation, but it has never been found. (Apparently several metapsychological treatises have been lost.)

Why are these first two vicissitudes so important that Freud should devote such lengthy and detailed discussion to them? Two factors are involved. First, Freud had a firm need to maintain dualism. This might have been in keeping with the scientific atmosphere of the time, or it may have been intrinsic to his cultural milieu. Still, he had to orient his conceptualizations in polarities such as ego and outer world, unconscious and conscious, autoplastic (internalized) psychic forces and alloplastic (externalized, action-directed) psychic elements, known also as acting out) and so on. His psychodynamic hypothesis depended upon conflicting polarities. Second, Freud was trying to postulate what he believed to be fundamental processes involved in psychic development, attempting to outline intrinsic patterns that are part of hierarchal sequences leading to secondary process developed structures. At the same time he was investigating what we might call the reverse direction—the course of regression and the genesis of psychopathology. Freud was able to apply these 4 vicissitudes only to sexual instincts.

The reversal of an instinct into its opposite can be subdivided into two processes: a change from activity to passivity, or a change from love to hate. Regarding the change of activity into passivity, Freud examined two pairs of instincts, sadism–masochism and scopophilia–exhibitionism. What actually occurs in these instances is a change of object, which Freud outlined as follows:

Sadism is at first directed toward another person, an external object. Freud was careful to point out that sadism initially consists of the exercise of power and control, and that desire for violence or for inflicting pain is not present then. (This would be in keeping with the observation that children wreak destruction when trying to establish autonomy, although this is usually not their primary intent.) Next, the external object is replaced by the self. The subject from which the instinct emanates becomes the object of the instinct. The instinct has changed from active (outwardly directed) to passive (inwardly directed). In the final step an external object comes back into the picture. Freud's description of this stage is confusing in that he stated the subject (the instigator of the instinct) becomes the object and the object becomes the subject. If we view the previous phase as an interaction between different parts of the self and if we then project into an external object that part of the self from which the instinct emanates, the result is an external object being sadistic toward the self. Freud put it differently in that he viewed the self and external object as being identified with each other, but I believe this is easier to understand in terms of projection, which, from the viewpoint of the self, is masochism. Freud added that here the self may experience sexual excitation associated with pain. When the instinct reverts back to its original sadism, this pain is, so to speak, brought back with it, and the wish to inflict pain becomes part of the sadistic impulse.

Freud also stated that, as opposed to scopophilia (voyeurism), sadism does not have a previous stage in which the instinct is initially directed toward the self. In other words, Freud is asserting that there is no such thing as primary masochism. Later, he changed his mind and made primary masochism a manifestation of the death instinct.

If we think in terms of psychic development, it makes sense to begin with preoccupation with the self before turning to external objects. Autoeroticism, followed by primary narcissism are the first stages of psychic development, in which the capacity to recognize external sources of stimuli has not yet developed.

The same developmental sequence can be outlined for scopophilia-exhibitionism with the addition of the preliminary looking at a part of the self before turning to an external object, something which, to Freud, must have seemed obvious. As was common with Freud, he described this sequence only in regard to males. First, the child looks at his penis, then he looks at another person's penis. Here the fluctuation of activity to passivity can be considered from several angles. For example, the self looking at a sexual organ becomes passive when it is put in terms of a sexual organ being looked at by the self. The next phase, also beginning as very active, that is, as the self looking at an extraneous object, then becomes the extraneous object which is identified with the self looking at the self, a passive position in which scopophilia has become transformed into exhibitionism. If we omit the specific instinct pairs that Freud wrote about and think just in terms of developmental processes, we can see how he developed a sequence from narcissism to beginning object relationships as the psyche directs its perceptions from the self and reaches toward external objects. Then when the psyche has achieved the capacity to identify, it again focuses upon the self, a process Freud called secondary narcissism (1914).

Freud's views are also consonant with structural hierarchies intrinsic to our current conceptual systems, which emphasize object relationships and ego systems. For example, he believed that early instinctual configurations are coexistent with later ones; he made a comparison to the eruption of lava where earlier layers push forward with later modified ones. The initial active drive persists with the later passive one. Freud speculated that the later passive stages of turning back toward the subject may be due to the persistence of the original narcissism, a factor that gives the psyche its characteristic stamp. I would assume that Freud meant that there is an innate tendency to retain one's libido, and that later defenses are designed to preserve the original narcissism. This is an interesting idea, which Freud did not pursue. It is most meaningful today as we treat patients whose narcissism is so low that they are hovering on the edge of existential collapse and who must hang onto whatever vestige of self-esteem they can.

These successive layers emphasize another quality of instincts—their fundamental ambivalence. As stated earlier, Bleuler first coined the expression and described three types of ambivalence: (1) emotional ambivalence, as exemplified by coexisting feelings of love and hate, (2) voluntary ambivalence, which is characterized by an inability to decide what action to take, and (3) intellectual ambivalence, which permits a person to tolerate antithetical ideas. In another sense, Freud was indicating that instincts are oriented in the direction of the primary process. He believed that archaic instincts (the instincts of primitive man) were more ambivalent than those of modern man. He conjectured that the initial instinct was strongly active. Therefore, when placed alongside later developed passive components, the contrast stands out sharply and is viewed as ambivalence.

The role of the object becomes negligible for the most primitive instinctual components. Here, the organic source of the drive coincides with the object that produces satisfaction. The object is part of the body in the autoerotic stage. Freud speculated that the organic source to some extent determines the qualities required of the object in order to achieve instinctual discharge. Could he have been referring to functional modes? For example, in male sexuality, the act is what we might call expulsive, whereas the stomach contractions that signify hunger are introjective.

Freud had some very interesting thoughts about reversal of content. He stated that this vicissitude applies only to the transformation of love into hate. However, love is not a component instinct. Rather, it is "the expression of the *whole* sexual current of feeling." Love belongs in a different frame of reference than hate. It is a highly complex, structured feeling or attitude characteristic of mature object relationships, and it involves whole objects. Hate, on the other hand, appears very early in psychic development. According to Freud, hate is the first response that accompanies discrimination of the inner from the outer world.

Nevertheless, even though love is not a component (in this instance I prefer the word elemental) instinct, it can still be studied in terms of polarities. Love admits three polarities: (1) love–indifference, (2) love–hate and, (3) loving–being loved. Again, I must emphasize that Freud was describing sweeping developmental trends that are fundamental to structuralizing processes. These polarities can be linked with the vicissitudes that have been described. Love–indifference corresponds to the antithesis of ego and the outer world and represents the earliest differentiation made by the structuralizing psyche. Love and hate are feeling states (they produce pleasure and pain). The psyche operates according to the pleasure principle, seeking objects that are pleasurable and rejecting, or as Freud said, ejecting, those that lead to "unpleasure."* Loving–being loved is another example of the instinct being turned toward the self, which focuses upon the antithesis of activity–passivity.

---

*Freud preferred the word unpleasure (*unlust*) rather than pain when describing the polarity of pleasure and pain. In many instances he was emphasizing the absence of pleasure rather than pain.

Freud discussed in detail the interrelationships of the polarities. Love–indifference and love-hate operate during early narcissistic developmental phases. Instincts are initially directed toward the ego. The outside world is not cathected, and the ego is therefore indifferent to it. Freud added that the ego coincides with what is pleasurable, and the outside world is viewed as indifferent or perhaps as unpleasurable.

Freud's formulation can be disputed on the basis that he attributed complex reactions to a very primitive ego. Freud (1900) had described the beginning psyche as an amorphous, unstructured mass, in which there are no distinctions between inner and outer world. At this time the infant has no concept of source; pleasure and pain (or, to put it better, states of equilibrium or disruption) cannot be located in any particular place, but are simply felt.

Although Freud's metapsychology is id-oriented, he recognized the importance of the external object for psychic development. He explained that part of the sexual drive is autoerotic and under the dominance of the pleasure principle, whereas another part is dependent upon external objects for gratification, something that is true for all the ego instincts. The sexual instincts dependent upon external objects and the ego instincts disturb this original narcissism and are responsible for development and, later, for the establishment of the reality principle (Freud 1911).

According to Freud, the reality ego *precedes* the pleasure ego. This seems to be a contradiction, but it is quite compatible with Freud's concepts. As far back as his first anxiety paper (Freud 1895), Freud believed that muscular motion, (flight) distinguished whether a feeling or perception originated from within or without. In this paper, he said that one distinguishes between an instinct and an external stimulus by muscular action. It is clear that Freud was describing reality testing, and that this is the basis of the initial reality ego. Thus, all those sensations that lead to pleasure would be attributed to the inner world and those that create unpleasure or pain would be placed in the outside world. This is the concept of the purified pleasure ego.

The sources of pleasure are located within the psyche, and everything else, is at first perceived with indifference. Freud next refined some of these statements, which he felt was justified as the ego structuralized further. The satisfaction of self-preservative drives does not lead to love; the ego needs but does not love the care-taker.

Freud was careful to point out that it is the ego, not the drive, that loves, hates, or needs. This is an extremely important point because, in view of the psychoeconomic hypothesis, it is easy to give drives concrete attributes. The tension-discharge model permits us to ascribe goals and motivation to drives as they seek discharge. Freud was quite right in stressing that only the ego is capable of such complex mentation; drives are the mental representatives of inner needs.

The satisfaction of sexual needs, which is perceived as pleasurable, leads to love. What is not pleasurable is first felt by the ego as indifferent and as belonging to the outside world. The transformation of the ego into the final reality ego occurs when pleasure is postponed because the requirements of the external world take precedence for the first time. So we have a sequence from initial reality ego to purified pleasure ego and then to reality ego which has achieved the capacity to make judgmental discriminations.

Love is derived from the satisfaction of sexual instincts and everything that produces unpleasure is hated. Regarding hate and unpleasure, it makes no difference whether sexual or self-preservative instincts are involved, but the prototype of hate is not related to the sexual instinct. Instead, it is connected to the ego's struggle to survive. Thus love and hate develop from different sources. They become opposites only when the influence of the pleasure–pain principle becomes effective.

What follows is an extremely pithy description of Freud's psychosexual theory of development. In a sense, he developed an hierarchal sequence of the structuralization of love. Freud placed love, a complex, structured feeling, at the very beginning of psychic life. Although this appears to be a clear contradiction, it is not necessarily, if we maintain the hierarchal viewpoint. The most complex emotions must have their antecedents, and here Freud was describing what could be called the forerunners of mature love. Perhaps it might have been better if he had used another word beside love when dealing with early pregenital stages.

Freud began the developmental sequence by going back to the autoerotic phase. He made the vague statement that love is the outcome of the ego's ability to satisfy its instinctual impulses autoerotically. Where does love enter the picture? Freud's next statement gives us a clue. He added that love is originally narcissistic. This means that the ego loves itself. Then the ego becomes directed toward pleasure-giving objects that have become incorporated into it; that is, the ego loves its introjects. This is secondary narcissism. Then love becomes part of later sexual instincts, which, when synthesized, become incorporated into genital sexuality. Freud was careful to point out that in his formulations about early development, he was conceptualizing "preliminary stages of love," which are connected with "provisional sexual aims."

Hate is older than love. This makes sense, intuitively, since so much of the hatred we observe seems primitive, whereas love with its tenderness and delicacy impresses us as being on a higher level. Freud believed that the narcissistic ego feels hatred toward the outpouring of stimuli from the outer world. Again, this emphasizes that hatred is created when the ego experiences unpleasure as its narcissism is threatened. This sets up a dichotomy between the ego and the outer world which creates a similar dichotomy between ego and sexual instincts. When the ego instincts dominate the anal stage, they acquire hate—this constitutes the anal-sadistic phase. Freud emphasized that the ego hates but then referred to sadism as an instinct. This is confusing because an affect is equated with an instinct.

These connections between love and hate explain why so many relationships are ambivalent. There are many situations in which the desires of love are opposed by the self-preservative drive. Frustrated love is frequently followed by hate, which strengthens Freud's theory that love can be transformed into hatred. Freud also believed that much hate occurs through the regression of love to the anal-sadistic stage, thus giving hatred an erotic quality.

6

Three Essays on the Theory of Sexuality (1905)

SYNOPSIS

The cornerstone of psychoanalysis is the theory of sexuality, which is presented in its most comprehensive form in these essays. Freud believed that this monograph and *The Interpretation of Dreams* represented the totality of his thinking and he valued them more than anything else he had written. Consequently, he kept them up to date, made many revisions, and added new sections. As we might have expected, Freud began this monograph by discussing aberrations rather than normal development.

Sexual Aberrations

Freud discussed different types of homosexuality, emphasizing the contribution of constitutional bisexuality and stressing the role of projection. For example, in certain homosexuals the feminine parts of the subject are projected onto the object. This formulation is essentially based on structural considerations insomuch as Freud referred to a part of the self rather than to the projection of id impulses, as he usually did.

Early in life, there is no fixed connection between sexual instincts and the objects that produce satisfaction. Even though psychoanalysis has, to some measure, a biological foundation, in this section Freud concentrated upon psychological aspects. The sexual instincts, as is true of all psychic elements, can be traced back to their antecedents, which are known as component instincts.

Component instincts cause perversions if they remain fixated, that is, if they do not develop further and are expressed directly. Freud called these fixated component instincts polymorphous perverse, and since perverse acts are their outward manifestations, he considered perversions to be the negative of the neuroses. In the neuroses the psyche defends itself against the polymorphous perverse component instincts, whereas in perversions these instincts express themselves in behavior.

Infantile Sexuality

This second essay was the most controversial of the three, and the opponents of psychoanalysis rallied against it. It was bad enough in mid-Victorian times that Freud placed such an emphasis on sex, but to attribute sexual feelings to children was outrageous.

In adults the period of infantile sexuality is repressed, which helps reinforce the denial that it ever existed. This is the familiar *infantile amnesia*, which Freud felt had to be overcome if psychoanalytic treatment were to be successful. He explained that infantile amnesia is the outcome of shame and disgust, attitudes reflected by society. However, he also believed that there was something intrinsic about the course of sexual development that causes it to be interrupted, as during the latency period. He stated that this interruption is organically based and "fixed by heredity." Frued traced the sequence of psychosexual development from autoerotism through orality, anality, the phallic phase, and the Oedipus complex. He did not develop these stages in the same chronological sequence in which he identified them, and because of addendas and footnotes the essay covers a number of years.

Transformations of Puberty

Sweeping physical changes occur during puberty that enable the adolescent to complete the sexual act. By this Freud meant that the sexual instinct can now achieve complete discharge—total satisfaction. This is an early version of what he later described in "Instincts and their Vicissitudes" (Freud 1915b).

The organic source of the sexual instinct in pubertal and postpubertal males is the interstitial tissue of the testes, which transmits a stimulus to a central site (neurologically, Freud probably meant the spinal cord). In any case, the impulse then reaches higher centers, cathecting memory traces of sexual experiences and producing conscious desire, which causes the subject to seek an object that will provide satisfaction.

Summary

In the final section Freud discussed concepts that he had developed through the years. The most important of these is *complemental series*, a term Freud did not use until 1920, but the idea is pertinent to the theses in the *Three Essays*. To repeat briefly, complemental series represents the nature–nurture dichotomy. The greater the organism's constitutional vulnerability, the less intense the environment's contribution has to be for psychopathological decompensation, and vice versa.

Freud's ideas regarding the occurrence and effects of sexual trauma changed over time, in that whereas he once felt that a traumatic incident or childhood seduction must have actually occurred, eventually he decided that this need not be true. This change of mind has important implications regarding his ideas about infantile sexuality.

During the years when Freud believed that sexual traumas were historical facts, he accepted the view that children, in a sense, were sexually innocent. That may seem to be a drastic thing to say about Freud, who put such an emphasis on sexual feelings. However, although he accepted that children had sexual impulses he felt that, for the most part, they were dormant, and that the seducing adult stimulated what otherwise would have remained latent. This put the child in the role of the passive, helpless victim. Even in the 1896 paper "Further Remarks on the Defense Neuro-Psychoses," in which he postulated that the obsessional male was the active seducer in late childhood, he also postulated that the obsessional male had been seduced in early childhood by an older person.

As Freud moved away from this theory, he made the child more responsible for his feelings, and the child's interest in sex was viewed as considerably more active then previously. Interest in sex can reach pathological intensity, as Freud discusses in his first essay, "The Sexual Aberrations," which deals with perversions.

The Sexual Aberrations

The first paragraph of this essay contains the roots of his formulations about instincts. In "Instincts and Their Vicissitudes," Freud postulated the existence of a sexual instinct alongside an instinct of nutrition, (what was later referred to as the self-preservative instinct). Freud was writing about basic needs, in this instance of hunger and sexual needs. Hunger is the felt need, a manifestation of the self-preservative instinct. As Freud could find no analogous word to express the need associated with sexual instincts, he once again suggested libido. He then postulated that an instinct has an object and an aim, the object being the person who will gratify the need and the aim being the act which brings satisfaction. There can be deviation of both object and aim, and Freud began by discussing deviation of the sexual object.

Deviation in Respect of the Sexual Object

He began with a group which he called inverts, homosexuals, who choose members of the same sex as sexual objects. Freud described different types of homosexuals; those who are "absolute" in that they seek only members of the same sex, and those who are "amphigenic" or bisexual. He also differentiated between homosexuality that can be traced back to disturbances of psychosexual development in childhood, and "contingent" homosexuality which is related to some precipitating factor, such as being isolated from members of the opposite sex. Would such inability to practice heterosexual sex lead to an anxiety neurosis? According to Freud it might, as we learned in his paper on the anxiety neuroses (Freud 1895). However, by seeking a sexual object of the same sex, a person can achieve discharge and thereby alleviate any buildup of tension that could lead to anxiety.

Freud made a curious statement that was intended to refute the idea that homosexuality is constitutional and innate: he stated that, in some cases, inversion can be removed by hypnotic suggestion. However, in view of the rigidity of the homosexual orientation, it is doubtful whether hypnosis would have any influence on sexual behavior. Perversions are now understood to be characterological adaptations that, for the most part, are ego syntonic, and not easily abandoned.

In attempting to explain inversion, Freud considered theories that included early developmental phases as well as psychodynamic explanations. He referred to constitutional bisexuality, an idea that Fliess had stressed, which could account for male inverts who seek female qualities in male partners—this involves projection of the invert's feminine component onto a male. In a footnote written in 1915 Freud concluded that a narcissistic object choice and a retention of the erotic significance of the anal zone are important factors in the development of inversion. Ferenczi, quoted by Freud in 1920, distinguished between "subject homo-erotics," who behave like women, and "object homo-erotics," who are entirely masculine.

Freud acknowledged that no explanation of inversions has proven completely satisfactory. He concluded that the connection between sexual instinct and object is not fixed from the beginning. He believed that early in life the sexual instinct is independent of the object and is not created by the stimulus of the object's attraction. This is interesting in view of the current idea that object relationships in themselves create needs. Loewald (1941) discussed how the mother helps the child structuralize needs that go beyond simply expressing biological requirements. The external object makes it possible to refine crude instincts into organized, sophisticated needs that involve sensual and esthetic feelings.

Deviations in Respect of the Sexual Aim

The normal sexual aim is intercourse, which leads to satisfaction in the same way that eating alleviates hunger. Freud now defined perversions as sexual activities that involve areas of the body other then the genitals and that stop there rather than leading to intercourse. Convention, that is, factors extraneous to biology, determine what will be labeled a perversion. Because of this, it is difficult to remove entirely moral implications from the term. For example, in Victorian society it was considered disgusting to kiss the genitals. Freud was aware that similar practices have been common since prehistory. I recall having seen small pre-Columbian statuettes, several hundred years old, of Indians having all kinds of sexual activities, including fellatio, cunnilinguism and pederastery at the Pornographic Museum in Lima, Peru.

After discussing fixations on various parts of the body, Freud briefly discussed fetishisms. He believed that, to some extent, fetishism is normal. The lover cherishes some belonging of his beloved, a ribbon, garter or lock of hair. The preoccupation becomes a perversion if it replaces the sexual act.

In footnotes, Freud added that the fetishistic object, commonly a foot or shoe, is sexually exciting in that it embodies the repressed olfactory sense. Smells are sexually stimulating, but they are repressed throughout the course of emotional development. The fetish, which is often dirty and smells, represents the return of the repressed. According to Freud, the fetish is also a symbol for the penis. To give a sexually desirable woman a penis protects her lover from the threat of castration. Freud was emphasizing that children have the fantasy that women are castrated. This viewpoint is now, for the most part, considered to be invalid, both by feminists and psychoanalysts.

Some clinicians explain fetishism in terms of structural defects; the fetish has been considered to be a part object and in some instances a transitional object. These formulations take us further back on the psychosexual developmental spectrum. Instead of being a manifestation of castration anxiety, which connotes a phallic or oedipal level, preoccupation with a fetish is the manifestation of pregenital fixation, perhaps symbiotic fusion, and it is asociated with fairly primitive defensive mechanisms such as splitting and denial. Freud (1926) discussed these defenses as being part of the fetish, while still retaining his ideas about castration anxiety.

In this section, Freud concentrated on activities that are associated with the sexual act. Touching and looking are important determinants in producing erotic feelings and the attraction that draws two people together. The scopophilic impulse can be extended to the body in general, and finally to aesthetic areas, such as interest in beauty and art. Freud called this process of diversion of sexual interest into nonsexual pursuits *sublimation*. This is the first time he used the word in his published writings, although he mentioned the term in a letter to Fliess in 1897. Sublimation leads to socially acceptable behavior. Inner forces, presumably emanating from what Freud later called the superego, or more accurately the ego ideal, oppose scopophilic impulses, causing shame.

In "Instincts and Their Vicissitudes" Freud paid considerable attention to the instincts of sadism and masochism. He examined them in detail for the first time in this section on perversions. Sadism and masochism can become perversions if they dominate sexual activity, but they are viewed as being primary and innate to the sexual drive. In 1905 Freud postulated that sadism is a component of sexual impulses in that the male wants to subjugate the woman and possess her without wooing her. He considered this to be part of natural masculine aggressiveness. Only after sadism has undergone some vicissitudes, as discussed in "Instincts and Their Vicissitudes," does it become associated with the infliction of pain. For a long time Freud considered masochism to be sadism turned toward the self. He did not view it as a primary instinct. In

1920, however, he formulated the existence of primary masochism in *Beyond the Pleasure Principle* which we will discuss shortly.

Returning to the clinical focus, Freud compared perversions with the psychoneuroses, stating that the neuroses are the negative of the perversions. He meant that whereas in neuroses, sexual feelings are repressed and replaced by symptoms, in the perversions they are acted out. These sexual feelings are infantile feelings that contain what Freud called the "polymorphous perverse." At the beginning, the sexual drive consists of component instincts (this is the first time the term appears), which consist of pairs of opposites, such as scopophilia and exhibitionism or sadism and masochism. In 1920, Freud added that in the psychoneuroses as well there is a universal tendency toward inversion.

This statement invalidates his hypothesis about perversions being the negative of neuroses, as they appear side by side rather than replacing each other. Furthermore, psychopathology can not be so simply explained on the basis of repression and the return of the repressed. Repressed feelings seek substitute outlets, which may cause perverse behavior as well as symptoms. In the perversions there are also many defensive mechanisms operating, such as splitting and denial, which Freud discussed in a later paper (1926). Today we emphasize structural defects and the primitive ego states that are so frequently found in patients who exhibit perverse behavior.

Infantile Sexuality

I believe Freud considered this essay to be one of his most important and controversial contributions. Ellenberger (1941) stated that Freud exaggerated the vehemence of his opposition. When he presented an account of his experiences in Paris with Charcot as well as some of his own conclusions on sexuality and hysteria to the Vienna Medical Society, he was not, as he later stated, denigrated and hostilely rejected. Ellenberger produced copies of the discussions, and although the medical community was skeptical and critical, it was not vituperative, at any rate not to the extent that Freud could feel justified in never attending another meeting of that society.

The reactions of mid-Victorian society against acknowledging the existence of infantile sexuality, however, were strong, and it is understandable that Freud withdrew from the scientific community during his years of "splendid isolation" (Freud 1915a), while he continued his explorations and even investigated the reasons why such opposition was inevitable.

Freud began this essay by calling attention to infantile amnesia. He asserted that the first six to eight years of life are ordinarily eradicated from our memory. This seems somewhat longer than reasonable, as most of us can remember back to four or five, and some claim even earlier verifiable memories. It would make sense, especially in Freud's schema, to place the beginning of infantile amnesia around the fourth year, since repression is the psychic mechanism that causes it, and in Freud's sequence of psychosexual development, there is a wave of repression during the oedipal phase, which occurs at this age. Infantile amnesia, therefore, would be the outcome of the repression of the Oedipus complex.

Freud saw a similarity between infantile and hysterical amnesia. The latter is due to the repression of oedipal sexual impulses. He then went on to discuss sexual latency, which follows the repression of oedipal feelings. Around age 3 or 4 the sexual life of children becomes manifest, but then there follows a period of sexual inhibition which impedes the expression of sexual instincts. This inhibition is the outcome of shame or disgust which is partially due to the moralizing influence of the environment and education, but which is primarily organically based and "fixed by heredity."

As an example of infantile sexuality, Freud discussed thumb-sucking. Despite the familiar criticism that thumb-sucking is not sexual, Freud maintained that it is sensual. He noted that the thumb-sucker is completely absorbed in the activity and that it leads either to sleep or some reaction that resembles an orgasm. Others, such as the pediatrician Lindner, also believed that thumb-sucking was fundamentally a sexual experience. Since the sexual instinct in thumb-sucking is not directed toward other people but rather toward the child's body, Freud called it autoerotic. Oral gratification at first involves nurture. Sexual activities then become attached to activities of self-preservation. The child's lips and oral mucosa have become erotogenic zones, and not until later do oral gratification and sexuality become separated.

The concept of erotogenic zones seems fuzzy. What did Freud actually mean when he stated that such zones lead to sexual pleasure? In fact, what did he mean by erotogenic zones? Simply, an erotogenic zone is a part of the body which, when stimulated, produces pleasure. Freud equated this pleasure with sexual pleasure even for infants. Apparently, any pleasure other than that which is the outcome of a satisfactory nurturing experience or, more broadly, anything related to self-preservation, is sexual pleasure, according to Freud. Alexander (1961) incorporated this assertion in his "surplus energy theory," in which he stated that any libido remaining after basic survival needs are met is used in play or sexual activity. Alexander, like Freud, based his concept on a quantitative energy model, which is no longer given much credence by many analysts.

Returning to erotogenic zones, any part of the body can become a source of sexual excitation, but particularly the skin and mucous membranes. The stimulus is always characterized by rhythmicity, and Freud suspected that the ensuing pleasure does not contain any specific quality. (This is a confusing statement, which I take to mean that regardless of which erotogenic zone is stimulated, the rhythmic quality of the stimulation evokes a similar feeling.) In hysteria, other parts of the body besides the genitals become erotogenic zones. These are then called hysterogenic zones, and they become substitutes for the genitals.

Freud concluded that the sexual aim of the infantile instinct is achieved through the stimulation of erotogenic zones, and then he proceeded to explain how this comes about. Satisfaction has to be a repetition of a previous satisfaction; that is regarding the lips and mouth, the previous satisfaction was the outcome of satisfactory feeding. Freud conceptualized sexual needs as being initially centrally located (or in his own words, "centrally conditioned") and then projected onto erotogenic zones. This projection leads to a state of tension or unpleasure, which is removed by an external stimulus, a manipulation analogous to sucking. Freud did not elaborate on what he meant by centrally located, but most likely, he was referring to the inner source of the instinct, as he discussed in "Instincts and Their Vicissitudes". However, he also stated that the instinct arises from the erotogenic zone. On page 185 of this essay he wrote, ". . . once we have understood the nature of the instinct arising from a single one of the erotogenic zones," a phrase which implies that the instinct has not been projected on such zones.

Infantile sexuality manifests itself by masturbation, which Freud divided into three phases: (1) early infantile masturbation, (2) a re-emergence of masturbatory behavior around the age of 4, followed by latency, and (3) pubertal masturbation.

This essay outlined the sequence of the various psychosexual stages of development, although they were not all formulated at the same time. Sucking is followed by the anal phase, which Freud equated with control. This is the first time the child is confronted with a prohibition: an instinct—to soil—cannot be gratified. Consequently, the child learns that a world exists that is contrary to his interests. This is an example of Freud's belief that psychic development is the outcome of frustration. In terms of ego psychology, Freud was asserting that the emergence from a fused state to beginning recognition of external objects is based upon the prohibition of instinctual gratification. Freud assumed that the fusion state would persist without this frustration. Winnicott (1953), in contrast, believed that there has to be a complete fusion in which the child does not recognize the external source of nurture before object relations can be established.

Freud believed that anal activity is related to control. The child controls his bowel movements, that is, he will soil, or retain his feces, when he wishes to counter the external world that is controlling him. Later, as we know, Freud connected this kind of control to the obsessive-compulsive patient's need to control his inner feelings.

When Freud wrote this monograph, he had already given up his seduction hypothesis, but he felt that sometimes childhood seductions occurred and that these could lead to neuroses as well as the reappearance of infantile sexuality in later childhood. However, this was not invariably the case. He stated that enuresis is equivalent to nocturnal emission, an interesting thought and one that possibly could be explored with the technical innovations of the sleep laboratory.

Scopophilia, exhibitionism, and cruelty are component instincts. The energy attached to scopophilic impulses can supply the instinct for knowledge or research which, in turn represents a sublimated effort at obtaining mastery. Children's curiosity causes them to try to discover where babies come from—the riddle of the Sphinx, as Freud called it. Sophocles, however, told us that the riddle of the Sphinx was: what has four legs in the morning, two at midday, and three in the evening? The answer was of course Man.

According to Freud, the male child assumes everyone has a penis similar to his own. It is only when he begins to doubt this that he begins to experience castration anxiety. Little girls develop penis envy as they become aware that boys have penises and they do not. I do not believe we need to dwell upon these male-oriented concepts. Today, we view femininity as having its own developmental antecedents rather than being a vicissitude of masculinity.

Children carry out their research on sexuality in solitude. Because children cannot know about the fertilizing role of semen nor, as Freud also believed, about the female sexual orifice, they will not be successful in their quest for knowledge. This failure might damage their instinct for knowledge later. (This interesting idea might have some relationship to learning difficulties.) On the other hand, this early solitude may also lead to independence, in that the children keep some things to themselves and do not completely confide in adults.

The next section, which was written in 1915, outlines the well-known oral, anal, and genital phases of sexual development. In a footnote, written in 1924, Freud mentioned that the phallic phase precedes the genital phase. It is interesting that he conceived these stages at different times and not in the sequence in which they were postulated. For example, the oral phase was first mentioned in 1915, whereas the later anal phase was formulated in 1913 in "The Predisposition to Obsessional Neurosis," and the phallic phase was formulated in his 1923 paper, "The Infantile Genital Organization of the Libido."

In discussing the sources of infantile sexuality, Freud referred to certain activities that are intrinsically stimulating, for example, being swung or thrown in the air. Any strong affect can be experienced as sexual. From this, we can conclude that activities that are not ordinarily sexual can become sexualized. The phases that we have just mentioned refer to body parts, such as the mouth or anus, that were initially involved in nonsexual functions. Freud viewed oral, anal, and urethral erotism as part of the normal sexual constitution. They become abnormal only when they become dominant, a quantitative rather than qualitative distinction.

The Transformations of Puberty

At puberty sexuality takes its final form. Freud stated that up until then masculine and feminine sexual development follow a similar course, but with the acquisition of secondary sexual characteristics, they diverge. This seems odd in that Freud had clearly indicated differences in boys and girls regarding the resolution of the Oedipus complex and castration anxiety. He did not discuss this divergence further, but proceeded to describe how he believed mature masculine sexuality is achieved.

The convergence of affectionate and sexual feelings, both directed toward a sexual object in order to achieve the sexual aim, leads to a normal sexual life. The affectionate feelings, or current, as Freud called it, represent the residual of the efflorescence of infantile sexuality. Here is another example of how feelings and attitudes characteristic of early developmental phases become incorporated into later adjustments and adaptations. A loving relationship based upon infantile dependence becomes further structuralized and, with the physiological maturation of the gonads, leads to the establishment of a mature object relationship in which both partners value each other and are capable of receiving and giving sexual gratification. Thus, each developmental stage contributes to later stages, which is another expression of the principle of structural hierarchy.

Much can go wrong in the process of psychic development, and Freud thought that, any disturbance in sexual development is the consequence of inhibition. This seems to be a somewhat constricted viewpoint, as it explains complex psychopathology simply on the basis of inhibition. Today we would think of ego distortions, defective development, and the manifestations of such disturbed fixated psychic states as all being involved in the production of sexual problems. Freud was conceptualizing almost exlusively on the basis of drives at this time, and structural factors remained in the background if they were considered at all.

Next Freud discussed the types of stimuli that cause sexual excitement. He believed that such stimuli come from three directions: (1) the external world, which stimulates erotogenic zones, (2) the interior of the body, which represents the inner organic source of an instinct, and (3) the mind, which refers to memory traces of past stimuli and gratifications. The resultant sexual excitation has a mental and a somatic component. In the psychic sphere, there is a peculiar and compelling feeling of tension, and in the somatic there are changes in the genitals, which are preparatory for copulation.

Again we are faced with the question of pleasure and unpleasure. Freud had postulated earlier that a rise in tension causes unpleasure. Sexual tension is, as Freud stated, "undoubtedly felt as pleasurable." This raises the perplexing question of how something unpleasurable (increase in tension) can be pleasurable. Freud did not answer this question, but he did rephrase it by asking how an experience of pleasure can give rise to a need for greater pleasure.

Freud was, in fact, referring to forepleasure. An erotogenic zone is stimulated, and this is perceived as pleasurable. This cathected erotogenic zone acts as a stimulus to another zone, the genitals, which are subject to tension. The latter leads to erection in men or secretions of the vaginal mucosa in women, making intercourse possible. The act of intercourse leads to the final pleasure, which is experienced as orgasm and leads to the discharge or reception of semen. There is danger when the forepleasure becomes too intense and the degree of tension is too small, in that the genital zone is not activated to the point of requiring the sexual act for discharge. This may lead to a fixation of the forepleasure that never goes beyond a nongenital erotogenic zone, a factor that is always found in perversions.

Again Freud equated the heightening of tension to unpleasure and discharge, and the lowering of tension to pleasure. We need not belabor this point inasmuch as in the previous section, Freud himself recognized the difficulties in thinking just in terms of quantitative vectors. However, he emphasized that the end result of the sexual act—the discharge of sexual substances—is the ultimate pleasure. He outlined a sequence, from an accumulation of semen in the gonads exerting tension on the interstitial tissue of the testes which then sends impulses to a central neurological site initiating a reflex, which is completed by ejaculation. This central site has connections with higher psychic centers, which become activated and enter consciousness. He amplified this sequence by postulating a chemical theory involving what he called an accumulation of sexual products. The stimulation of the interstitial tissue produces what we might call hormones, which enter the bloodstream and stimulate both spinal centers and psychic areas, presumably memory traces of satisfactory sexual experiences. This stimulation is experienced as sexual excitation.

However, there is a basic weakness in these conjectures: Freud called attention to children, women, and mature men who have been castrated, and in whom there is obviously no accumulation of sexual products, yet they are capable of experiencing sexual excitation.

Freud wondered whether the interstitial tissue is initially hermaphroditic. He also conjectured that there may be other organic structures besides the interstitial tissue of the gonads—perhaps glands—that are instrumental in determining sexual excitation and gender.

Freud next proceeded with the libido theory, but this section was written in 1915, and these concepts will be discussed in detail in Chapter 7. Briefly, Freud directed our attention to the balance between ego libido (narcissistic libido) and object libido: the more ego libido the less object libido, and vice versa. He traces a continuum between a narcissistic ego, in which the libido is mainly directed toward the self, and a state of psychic depletion, in which the libido is attached to the idealized love object.

Freud then returned to the topic of the differences between men and women. I suppose these views are one of the reasons why some have considered the Three Essays to be anachronistic. For instance, Freud believed that women repress their sexuality earlier and more intensely than men. Freud stated that women are no different than men regarding infantile sexuality and masturbation, but then he called these activities masculine sexuality. Feminine sexuality is essentially passive in that the female is receptive, the ovum receiving the sperm. Males, however, are sexually aroused by the female's passivity and even by her repression of sexuality.

The last ten pages of this essay recapitulate much of what Freud wrote in "On Narcissism." He mentioned here how sexual object choice is patterned after early infantile objects that were responsible for nurture. He also emphasized how infantile objects, the parents, stimulate their children sexually through such ordinary activities as bathing, hugging, and caressing, and how an excess of such stimulation can lead to disturbances of the sexual life later. Because of the incest barrier, an innate inherited quality, the pubertal child has to abandon infantile ties and seek heterosexual object relationships elsewhere. Consequently, there must be an inevitable opposition to parental authority to make this detachment possible. Adolescent rebellion, therefore, is unavoidable and independent of cultural factors, so Freud believed. Nevertheless, he did not abandon cultural relativism. He alluded to the homosexuality of highly developed cultures such as the ancient Greeks and how, although their early upbringing of children could lead to inversion, this was compatible with the values and standards of that civilization.

Freud covered many topics in these essays. He constructed a developmental continuum by discussing deviations and vicissitudes of sexual drives. This is the approach of the clinician. We will now trace Freud's further development of these ideas in the next paper "On Narcissism" in which he introduced us to extensions that today are relevant to structural psychopathology and object relations theory.

7

"On Narcissism: An Introduction" (1914)

SYNOPSIS

Freud's clinical observations of schizophrenic patients caused him to formulate the concept of narcissism. Although he first observed narcissistic phenomena as perversions, in that the patient treated his body as if it were a love object, Freud also understood that these phenomena were related to psychic development and represented an instinctual vicissitude. Freud defined narcissism as the libidinal supplement to the egoism of the self-preservative drive and formulated the existence of ego libido; this concept made it difficult to maintain the dualism of ego and sexual instincts, since sexual instincts were now also thought to be directed toward the ego. He concluded that narcissistic patients could not be treated psychoanalytically, since their libido cannot be directed toward external objects, which must occur in the formation of transference. Freud also distinguished between the narcissistic and the transference neuroses.

There is a balance between ego libido and object libido. In megalomania, libido remains within the ego. In the opposite state, being in love, the ego is depleted as the external object is invested with large quantities of libido.

These formulations about distribution of libido are relevant to the developmental sequence Freud postulated. He traced a continuum beginning with autoerotism through primary and secondary narcissism, and ending with whole object relationships. In this monograph Freud did not discuss whole object relationships, as he was more interested in the early phases of the developmental spectrum.

Narcissistic phenomena, as manifested in megalomanic orientations and by attitudes about the omnipotence of thoughts, are frequently observed in savages and children, according to Freud. Narcissism can be studied further by investigating (1) the psychic states accompanying organic disease, (2) hypochondria, and (3) the erotic life. Freud commented that hypochondria is similar to organic illness in terms of libido distribution. In fact, hypochondria can be thought of as being the third actual neurosis. Whereas in neurasthenia the libido is depleted and in anxiety neurosis libido that would have been directed toward objects is dammed-up and never reaches higher mentational centers, in hypochondria ego libido is dammed-up. In the psychoneuroses the anxiety resulting from dammed-up libido reaches higher centers and is defensively worked over by fantasies. In hypochondria, megalomania works over dammed-up ego libido.

Freud next discussed object choices as he focused upon the third area—erotic life. In the young male, sexual instincts attach themselves to the first object attachment, the nurturing mother. Sexual instincts lean on self-preservative instincts, a masculine type of object choice known as *anaclitic*. Freud also described narcissistic and non-narcissistic object choices.

There are many factors involved in the maintenance of narcissistic equilibrium, which may also be referred to as self-love or self-esteem. Repression proceeds from the ego and drives out of the field of awareness psychic elements that threaten self-love, self-regard, and self-respect. These latter elements reside in the ego ideal, which Freud believed retained the lost elements of infantile narcissism. Self-regard is linked to narcissistic libido. In schizophrenia, self-regard is pathologically enhanced (as evidenced by megalomania), whereas in the transference neuroses and the state of being in love it is lowered.

If libido that would lead to self-regard on the one hand or to object relationships on the other is repressed, there is a diminution of narcissism. Though cathecting an external object may deplete narcissistic libido, reciprocation—being loved—restores it. If loving –being loved is not an aspect of psychopathology, then it is implied but not stated explicitly that narcissism has both psychopathological and healthy elements.

By the time Freud wrote this work, he had already given the topic of narcissism considerable attention. He outlined its importance in formulating the psychodynamics of paranoid psychoses when writing about the Schreber case (Freud 1911a). In 1909, Freud had told Ernest Jones that he considered narcissism to be a normal stage of development between autoerotism and object relationships.

Freud at first attributed the term narcissism to Näcke, although later, in one of the numerous addendas to the "Three Essays," he corrected himself and credited Havelock Ellis for having coined it. Ellis, in turn, wrote that Näcke did have some claim to the term in that he had first described narcissism as a perversion, whereas Ellis had described a "narcissus-like" mental state.

Freud began by noting that some persons treat their body as if it were a love object, stroking and fondling themselves or regarding their body with fondness and admiration. If this attitude becomes fixed and intense, it becomes a perversion.

However, this does not necessarily happen. Freud defined narcissism as the libidinal supplement to the egoism of the self-preservative drive. This formulation creates difficulties for the dual instinct theory. First, narcissism, or ego libido, upsets the pairing of self-preservative or ego instincts and sexual instincts. Libido is defined as the energic component of the sexual instincts. If libido can also be directed toward the ego in the same way as the ego instincts are, what is the advantage of separating ego and sexual instincts? This is confusing because ego instincts are directed toward external objects and thus, unlike ego libido, they are not directed toward the ego. In "Instincts and Their Vicissitudes," Freud made this point explicit, indicating that self-preservative instincts (ego instincts) require an external object, whereas some sexual instincts do not. The latter may be either autoerotic or directed toward the self, as in narcissism. Even though an external nurturing object is required for an infant's survival, is the neonate aware of this? Would not both ego and sexual instincts be directed toward an amorphous self or a rudimentary ego that does not yet have the capacity to make distinctions between the inner and outer world? During these early phases we cannot think of any drive being object-directed. Object direction is achieved later.

When Freud discussed the egoism of the self-preservative drive, he was referring to that part of the drive that cathects the ego. Narcissism as a libidinization of that egoism leads us to think in terms of three rather than two types of instincts: (1) self-preservative instincts; (2) a confluence of self-preservative and sexual instincts directed toward the ego and defined as narcissism; and (3) sexual instincts as object libido. These theoretical speculations are the outcome of Freud's attempts to cling to a dual instinct theory.

Freud now returned to the clinical area. The concept of narcissism was forced upon him by his observations of schizophrenic patients. Freud had referred to this group of patients as "paraphrenics," but he later adopted Bleuler's term, "schizophrenia," which was coined in 1911. Freud had direct contact with two schizophrenic patients that we know of: the paranoid woman he discussed in the latter part of his second paper on the defense neuropsychoses (Freud 1896, Ch. 3) and another paranoid woman whom he discussed much later (Freud 1920a). His most comprehensive formulations about psychoses came from his study of the Schreber case, which he learned about by reading the patient's memoirs. He never met Dr. Schreber. Similarly, he only saw Little Hans once, and yet, from that one meeting and consultations with his father, he made his most cogent formulations about phobias. I doubt that Freud would have thought he had had much clinical familiarity with schizophrenic patients.

He outlined here why psychoanalysis has very little influence on schizophrenic patients, who he considered as belonging to a subcategory of the narcissistic neuroses. (As mentioned earlier, the other group consists of depressive disorders.) The schizophrenic withdraws libido from the outer world, detaching it from external objects and returning it to his ego—an example of narcissism. This is different from what happens in the psychoneuroses or, as Freud called them, the transference neuroses. In these conditions the libido is also returned to the ego from the outer world, but it does not become detached from the object; it remains attached to the memory trace of the object, the fantasied object. Freud reluctantly acknowledged that this process can be considered an example of introversion, a term that Jung first used. [It seems strange to think of libido being completely without an object.]

Freud defined drive in operational terms as having a source, aim, and object. Inherent in a drive (or, for our purpose, the energic component of the drive, libido) is the object that will satisfy it. Thus, it is conceptually meaningless to speak of free-floating libido. These distinctions are not just exercises in theoretical hair-splitting; they are crucial to our understanding of the therapeutic process and of what disorders are psychoanalytically treatable. If there is no such thing as objectless libido, then transference *is* possible, and, of course, it does occur in the entities Freud labeled narcissistic neuroses.

Again we have to think in terms of hierarchies. The schizophrenic object is much more primitive than the object of the structured neurotic. As Freud (1915) pointed out, schizophrenics relate to external objects as if they were things, that is, in a concrete manner. When libido is pulled back from the external world, the archaic object to which it is attached is also withdrawn. In fact, for the most part, these objects remain internal and are weakly projected outside the psyche. Furthermore, they are merged with primitive parts of the self, so that in the schizophrenic patient it is often difficult to determine what belongs to the external world in what is part of the psyche.

Freud next postulated a balance between ego libido and object libido. Megalomania is the result of libido being primarily contained within the ego. The opposite condition—libido being predominantly invested in the external object, as occurs in the state of being in love—is experienced as depletion and leads to the idealization of the beloved. Ordinarily, there is a balance, a reciprocal relationship, between ego libido and object libido.

The accumulation of libido withdrawn from the external world into the ego leads to omnipotent feelings, which are superimposed upon previous omnipotent states. Freud expressed this rather clumsily, and it is not at all clear what is meant by a previous omnipotent state. Freud was thinking primarily in developmental terms. I wish to emphasize that he was discussing narcissism in the context of *normal* development. He traced a progression from autoerotism through primary narcissism to secondary narcissism as a pathway to object relationships. During the autoerotic stage, the psyche has very little structure; it is amorphous. Primary narcissism is distinguished by the formation of a rudimentary ego toward which the component instincts now direct themselves. Freud introduced us to the amoeba metaphor to explain secondary narcissism. He viewed the psyche as an amoeba, which extends pseudopodia toward the outer world and then retracts them. This is a depiction of how the libido seeks objects and then returns to the ego.

What is missing here is the fate of the external object. To understand its significance, we need another model. Today, we postulate the existence of self and object representations within the ego system. In secondary narcissism, the object representation becomes cathected but then fuses with the self-representation. With this merger, both self and object representations are cathected. Primary narcissism, on the other hand, involves only the self-representation, although at these early stages there is not much of a cohesive sense of self.

Savages and children, according to Freud, exhibit manifestations of narcissism. They believe in the omnipotence of thoughts and magic presumably because of increased ego libido, which is a megalomanic phenomenon. Anthropologists would be quick to say that "savages" cannot be thought of as being simply fixated at primitive developmental levels. So-called savage societies can have extremely intricate organizations, indicating that the minds of the members are correspondingly complex. Perhaps, the sense of omnipotence and belief in magic is more overt than it is in our society, but much more than narcissism is involved.

The remainder of this first section is devoted to saving the dual instinct theory and to expressing anger at Carl Jung, who had postulated that a monistic theory would resolve many of the dilemmas Freud faced. Freud himself (1914, p. 76) raised the question that, since psychic energies of ego instincts and libido exist together during narcissism, ". . . why is there any necessity for further distinguishing a sexual libido from a nonsexual energy of the ego instincts? Would not the postulation of a single kind of psychical energy save us all the difficulties of differentiating an energy of the ego-instincts from ego-libido, and ego-libido from object-libido"? In fact, Freud stressed that we cannot know about the existence of ego libido until we can recognize object libido.

What follows contains some interesting arguments, but they are impassioned and at times resort to tautological thinking. This is evidenced by Freud's attempt to justify himself by presenting a methodological argument. He emphasized that any science has to begin with loose and indistinct hypotheses. As we gather more observational data, these hypotheses will be modified and become more precise, allowing for a more organized approach. He stressed that these indistinct hypotheses are not basic concepts, that is, they are not the foundations of our science, but rather are surface concepts. Freud's methodological digression is an example of his familiarity with scientific principles and confirms once again that he is a scientist. However, his bringing this topic up at this juncture could indicate defensiveness on his part.

The treatment and investigation of the transference neuroses strengthened Freud's conviction about a basic dual instinct theory. In the clinical setting, he could make psychodynamic formulations on the basis of conflict between sexual desire and the need to survive. His theory also conforms to the well-known antithesis of hunger and love.

Freud's basic justification of dualism rests primarily on biological principles. Man functions in two fundamental ways. First, he is the carrier of an immortal germ plasm that ensures the survival of the race. This is an expression of the self-preservative instinct. Second, he derives pleasure from the sexual act which is the outcome of the gratification of the sexual instinct.

Freud believed that someday we would find a chemical basis to support the division between self-preservative and sexual instincts. However, he hoped that we would be able to replace chemical substances with psychic forces. In essence, he was tracing a continuum between organic substrata and psychological processes. If the former can demonstrate two basic elements, then these different substances will create two fundamental instincts. This argument borders on tautology.

Next, Freud proceeded with vehemence against Jung, who had stated that Freud had to extend the concept of libido to a general psychic interest and divest it of the sexual factor. Jung also claimed that Freud should retract his libido theory because of the difficulties he encountered in formulating the Schreber case. Freud vigorously denied this claim, but Jung had a good point. It is difficult to formulate the problems of patients suffering from structural defects in terms of Freud's dualistic libido theory. However, I doubt that Jung was thinking in an ego-psychological perspective.

Freud also took issue with Jung's assertion that the loss of reality following the withdrawal of libido from the outer world best describes as anchorite rather than a schizophrenic patient. Freud here demonstrated his striking ability to find another's weak spot and use it to his advantage. An anchorite has not withdrawn his interest into himself; he has renounced sexual and material needs but has displaced them to the spiritual realm. Still, Freud's criticism of Jung's statement had little to do with validating a dual instinct theory.

This second section of the paper, in my mind, is one of the most exciting chapters in psychoanalysis, and is particularly relevant to current studies of primitive mental states and their accompanying agitation. Furthermore, the connections Freud made between neurotic and psychotic processes brilliantly demonstrate what might be called the universality of psychic mechanisms.

Freud began by stating that we can obtain a better knowledge of narcissism by studying (1) the psychic states accompanying organic disease, (2) hypochondria and, (3) erotic life.

It is well known that when a person is sick he is no longer interested in the surrounding world. Freud added that both libidinal and general interest is withdrawn, again emphasizing dualism. He admitted that since the fate of libidinal and nonlibidinal interests are the same (both are withdrawn from the external world back onto the ego), they are indistinguishable from each other. These are examples of a redistribution of libido, as also occurs during sleep when the libido is also withdrawn back onto the self, or specifically, back onto the wish to sleep.

Hypochondria and organic illness are both characterized by painful bodily sensations. Unlike organic illness, however, hypochondria is supposedly not accompanied by organic changes. Freud, however, believed that the introversion of libido in hypochondria does, in fact, produce physical changes, and here he made a fascinating connection, which he had discussed as early as 1911 when he was formulating the Schreber case (Freud 1911). He postulated that the anxiety found in patients who might form transference neuroses also caused organic changes, which occurred as a result of a damming-up of object libido. In hypochondria there is a similar damming-up of ego libido. Consequently, in addition to the anxiety neurosis and neurasthenia, hypochondria can be classified as a third actual neurosis.

The comparison can be extended further. Freud postulated that in the actual neuroses libido cannot gain access to higher psychical structures; that is, it cannot reach ego levels where it could be worked through, or in his phrase, "worked over." Consequently, libido is deflected and experienced as anxiety. We can think of this state of affairs as representing a kernel around which a neurosis can be formed. The ego sets defenses in motion to alleviate anxiety, resulting in a transference neurosis or psychoneurosis. From this viewpoint, we think of the actual neuroses as transitions in the process of formation of a neurosis. Freud would not have agreed completely with this formulation, because he also viewed the actual neuroses as distinct, stable, clinical conditions.

In hypochondria, something similar happens. First we have to discuss why withdrawn libido, as the dammed-up libido of anxiety, has to be painful. In *The Three Essays* (Freud 1905), Freud wrestled with the question as to what constitutes pain, and he speculated that increased tension is responsible for unpleasure. Then he added that pleasure becomes unpleasure when it cannot be mentationally worked over. If a state of tension cannot be relieved or discharged, by an appropriate act, then it becomes painful. For every change in the erotogenicity of an organ, there is a parallel change in the ego's libidinal cathexis, unless psychopathology interferes. In paraphrenia there is a damming-up of ego libido, which leads to hypochondria in the same way that damming-up of object libido leads to anxiety neurosis. The accumulations of ego libido caused Freud to consider paraphrenia as the third actual neurosis.

This is a problem of terminology. Freud used the word ego in several ways, sometimes loosely to signify the self and at other times to identify the ego as a system. He became increasingly aware of the imprecision of the concept, and in 1923 he wrote "The Ego and the Id" to clarify his ideas and to introduce the structural hypothesis. In "On Narcissism," when he referred to damming-up of ego-libido, he meant the more primitive somatic levels of the ego organization. Ego is not synonymous with mental representation or mentational processes, which belong at higher levels of the ego organization. As with all psychic structures, the ego can also be viewed in terms of an hierarchal continuum. The ego libido is not permitted access to psychological structures that contain memory traces of satisfying experiences. We concluded that in the anxiety neurosis libido cannot cathect memory traces of sexually satisfying object representations, which thus cannot stimulate the executive apparatus to seek sexual gratification in the outside world.

To be consistent, we would have to assume that libido bound in the soma cannot cathect memories of past experiences that elevated self-esteem. Although Freud did not say this directly, he implied it by stating that megalomania is a way of "working over" the accumulated libido of hypochondria. The megalomanic state is pleasurable in contrast to the hypochondriacal state. The grandiosity and self-aggrandizement of megalomania are the consequences of ego libido that is no longer dammed-up, and they represent a first stage in a process that will re-establish psychic equilibrium. In the anxiety neurosis, the equilibrating process results in a psychoneurosis, whereas in hypochondria, the end result is paraphrenia or schizophrenia, as we would say today.

These formulations are not altogether accurate, and the parallelism between the genesis of the psychoneuroses and paraphrenia cannot be maintained entirely. The megalomanic state achieves a type of equilibrium. Paraphrenia occurs when equilibrium fails, that is, when it does not work over the painful hypochondriacal tension, in which case libido has to be disposed of and is once again directed to the external world. In the anxiety neuroses, libido is somatically discharged. If it gains access to the ego and begins to cathect higher mentational centers, it creates anxiety.

Defensive and repressive processes are set in motion, causing psycho-neurosis. Freud did not modify this sequence, and later changed his formulation only in regard to where the anxiety came from; rather than attributing it to converted libido, he viewed it as the higher ego system's reaction to libido that threatens to intrude itself into forbidden areas of the mind (Freud 1926).

Damming-up of libido causes changes in the erotogenic zone similar to those in the genital zone: congestion of the vaginal mucosa, or an erection. Normally the erotogenic zones are libidinized as part of the foreplay and then cathect higher ego centers that are also associated with the genitals. These higher centers become cathected and the psyche seeks discharge through sexual gratification. In the actual neuroses these higher centers do not work over the accumulated libido, and painful tension is created. There is further confusion here; we spoke of libido being "bound" in the soma but we actually meant that it was contained there in a state of painful tension. If we think of binding tension as the conversion of a disruptive, agitated state to one of harmonious balance, then this libido is unbound.

What is the relationship between the damming-up of libido in eroto-genic zones, which causes hypochondria, and the autoerotic instincts, which also involve erotogenic zones? In the former, there is no discharge, whereas in the latter the instinct is gratified and libido discharged. What is responsible for this significant difference? Autoerotism is a phase of development in which the psyche is progressing to higher structural levels. The libido involved in hypochondria, however, has moved backward, due to regression from an attachment to an external object to a cathexis of the somatic part of the ego.

This has an interesting implication. During the autoerotic phase, instincts can be gratified (that is, achieve discharge) through the erotogenic zones without the working over of higher psychic centers. In fact, there are no higher centers. Apparently, once development has proceeded to the point that libido can be satisfied by objects, then it cannot be discharged when it regresses back to erotogenic zones. Thinking in terms of degrees of satisfaction causes difficulties, because hypochondria is a form of psycho-pathology and not simply another method of instinctual discharge. The acquisition of psychic structure makes previous modes of obtaining gratification ineffective. As a concrete example, although mother's milk is satisfying to an infant, the adult requires something more savory.

We have been discussing very complicated and, because of imprecise terms, confusing concepts. Some of these ideas are summarized in Table 1.

Freud then discussed further different types of object choices. He introduced a positive note in that he also viewed the formation of object libido as a way of enhancing oneself. Withdrawn libido has to be returned to external objects, and this regularly occurs when a person is being creative. The creative act is a healing process; turning toward the outer world can re-establish psychic equilibrium as well as lead to a depleted psychic state. Some psychoanalysts would agree that this is a valid view of creativity, the creative person is basically depressed and uses his talents to heal himself.

This theory implies that creativity is a reaction to psychopathology. I believe, however, that the creative person has an unusual capacity to relate to the inner world of the mind and the outer world of reality intensively and often at the same time. The scientists I have analyzed had a strong tendency to idealize, and when working they were still very actively involved in their object relations and other aspects of reality. They were not withdrawn while creating; on the contrary, they lived life to their fullest and were very

Table 1. Parallels Between the Psychoneuroses and Narcissistic Neuroses (Paraphrenia)

Psychoneuroses	Narcissistic Neuroses (Paraphrenia)
Libido is worked over in fantasy, which contains defensive elements. As in a dream, there is sufficient disguise so that the ego is not threatened by libidinal impulses.	Libido is worked over (megalomania).
Failure of above leads to anxiety.	Failure leads to hypochondria (libidinal regression).
Anxiety is resolved by neurotic defenses such as: 　Repression (hysterical mode) 　Isolation (control of sadism) 　(Obsessive neurosis)	Regressed libido is redirected to the outer world in an attempt at restitution: Projection and withdrawal (schizophrenia) Projection of rageful impulses causing persecutory feelings (paranoia)

much involved in all areas of their lives including sexuality. Some may have suffered from psychopathology, but it hindered rather than enhanced their creativity.

An argument frequently given for the curative aspects of creativity is that it occurs in inspirational spurts and is episodic in nature. I have not observed this in the scientists I have analyzed. It is true that most of them sought analysis because one of their symptoms was a certain degree of paralysis in their creative ability, and many had long fallow periods followed by bursts of activity. However, this changed as the analysis progressed, and in many instances the end result was what we might call continuous creativity. What happened was that the creative act became drawn into a defensive adaptation but this does not mean that it was a defense in the first place. The analysis in some instances helped make creativity autonomous once again.

We now return to specific object choices and the vicissitudes of narcissism. The erotic lives and object choices of men and women is the third area in which narcissism can be studied. Freud began by describing an object choice that regularly occurs in male development. The boy's sexual feelings attach themselves to the first object attachment, the nurturing mother. According to Freud, the sexual instincts lean on the self-preservative instincts, what he called the *Anlehnustypus*, the anaclitic type of object choice. He divided object choice into general categories, distinguishing between narcissistic object choice and anaclitic. In an interesting aside he asserted that the anaclitic type is a masculine object choice; therefore, by exclusion, the only type of object choice available to women is the narcissistic type.

Freud described certain women who are totally narcissistic. They are frequently beautiful, and their attraction is based upon their total self-contentment and independence. By independence, Freud meant that they are involved only in themselves and feel that their role in life is to be admired. He emphasized that, to some extent, we are all fascinated by persons who are immersed and comfortable in their narcissism. Certain animals, such as cats, intrigue us because of this quality. We relate to babies as idols and ignore their imperfections. "His majesty, the baby" rules the household in his exalted narcissistic position and our positive reactions to him are reflections of our longing to recapture our lost childhood narcissism. According to Freud, this is a typical feminine orientation. A woman gives up her narcissistic position when she has children of her own. As she continues to love the child who first is part of her body and then separate from her, there is a shift from primary to secondary narcissism.

Actually, Freud was not saying that those women achieve a non-narcissistic type of object love. Rather, he saw a progression from total involvement with the self to narcissistic preoccupation with an external object. Freud's opinions about women were not particularly charitable—still, is there any such thing as completely non-narcissistic object love? Even in those instances of idealization and depletion of ego libido in favor of object libido, there has to be a narcissistic element. This is probably the outcome of projective identification. In the best of relationships, one finds valued parts of the self in the love object.

We occasionally encounter clinically women and men such as Freud described. These patients may be difficult to treat and casue specific countertransference reactions. They require admiration, and in the analytic situation this usually takes the form of demanding feedback. I have found this to be true of the very few patients that I have been unable to put on the couch. One woman violently rejected the idea of lying down because she had to maintain eye contact. Another patient finally did lie down but frequently turned around to look at me. On the surface, these women had an intense need to be admired, but underneath they were hollow, and painfully isolated. Clearly, the narcissistic orientation represented an attempt to maintain a sense of aliveness. From another viewpoint, they were not narcissistic enough; that is, they did not have enough healthy narcissism.

Freud summarized the following types of object choice.

1. Narcissistic
   What oneself is
   What oneself was
   What oneself would like to be
   A person who was once part of the self
2. Anaclitic
   The nurturing woman
   The protective man

Freud next made some curious remarks about the role of castration anxiety. The castration complex is perhaps the most intense threat to the child's original narcissism. At the time of its formation, the ego and sexual instincts are still blended with each other, and together they form the child's narcissistic interest.

This is difficult to understand. What did Freud mean when he wrote about the comingling of libidinal and ego instincts within the context of the castration complex? He remarked about this in passing, as if it were self-evident. Since he did not elaborate it is impossible to tell exactly what he had in mind, but I suppose the ego-instinct element, that is, the self-preservative factor, is involved in the idealization of the phallus. The possibility of castration threatens bodily integrity. Mutilation would be a narcissistic injury, to say the least. Since libidinal impulses—more specifically incestuous feelings—create the castration complex, we can think of a confluence of libidinal impulse and ego instincts. To summarize, sexual feelings toward the mother lead to the fear of retaliatory castration from the father and later from the internalized father, (now part of the superego), thereby threatening self-preservative or ego instincts. Thus, the penis is, as can be easily understood, the organ of the expression of sexual instincts and, at the same time, a narcissistically prized possession.

Adler believed that the masculine protest is the defensive consequence of the vulnerability that accompanies castration anxiety. However, he based it upon social evaluation rather than upon libidinal factors. Freud and Adler were different in one particularly important respect: Adler based the cause of neuroses on how the patient adjusts to the environment or as to how external objects react to the patient. If the outside world can support rather than threaten masculinity, then the patient achieves psychic equilibrium. Of course, the support of the external world is important because this will determine how well our adaptations will work. Freud, however, based causation less on external factors than on the strength and fate of the instincts.

The next passage is strange, as Freud later acknowledged. He stated that Adler made the masculine protest the sole cause of neurosis, but that there are also neuroses not based upon the castration complex. Freud wrote, "Incidentally, I know of cases of neurosis in which the masculine protest, or as we regard it, the castration complex, plays no pathogenic part, and even fails to appear at all" (Freud 1914, p. 93). Later, he admitted he did not know what he had in mind when he made that statement. He was a firm believer in the universality of the Oedipus complex, which always leads to castration anxiety. Indeed, his whole theory of neuroses is built upon this premise.

Freud then continued to examine the fate of infantile narcissism. He began by discussing repression: as a person develops, he acquires certain standards by which he measures himself, and what is unacceptable is repressed. Freud reached the important conclusion that repression proceeds from the ego, or, to be more precise, from the ego's self-respect. Whatever impulses or wishes threaten self respect are barred from consciousness, or repressed. In this work he stated that the standards and ideals that lead to repression are conscious. However, clinical data reveal that this often is not so; in fact, many patients put up considerable resistance to bringing superego factors into consciousness. This means that the standards that lead to repression may be unconscious. Consequently repression is a process emanating from the ego, but at the same time it is unconscious. This represents a conceptual dilemma. It was necessary for Freud to define a structural hierarchy in which the ego also has unconscious parts, which is the essence of the structural hypothesis and which he outlined in its final form in "The Ego and the Id" (Freud 1923). The ego ideal is an ego subsystem that contains the self-respect factor responsible for repression. Freud viewed the ego ideal as containing the perfections of infantile narcissism. In other words, the lost infantile narcissism is displaced into the ego ideal, inasmuch as the ego never wants to give up a past satisfaction.

In the course of growing up, the demands of the outside world and the person's critical judgment disturb the original narcissism. The ego ideal later becomes the focus of self-love. In childhood, the ego is the actual ego ideal. Freud put it succinctly: "What he projects before him as his ideal is the substitute for the lost narcissism of his childhood in which he was his own ideal" (Freud 1914, p. 94).

This may be confusing in view of current thinking. Freud was here bringing the ego ideal together with what in 1923 he described as the superego. The ego ideal contains all the perfections of infantile narcissism, but also contains prohibitions since it is the instigator of repression. Today we separate prohibitive factors from values and ideals. Violation of superego demands causes fear and guilt, whereas not meeting the standards of the ego ideal leads to shame.

Freud must have been aware of the difficulties inherent in placing the locus of repression and idealization in the same psychic structure. He recognized that there were differences in the mental processes that involved drives and those responsible for idealization, and he discussed this specifically in reference to sublimation and idealization. Sublimation, which he had already discussed in the *Three Essays*, leads to the desexualization of sexual instincts: in other words, it is something that happens to an instinct. Idealization, on the other hand, concerns the object. Freud emphasized that subservience to an idealized object is not accompanied by sublimation of libidinal drives, and added, "It is true that the ego-ideal demands such sublimation, but it cannot enforce it . . . " (Freud 1914, pp. 94–95). Once more, Freud anthropomorphized when he stated that the ego-ideal demands repression but through sublimation the ego can avoid repressing instincts.

Freud proceeded further in what eventually became the formulation of the separate psychic structures of the superego and the ego ideal. As early as this paper, he postulated the existence of a special agency that watches over both the ego and the ego ideal, measuring the ego by the standards of the ego ideal. Freud acknowledged that he was describing conscience, a psychic agency that enables us to understand the mechanisms of the psychopathology underlying "delusions of being noticed." His formulations were especially interesting because he made them in a structural rather than a psychodynamic context. In this instance, he was very much in line with modern clinical orientation. Delusions of being noticed or watched are characteristic of paranoid patients. Freud reached the fascinating conclusion that their complaints were justified. He was referring to the historical truth underlying delusions, but rather than discussing this in terms of the infantile past and trauma, he viewed it in terms of psychic structure. He pointed out that there is, in fact, an agency in the mind, in patients suffering from psychopathology as well as in normal persons, that watches over the person and that discovers and criticizes all his intentions. This agency undergoes repression in psychopathology.

Unquestionably Freud was here discussing structural regression, a concept far ahead of that time. First he described the genesis of what we can call the superego. The tendency to form the superego is developed from the critical influence of the parents and then is supplemented by teachers and other authority figures. Finally, public opinion adds its influence and becomes internalized into the conscience. Of course, Freud could not give up focusing on drives, as evidenced by his conclusion that homosexual libido is drawn into the formation of the narcissistic ego ideal. He had already discussed the importance and developmental significance of the Oedipus complex (Freud 1900). Around the age of 3 or 4, boys develop sexual feelings toward their mothers and murderous feelings toward their fathers. These feelings must be repressed, and the consequence is a passive homosexual attitude toward the father. Finally, the father's prohibitions are internalized and become part of the superego, and the homosexual libido that was attached to him is now directed to the superego, or the ego ideal, as Freud called it here. Inasmuch as this libido cathects an intra-ego structure, it is also narcissistic.

Freud always seemed to be emphasizing negative factors. For example, a mother's love for her child is the outcome of narcissism; fathers, and adults in general, want to recapture their lost infantile narcissism by idealizing their children. Indeed, every feeling seems to be self-serving. Today it is recognized that there are benign and loving aspects to the superego. It is also recognized that a mother's attachment to her child goes beyond narcissism. Still, Freud's orientation was deterministic and clinical. In fact, we might conclude that everything we do or feel has a self-serving element.

Returning to the genesis of delusions of being watched and ideas of reference, Freud continued formulating in terms of a structural regression. Conscience is a structure formed by the internalization of external prohibitions and standards. First external objects watch over the child's behavior, both approving and disapproving. After the passing of the Oedipus complex, the child, having made the restrictions of the outside world his own, judges himself. In a paranoid psychosis, the process is reversed. What was internalized is once again placed into the external world. What was once part of the psyche is now perceived as being outside the self, as it has been in the past.

Again, Freud made interesting side comments. Watching over the self is part of a self-observing introspective process, a quality he believed to be especially prominent in philosophers. He did not feel that he was philosophically bent, and consequently did not consider himself to be particularly introspective. Could this be why he dismissed countertransference as something that has to be done away with as soon as possible? On the other hand, how could he have conducted self-analysis without being introspective?

This self-observing quality occurs in dreams (which Freud claimed he seldom had) that depict psychic structure rather than just conflicting psychic forces. In *The Interpretation of Dreams*, Freud noted that Silberer had described such dreams and labeled the dream process the "functional phenomenon." Freud (1900) described states between sleep and waking, in which the sleeper is aware of his mental set and this is translated into visual images. The sleeper dreams of his current emotional state, his fatigue, or, as Freud put it, willingness as he struggles against sleep. There are several varieties of dreams that we can discuss primarily from an ego-psychological perspective rather than just in terms of id psychology. In other papers, Freud's ambivalence toward Silberer emerged as his negative feelings gained dominance.

Silberer initially described dreams that were visual representations of states of mind. He conducted an experiment in which the subject was engaged with a particular task while falling asleep. This activity carried over into the dream. Silberer gave the example of a person involved in hard intellectual work dreaming of a saw cutting a log. I suppose that Kekulé's famous dream of a snake swallowing its tail, representing the benzene ring, is another example of the functional phenomenon. These are concrete depictions of the functioning mind.

There are other dreams in which the self-observing function operates vigorously. We might call these totally narcissistic dreams, although all dreams are basically narcissistic. In these dreams, the dreamer knows that he is dreaming. Consequently he is in omnipotent control and can do whatever he wishes because he knows that he cannot be harmed. If he wishes to fly off a building like Superman, he can. He can bury himself in primary process and enjoy it. The dreamer enjoys this state; sometimes he is ecstatic and does not want to wake up. These are called lucid dreams and apparently occur quite frequently among creative persons. This makes sense, since the creative act involves a blending of primary and secondary process without being submerged by either. From one viewpoint, creativity can be viewed as secondary process mastery of the primary process.

There is another type of dream, which is a variation of those just discussed and which occurs frequently in patients suffering from structural defects. These are again dreams that depict something about the status of the psyche. Similar to Silberer's functional phenomenon, the manifest content is a visual expression of part of the mind, but instead of representing just thoughts and feelings the images depict psychic structure. For example, a house with various rooms may refer to the ego and its subsystems. The orderliness or disorderliness of the house parallels the synthesis or lack of synthesis of the ego organization. I have heard many such dreams from my patients who have characterological problems. An abstract concept, which stands for psychic structure, is concretely represented in the dream.

Freud did not believe it is necessary to give the dream censor, and now we have returned to standard dreams, the status of a separate psychic structure. Rather, he viewed it as part of the repressive process, that part which is directed toward the emerging dream thoughts. In *The Interpretation of Dreams*, he explained that the ego, in order to remain asleep, distorts these thoughts under the dominance of repressive forces.

Freud then returned to the topic of self-regard in both normals and neurotics. (Today we speak of this as self-esteem.) Anything that raises self-regard enlarges the ego. This is an interesting statement, which, in my mind, indicates that Freud was once again thinking in terms of a structural frame of reference. He remarked that residuals of the infantile omnipotence that are confirmed by contemporary experiences always raise self-esteem.

Freud repeatedly referred to this infantile omnipotence as the consequence of primary narcissism. For example, his use of the phrase "his majesty the baby," which he quoted in English in the original German text, emphasizes how committed he was to this belief. However, can a 2-month-old infant really feel omnipotent? Omnipotent feelings are relatively sophisticated and presuppose at least the recognition of external objects and the outer world, something which is beyond the psyche that has not gone beyond primary narcissism. Freud was adultomorphizing here.

Of course, in analysis we observe material indicating the infantile, extremely primitive qualities of megalomania but we can understand this material in terms of regression. Such feelings are constructed during later ego states and are defensive adaptations against various vulnerabilities and ego defects. As the ego regresses backwards to states approaching primary narcissism, these adaptive defenses are brought into the regression and then become associated with ego levels that antedate their formation.

Kohut commits the same error when he states that the grandiose self and the idealized parental imago are normal accompaniments of primary narcissism. The formation of a parental imago presupposes the recognition of external objects and the capacity to introject, something that would be far beyond the abilities of the embryonic ego at the stage of primary narcissism. Freud, Kohut, and Melanie Klein (particularly Klein) could all be accused of adultomorphisizing.

Returning to the text, Freud linked self-regard to narcissistic libido, which helped him differentiate sexual from ego drives. In paraphrenia, self-regard is enhanced, whereas in the transference neuroses and in loving and not being loved, it is lowered. Freud outlined the role of repression in the loss of self-regard. If sexual impulses are excluded from the ego sphere, the ego cathexis is lowered. In turn, the capacity to love, that is, to produce object cathexis, is impaired. In this situation the retention of libido within the psyche does not enhance self-esteem. This is because libido is repressed and not available to the ego, as it is in the megalomania of paraphrenia. Furthermore, if a person is unable to love, then the external object cannot reciprocate, so another source of narcissistic satisfaction and self-enhancement is lost.

This makes sense in general but it is also, at least in one way, confusing. The enhancement of self-esteem constitutes a narcissistic gratification and involves the ego ideal, but the ego ideal also institutes repression, which lowers the ego's cathexis. Somehow it seems conceptually awkward to make the agency responsible for repression and the agency that leads to narcissistic gratification one and the same. Freud recognized this difficulty and later postulated the existence of two ego substructures, with the superego responsible for repression and the ego ideal responsible for regulating self-esteem.

The ego ideal receives help from the sexual ideal. What one is lacking in oneself is found in the love object, with whom one can identify and thereby satisfy the ego ideal. Here Freud made the assumption that sexual feelings are ego-syntonic. Perhaps he was not blending psychopathology with normal psychic processes, but he shifted rapidly from one to the other.

It is implied, but not altogether clear, that narcissism has both pathological and nonpathological aspects. The megalomania of paraphrenia is definitely psychopathological, but Freud was vague as to whether loving and being loved are desirable or undesirable. He discussed idealization, but at times I get the feeling that it usually involves personal sacrifice.

Both omnipotence and idealization are important in creativity. What is more megalomanic than Archimedes' boast that given a spot to stand on, he could move the world? The fact is, this is not really an idle boast because based on what he had discovered about levers, he actually could have moved the world, at least in principle. Concerning idealization, the scientists I have studied exhibited a series of idealizations, proceeding from early parental objects to revered teachers and finally to an abstract cause such as science. These idealizations led to self-idealization and what to the observer might seem to be a sense of omnipotence. In actuality, their self-assesments were consonant with their achievements, and in no way did they seem arrogant, only self-confident.

I believe that Freud's view of development as expressed here tends to diminish the contribution of earlier phases to more mature ego states. He pointed out that as the ego develops it leaves the original narcissism behind and expends much energy trying to recapture it. He summarized by stating that a primary part of self-regard consists of the remnants of infantile narcissism, that another part stems from the confirmation of successful gratifying accomplishments, that is, the fulfillment of the ego ideal, and a third part is the outcome of a satisfactory object relationship, one in which the person is loved.

It sometimes happens as the outcome of analysis that a patient will be able to form a love relationship which gives him narcissistic gratification. The sexual ideal becomes a substitute for the ego ideal, and the patient prefers the satisfaction received in a love relationship to further analysis. This is a "cure by love."

Freud concluded this very important paper by pointing out society's contribution to the formation of the ego ideal. Presumably the boy's passive homosexual relationship to his father is internalized and becomes part of the ego ideal. Homosexual libido invests the ego ideal, which eventually incorporates society's standards. This libido is desexualized. If sublimation breaks down and the libido is once again directed to the outside world, it is experienced as social anxiety.

Many of Freud's formulations in this article seem to have limited clinical usefulness. Still, as I have repeatedly emphasized, he had begun to construct the formulation of the structural hypothesis, which has proven indispensible for our understanding of patients suffering from characterological problems.

8

Beyond the Pleasure Principle
(1920)

SYNOPSIS

Pleasure is equated with the lowering of tension, and pain with its increase. Freud borrowed these concepts, which form the basis of the pleasure–pain principle, from Fechner.

The traumatic neuroses appear to contradict the theory of the pleasure–pain principle. In these neuroses, rather than seeking pleasure by lowering tension, the psyche focuses upon traumatic experiences and seems to create tension and produce unpleasure. Freud called attention to the fact that the victims of traumatic neuroses have repetitive dreams of the traumatic incident. We would expect that, if dreams are wish fulfillments these patients would dream of pleasant situations or the anticipated cure. It seems that in the traumatic neuroses, the wish fulfillment function of the dream is upset.

Freud described his 1½-year-old grandson's behavior, the famous incident of the game of throwing away a reel attached to a thread. When his mother was away the little boy would repetitively throw a reel in his curtained bed while hanging onto the attached string; the reel would disappear from sight. Freud viewed this behavior as a recapitulation of the mother's departure and return, since his grandson would pull the reel back. However, the child sometimes did not pull it back, yet he still derived pleasure from the game. This too seems to contradict wish fulfillment and to be "beyond the pleasure principle." Freud emphasized that the game represented an attempt to convert a passively experienced situation into an active one in the service of mastery.

Certain childhood situations are inevitably painful. The discrepancy between instinctual and structural development is a case in point. The body is unprepared for the efflorescence of sexual feelings during the oedipal phase around the age of 3. Such feelings are intrinsically disruptive, regardless of the environment's reaction, because the ego does not have the executive techniques to achieve satisfaction. More specifically, the immature gonads cannot function to discharge the sexual instincts. Freud concluded that there are elements of the human constitution that work against the pleasure principle.

Emphasizing development, Freud postulated that the mind, at first, is an amorphous mass. As it receives impingements from the outer world; a peripheral core achieves some coherence and structure and becomes the beginning rudimentary ego. The nurturing source, the mother, modulates incoming stimuli and supplies the ego with a protective shield, the *Reizschutz*. If the organism is flooded with external stimuli that break through the *Reizschutz*, then energy is withdrawn from other parts of the psyche to bind the incoming disruptive stimuli. The penetration through the *Reizschutz* defines the traumatic state. This redistribution of energy is also, according to Freud, beyond the pleasure principle.

The psychic system, in order to heal the breach and master the disruption, has to be energized. When the reaction to the traumatic situation is anxiety, that anxiety hypercathects the organizing systems that will deal with the trauma. Thus there is an adaptive purpose to the production of anxiety, which is experienced as unpleasure.

Freud discussed instincts next. Instincts are conservative in character and resist change. They try to restore earlier states, and in the case of the living organism, instincts attempt to restore the inanimate state. This reasoning caused Freud to revise drastically his concept about the function of the self-preservative instincts. Rather than being concerned with the preservation of life, their real aim is to permit the organism to seek death in its own fashion. Freud defined this as the *death instinct*. The sexual instincts, however, are in opposition to such forces. They are part of the germ plasm that strives toward unification and life.

Some biological experiments have relevance to these formulations. Weisman's work indicates that the tendency or striving toward death is a characteristic only of multicellular, not of unicellular, animals. If that were true, then it would be difficult to conceptualize a death instinct as basic and irreducible. Woodruff observed 3000 generations of Infusoria reproduce by fission, and the later animalcules were just as fresh as the first generation. This would also argue against a death instinct.

However, Freud was quick to point out that if the Infusorias' waste products were not removed from the surrounding media, the animalcules would die. This was true only of *their own* waste products; other protozoas' excreta would have no effect on their longevity, indicating that something inherent in the organism leads to its destruction—a death instinct. On the other hand, protozoa deteriorating in states of senescence become rejuvenated when they conjugate. According to Freud, this is evidence for the existence of the life instinct, conjugation being a forerunner of sexual union. The sexual instincts represent the life instincts which strive to unite.

From these concepts, we are able to trace the development of Freud's instinct theory. Bibring (1941) summarized Freud's progression of viewpoints by dividing them into four dualistic stages: (1) sexual and ego instincts, (2) ego and object libido, (3) sexual and aggressive instincts, and finally (4) life and death instincts.

Toward the end of this monograph Freud once again focused upon psychoeconomic factors as they are relevant to the pleasure principle. Both bound and unbound psychic energy can produce feelings of pleasure and unpleasure. Unbound feelings, however, are associated with more intense feelings. Eventually the pleasure principle becomes "restricted," which means that it becomes associated with bound energy. Inasmuch as pleasure is the outcome of the lowering of tension during a fixed period of time, the pleasure principle is also linked to the death instinct.

I

This monograph represents another step on the way to the formulation of the structural hypothesis. The penetrating insights Freud provided here have been extremely useful to me in understanding patients undergoing deep transference regressions. I am referring particularly to the repetition compulsion as it shapes the transference and also leads to characteristic countertransference responses.

There are also many controversial formulations in this essay. For example, the concept of the death instinct stirred up intense controversy in psychoanalytic circles. Many analysts found that postulating an innate instinct that leads to self-destruction is unacceptable because it contradicts fundamental biological principles in which the organism tends toward homeostasis and survival. Still, their loyalty toward Freud and their need to revere everything he said created considerable turmoil. The situation became further complicated because the Kleinians, who were thought of by so-called orthodox analysts as having left the mainstream of psychoanalysts, embraced the death instinct as fundamental to their conceptual scaffold, as they still do today.

Freud began by pointing out that we unthinkingly assume the organism is under the dominance of the pleasure principle, which holds that the purpose of life is to achieve pleasure. From a theoretical perspective, this is a psychodynamic viewpoint that along with the topographic and psychodynamic hypotheses, constitutes metapsychology. Freud first used the term *metapsychology* in the "Psychopathology of Everyday Life," which was written in 1901.

Pleasure is related to the quantity of excitation but is not directly proportional to it. As we noted in the *Three Essays on Sexuality*, Freud again connected the production of pleasure with the lowering of excitement and pain or, more precisely, unpleasure (*unlust*) with a rise in excitation. Freud added that there is a close association to time. This passage about time is not entirely clear. Probably, he meant that a rise or lowering of excitation must occur during a particular interval of time to be felt either as a pleasure or unpleasure. For example, an increase in the intensity of a stimulus over a short period of time would produce a greater amount of unpleasure than the same increase over a longer interval. To attribute such complex feelings only to one set of quantitative variables constitutes a fairly narrow viewpoint.

Freud next introduced us to Fechner, who stressed stability and instability as the significant elements involved in pleasure and pain.

Fechsner stated that as feelings reach consciousness, they either tend toward states of stability, which produce pleasure, or states of instability, which lead to unpleasure. However, Fechner was also confusing. He stated that ". . . every psychophysical motion rising above the threshold of consciousness is attended by pleasure in proportion as, *beyond a certain limit*, it approximates to complete stability . . ." (p. 8; emphasis mine) and the same limit applies to unpleasure as the impulse approximates toward instability. It is not completely clear what "beyond a certain limit" means. This phrase would make sense if consciousness is considered in terms of a quantitative energic spectrum. Instability would be associated with more intense sensations and stability with a lowering of feelings. This is consistent with what Freud just stated, and it makes Fechsner's next statement—that between these limits is an area of aesthetic indifference— understandable.

Both Fechner and Freud recognized that even if an innate tendency toward pleasure characterizes the psyche's strivings, this does not mean that all of our actions, thoughts, and dreams will lead to pleasurable feelings. There are forces working against such strivings.

In 1911, Freud introduced the reality principle. He maintained there, as he did in *Beyond the Pleasure Principle*, that the organism pursues pleasure but that this pursuit could prove inexpedient—in conflict with reality. Consequently, the pursuit of pleasure might have to be postponed or substitutive outlets sought. This reality principle is not basically in opposition to the pleasure principle, as it is also working toward the goal of obtaining pleasure, but in a reality-oriented fashion. We could say it is primarily concerned in protecting the psyche from unpleasure.

In "Instincts and Their Vicissitudes" (Freud 1915b), Freud postulated a developmental progression from original reality ego to pleasure ego and then to reality ego again, which could be described as an ego in which the reality principle has gained dominance. Briefly, the ego's early task is to distinguish an inner impulse from an external stimulus. If the infant can alleviate pain through muscular movement, then he learns that pain comes from the outside world. Only after dealing with pain or unpleasure does the ego become dominated by the pleasure principle, what Freud called a pleasure ego (1911, 1915b). Then the reality principle takes over with further emotional development. It is interesting that Freud concentrated on painful sensations.

In this monograph Freud discussed further the vicissitudes of the pleasure principle in the context of instinctual development. As instincts develop, some gain access to the ego and are experienced as pleasurable.

Other instincts are repressed; which means they are barred access to the ego, and their progressive structuralization is also halted. When these instincts return from repression in their quest for pleasurable discharge, they cause unpleasure, that is, the ego reacts to them with displeasure.

Here Freud was distinguishing between the aim of an instinct and contrary forces associated with higher psychic structures such as the ego. Since he had not yet formulated a definitive structural hierarchy, he was not clear as to what he meant by ego, but he both implicitly and explicitly indicated that he was discussing consciousness. He stressed that both pleasure and unpleasure are ego reactions, conscious feelings. We get the impression from previous formulations that the instinct itself seeks pleasure; this implies that it feels pleasure. This causes conceptual confusion because it is difficult to understand how a driving force such as an instinct would be capable of feeling anything. It can only cause other sensory systems, systems that have attained a certain degree of structure, to react with such feelings as pleasure and unpleasure.

The situation of repressed instincts, which were once experienced as pleasurable, causing unpleasure can be viewed in terms of ego-syntonicity and developmental levels. Throughout the course of development, the ego integrates certain instinctual patterns within its organization as ego-syntonic. If all of the psyche is considered in terms of a structural hierarchy, then we could state that both instincts and ego have had parallel development and have achieved the same degree of structure. During infancy and childhood, needs become increasingly sophisticated and varied. The child enjoys much more than just mother's milk and the ego acquires executive techniques designed to achieve these more structured desires, which then are experienced as pleasurable satisfaction. There is a synchrony between structured needs and the structured ego apparatus, a situation we refer to as ego-syntonic.

Freud described a situation in which different needs, or as he called them, instincts, develop at different rates. Those that remain behind, as he described in his advancing army metaphor (Freud 1916) which explains fixation and regression, are barred from consciousness. Freud stated they are repressed; today we would be more prone to speak of them as being split off from the main psychic current. If these instincts achieve ego levels, which, in this section of the monograph are equated with consciousness, they cause unpleasure.

The structured ego is unable to integrate impulses that belong to more primitive ego levels. They are ego dystonic and cause pain and have to be defended against much in the same way the soma reacts to a foreign body. Inasmuch as there is a structural differential between the ego and the instincts, the instincts cannot be smoothly incorporated into the ego organization. Thus, they are experienced as displeasurable.

II

There are other experiences that run counter to the pleasure principle that also cause unpleasure. Freud here introduced the topic of the traumatic neuroses by defining three important terms: anxiety (*Angst*), fear (*Furcht*), and fright (*Schreck*). Anxiety is an awareness and preparation for danger; it has an evaluative component. Remember once again that Freud (1915b) wrote in "Instincts and Their Vicissitudes" of how the first reality ego acts toward danger. If flight can remove the danger, then the danger was external. Freud called such reaction to external danger fear. If danger persists after flight, then the danger is internal and felt as anxiety. Fright, on the other hand, is a reaction to a traumatic situation that a person is totally unprepared for; the emphasis is on the factor of surprise. Freud was developing a thesis that he stressed further in this monograph and discussed, specifically in "Inhibitions, Symptoms and Anxiety" (Freud 1926a), that anxiety has a protective function and serves as an adaptive mechanism by calling into action appropriate defenses.

Psychoanalytic investigators have always relied heavily on the study of dreams. In the dreams of the traumatic neuroses, the patient is always brought back to the painful, dangerous event. Freud found this to be extremely interesting and wondered why others were not as astonished as he was. He said that most likely, they had explanations which seemed obvious but were not necessarily adequate.

For example, some clinicians explain the fact that, by its sheer intensity, the traumatic experience constantly forces itself upon the person during sleep. Others, such as Ferenczi and Simmel (Simmel 1918), emphasize fixation on the traumatic moment.

Although Freud did not discount these theories he did not believe they explained the subtle factors involved or account for some of the data. In their waking lives these patients are not preoccupied with memories of their accident; they seem rather, to be concerned with not thinking of the trauma. Similarly, in dreams, which are considered to be the products of wish fulfillment, we would expect the patient to dream of the healthy past or the hoped-for cure. In the traumatic neuroses, the wish-fulfilling function of the dream is upset, although here Freud went on to introduce us to data that could account for these dreams in a fairly conventional fashion. Freud presented his argument here in an ingenious fashion.

Freud described the game played by his 1½-year-old grandson. As mentioned earlier, when the mother was away, the child would throw a spool, a wooden reel, around which a string was attached, into his curtained bed. He hung onto the string, but the reel disappeared. As he threw the object away, he would murmur "o-o-o-o-," and when he pulled it back, he would joyfully say "da." Freud interpreted "o-o-o-o" as meaning *fort* (the German word for "away") and "*da*" as meaning "there." Freud argued against the interpretation that the child plays the game to experience the joyful return of the mother, as this interpretation would not explain that sometimes the child played only the throwing away part of the game, and that he usually played that portion of the game more intensely than that of pulling the reel back into view.

Freud explained this repetitive play on the basis of the child needing to turn a passive experience of unpleasure into an active one; this is a way of achieving mastery. It could also be explained on a wish-fulfillment basis, an idea that occurred to Freud a year later when his grandson threw things away while saying, "Go to the fwont." His father was away in military service. Earlier the child was expressing his angry revenge toward the mother much in the way of saying "Go away—who cares?" and wished that his father would stay away so that he could remain in sole possession of his mother.

III

Freud now considered repetition in the clinical setting. He emphasized the differences between remembering and repeating, the analytic task being to make the patient remember rather than repeat. The analytic task does not consist of just discovering the unconscious and then interpreting it, but rather of having the patient confirm his discoveries with his reconstructed memories. This is accomplished by discovering the resistances "as quickly as possible" and then using the power of suggestion, which is the outcome of transference, to get the patient to give them up. This creates a setting in which repressed memories will emerge rather than being repeated in acting-out behavior.

It is obvious that Freud's ideas about resistance were considerably different from those many of us subscribe to today. Some psychoanalysts view resistance as part of the patient's adaptive modalities, as a modality that is directed against treatment. Resistance must be considered in the same way as any other manifestation of psychopathology: It is not something simply to be done away with, but should be analyzed. Freud would have been the first to stress that resistance has to be analyzed, but the purpose of such analysis is to get rid of resistance. We would not necessarily expect the patient to give up behavior simply because we have interpreted it; the patient will continue using whatever adaptive modes he has as long as he needs to.

The idea that transference should be used to persuade the patient to relinquish resistance is confusing, because Freud has repeatedly stressed that transference is in itself a resistance. This leads to the absurdity that a resistance can be used to do away with another resistance. Freud, however, divided transference into two categories, positive and negative, and it was negative transference that constituted resistance. Positive transference on the other hand, could be used as an ally for the therapeutic process. However, positive transference includes the erotic transference, which also leads to resistance by trying to convert the analyst into a lover.

At this juncture, Freud once again referred to the "transference neurosis," a term that first appeared in "Remembering, Repeating and Working Through" (Freud 1914a). He discussed this concept further in the "*Introductory Lectures on Psycho-analysis*" (Freud 1916).

Freud did not, in any of these references, confine the transference neuroses just to an oedipal re-enactment. It certainly includes Oedipus, but it also involves, as he stated here ". . . some portion of infantile sexual life—of the Oedipus complex, that is, and *its derivatives*" (emphasis mine). In other references, Freud made it clear that he considered the pregenital elements of the infantile sexual life just as likely to determine the content of the transference neuroses as material solely derived from the oedipal level.

Regression and resistance arise from the ego, which seems clear enough, but it must be remembered that in the past some analysts have talked about the resistance of the id. We need not pursue this further, inasmuch as Freud continued to discuss the topographical hypothesis but he indicated a need to go beyond it, which he did by formulating some of the beginning concepts of the structural hypothesis.

Freud needed a structural hypothesis to stress that both conscious and unconscious ego operate under the sway of the pleasure principle and that the liberation of the repressed would cause unpleasure. He now repeated "unpleasure for one system and simultaneous satisfaction for the other." However, he pointed out that some past experiences are recalled that never had any possibility of producing pleasure.

Freud viewed certain childhood situations as being inevitably painful. Early infantile sexuality, for one, is doomed to failure. In terms of the Oedipus complex, the child cannot possibly possess his mother and defeat his father. This would be true even if the father were not bigger and stronger, since the child's body is not equipped (in terms of ego psychology it does not have the integrative and executive apparatus) to gain pleasure by gratifying sexual instincts. Because of the asynchrony between the psyche and the soma, the mind faces situations that have to be experienced as traumatic, and from this viewpoint, are beyond the pleasure principle.

In psychoanalytic treatment, this inevitable failure to achieve instinctual satisfaction is repeated in the transference. Freud pointed out that patients repeat these painful situations in their relationship to the analyst. They want to break off the treatment before it is completed, and they do everything possible to be reviled and rejected. We could easily get the impression that Freud believed that, as the patient's behavior and associations are the inevitable consequence of a repetition compulsion beyond the pleasure principle, the analyst's reaction is also inevitable, in that the patient forces the analyst to conform to his material. In any case, Freud did not blame the analyst, placing the responsibility instead on the patient. Consequently, we have to assume that in this situation the analyst's feelings and responses are not the outcome of countertransference, since Freud (1910a) was very critical of analysts who had countertransference feelings, attributing them to the therapist's personal neurosis, which should be resolved through further analysis rather than being a reaction to a fundamental attribute of the psyche.

Freud described certain types of behavior that occur outside of analysis in both neurotic patients and normal persons. He was referring to what today might be called fate neuroses. The lives of persons suffering from fate neuroses seem to be an endless series of similar self-defeating events. For example, I am now treating an intelligent, attractive, competent business woman in her middle thirties who has had three bad marriages. All of her husbands were doctors, apparently rigid, obsessive-compulsive character types who dealt with her as a narcissistic object choice in that they used her as someone to display proudly but were unable to relate to her at a feeling level. Since these marriages, she had several relationships, all with men who could not make a commitment and who seemed to be afraid of becoming involved in an intimate relationship. Freud gave a similar clinical example of a woman who married three husbands, all of whom died, repeatedly leaving her a widow.

Freud grants that the repetition compulsion can very soon become enmeshed with other motives that are presumably of a wish-fulfilling nature under the influence of the pleasure principle. Child's play, for example, which begins by being impelled by the repetition compulsion, quickly gains other meanings, such as an attempt to achieve gratifications that had previously been provided only by adults.

Toward the end of this section of the monograph, Freud established more firmly the existence of the repetition compulsion. An active repetition compulsion can be viewed as being in the service of mastery by converting a passively experienced trauma into an active situation in an attempt to overcome what had been initially perceived as dangerous. The repetition compulsion has also been viewed as more primitive, elemental, and instinctual than the pleasure principle, which is acquired later during the course of development.

IV

In this section Freud described his formulations about the system perceptual-consciousness, which does not form or retain memory traces, since that would be incompatible with its function. This occurs in the adjacent system, the preconscious. Once again Freud was making formulations in the frame of reference of the topographical hypothesis. As the name perceptual-consciousness connotes, the function of this system is conscious awareness of percepts. This subject could be discussed at considerable length, but for our purposes as well as for Freud's, the location and development of perceptual-consciousness is of primary importance. Anatomically, the function of consciousness resides in the cerebral cortex, the outer layer of the brain. It could be located in the interior of the brain where it would be better protected but, nevertheless, it is on the surface. This allowed Freud to postulate the developmental sequence of how the ego develops from the id. At first, the mind can be compared to an amorphous structure, an undifferentiated vesicle. As stimuli impinge upon it from the external world, at some point on the periphery of the mind, where stimuli enter, it begins to organize itself and form structures. The mother protects the infant from the full force of external stimuli by monitoring and modulating the stimuli her child receives. She provides a stimulus barrier (*Reizschutz*), which permits further structuralization.

Hartmann constructed a different model: an initial undeveloped state containing both id and ego elements structuralizes into the id and the ego. This is confusing because it implies different lines of development for the id and the ego, and by so doing obscures the principle of a structural hierarchy, which is useful in understanding the processes of biological maturation. Inasmuch as emotional development runs parallel to biological maturation, the concept of hierarchal elaboration would also be useful for our understanding about the acquisition of psychic structure. Furthermore, viewing the id as the product of structure seems to be a contradiction. Granted that the id has a structure of its own, it is, nevertheless, a primitive structure dominated by the laws of the primary process. If it goes beyond this development, it would no longer be id. It would be encroaching upon ego territory, a point Freud elaborated on in "The Ego and the Id" (Freud 1923).

The concept of the *Reizschutz* has some interesting implications. If we follow Freud literally, the external world is assaultive from the beginning of life, and the neonate has to be protected from this world. The mother initially supplies this protection, and later the child forms a protective barrier of his own. Winnicott (1960) postulated that, as the child has to protect himself, in a sense mold himself, to the impingements of the external world, he will develop a false self. Because psychic energies are so concentrated on dealing with outside disruptive stimuli, he will lose contact with his inner core or true being. The true self develops only when the environment is compliant to the child's needs.

Thus, the establishment and further elaboration of the stimulus barrier can be considered the beginning of the false self. Protection implies a defensive orientation. Conceivably the mother could protect the child from disruptive stimuli while at the same time relating to inner needs. The child would then develop the stability and integration to permit him to deal harmoniously with the external world of infancy, which basically does not impinge upon his developing psychic structure. As he acquires further structure and grows older, he can allow himself to experience a larger range of stimuli in a harmonious way. Freud referred to Roux, the embryologist who stated that, to an embryo, a pinprick represents a tremendous trauma and leads to serious malformation, but to an adult, a pinprick is trivial.

As stated, the *Reizschutz* is not directed toward inner stimuli, which seek direct access to consciousness and are governed, so to speak, by the pleasure principle. Freud's psychodynamic hypothesis was up to this point based upon the control, through repression, of impulses that will cause unpleasure if they reach higher psychic levels. Now he introduced another mechanism. If an unpleasurable impulse reaches a certain intensity or amplitude, as he put it, it is treated as if it came from the outer world and the psyche can be protected from it by the stimulus barrier. Freud called this defensive maneuver projection. He did not discuss how the psychic apparatus "decides" what is internal and what is external. Even modern metapsychology does not help us understand how internal and external stimuli are distinguished, although quantitative factors are undoubtedly involved.

Defenses maintain psychic equilibrium. The achievement of emotional stability may not necessarily be a pleasurable experience—another instance of "beyond the pleasurable principle." Specifically, Freud was referring to the redistribution of energy when the organism is flooded by external stimuli breaking through the stimulus barrier. This disruptive situation requires shifting cathexes so that unbound stimuli may become bound and aberrant stimuli mastered.

Freud did not develop this in a clinical context. However, as so often happens with Freud, ideas that at the time seemed to have no particular clinical usefulness can be applied to clinical phenomena that have puzzled or have been ignored by clinicians. I am referring specifically to patients who suffer from states of disruptive agitation. We have tried to explain this agitation in psychological terms, perhaps in terms of intrapsychic conflict or ego defects, as disturbances of mentation. The traumatic states Freud described here would appear to antedate mentational elaboration, what I have referred to as a prementational phase (1979). He was discussing disruptions brought about by unorganized percepts that cannot be contained by the psyche. I believe we sometimes encounter patients whose psychopathology can be traced back to such early states and whose treatment is complicated and difficult because we try to fit them in a familiar but unsuitable mold (Boyer and Giovacchini 1980). These patients have had early traumatic experiences in which inner excitement was uncontrolled and was felt as disruptive agitation. These patients cannot be soothed.

Stimuli breaking through the protective shield define the traumatic state. Freud focused upon energic shifts, rather than emphasizing the breaking-through itself, which caused some theorists at that time to postulate that trauma is the outcome of an impact, of shock in a mechanical sense. To deal with disruptive stimuli requires energizing of psychic systems that will heal the breach and master the disruption. The effects of the incoming stimuli are indirectly proportional to the cathexis of the adjoining systems. When an organism reacts to traumatic situations with anxiety, that anxiety hypercathects the organizing systems that will deal with the trauma.

Freud here was still referring to his first anxiety theory. He implied that the energy produced by anxiety is directly transferred to that part of the psychic apparatus adjacent to the area in the protective shield where the breach occurred. Somewhat mechanistically Freud was saying that trauma occurs when the organism is not prepared to deal with an overwhelming situation, because it is unable to experience anxiety at the time of the trauma. Recall that this idea had already been formulated in the *Studies on Hysteria* (Breuer and Freud 1895). However, here Freud extended this formulation and placed the production of anxiety for the purpose of mastery beyond the pleasure principle. Again, he referred to anxiety dreams and called into question a theory that he had devotedly adhered to, that is, the wish-fulfillment theory of dreams. He postulated that the purpose of the dreams of the traumatic neuroses is to generate anxiety that was not experienced at the time of the trauma. Here there is no question of the pleasurable fulfillment of a wish. The task of the dream is reconstructive. Later, when it is under the dominance of the pleasure principle, it acquires its wish-fulfillment aim.

The feeling of pain may exist from the beginning of life, but the concept of pleasure develops later. This may be the reason why Freud felt that hate, as a reaction to pain, was a primal feeling, whereas love was a reaction to a confluence of gratifying experiences and represented a later developmental acquisition (Freud 1915b). Similarly, the pleasure principle is established after a certain degree of psychic structuralization has been achieved. To feel something as organized and cohesive as pleasure requires the capacity to go beyond simply experiencing physiological tensions. There has to be some ability for mentational elaboration, as we believe occurs around the age of 2 months, the usual time of appearance of the smiling response.

Again, we can refer to these formulations in a clinical context. First, we might ask if some patients' dreams are pictorial representations of regressed states that have gone far backwards in the psychic developmental scale to a stage before the pleasure principle was established. I believe that this occurs, but only to a limited degree, because, as we know, no regression can exactly recapitulate the developmental level the ego has regressed to. Some later developmental acquisitions are always retained.

In fact, the very act of dreaming, that is, to be able to put the operations of the mind in visual images, is a fairly sophisticated form of thinking. However, dreams use later-acquired levels to express various interactions that are characteristic of primitive mental states.

Freud's energic formulations enabled him to explain why a simultaneous physical injury with psychic trauma has a paradoxical beneficial effect. The traumatic situation of breaking through the protective shield releases unbound sexual energy—libido. The injured site, which is in a state of lowered cathexis, draws this free energy to itself, and binds it. A wound, for example, causes a person's attention to be riveted on his own body, resulting in narcissistic replenishment. Freud called attention to a fairly common clinical phenomenon in which a depressed patient recovers after incurring an organic illness.

Freud returned to instincts in this section, discussing inner stimuli rather than external impingements and trauma. The organism's primary task is to master these stimuli, which are instinctual in nature and operate according to the laws of the primary process. Inner stimuli are unbound forces which have to be bound in order for the psyche to establish equilibrium. The achievement of homeostasis is a principal aim that antedates the establishment of the pleasure principle. It is not in opposition to the pleasure principle—it is independent of it. However, Freud pointed out that the mastery of instinctual forces creates a setting in which the establishment of the pleasure principle becomes possible.

The repetition compulsion also operates on the basis of instinctual energy. There is an innate, primitive quality to repetition. Children tend to repeat all kinds of experiences, even unpleasurable ones. A child binds unbound traumatic feelings by repeating the trauma; this is more easily accomplished when the child is in active control rather than being the passive victim.

Instincts are conservative in character and resist change. To further justify his formulation of the existence of a death instinct, Freud stated than an instinct is an inherent urge of living matter to restore an earlier state, one that the organism was forced to abandon because of both inner and outer disturbances. An instinct represents the inertia inherent in the living organism. He recognized, however, that he had stressed in the past the importance of the self-preservative instincts, whose aim seems to be the preservation of life. Now he reversed his position, stating that the concept of self-preservative instincts has lost its theoretical importance. The self-preservative instincts seem to cling to life, but their real aim is to permit the organism to seek death in its own fashion. As such, they prolong the road toward death, as they represent reactions to outward disturbances and the external impetus for change. Immanent (Freud's term) within the living organism are forces that seek death, or a return to the inorganic state. If outside forces threaten to disrupt the natural course toward death, then the self-preservative instincts oppose them so that the organism cannot follow its predestined path. Freud questioned whether there really is an instinct for change and higher development. He viewed this as a reaction, actually as a defense, against intrusive and assaultive outer stimuli.

These ideas are presented in a complex and convoluted fashion, which I believe is a reflection of Freud's ad hoc reasoning. He slanted everything, sometimes to an absurd degree, to support an assumption which he was quickly turning into a universal law. Still, his development of this thesis is interesting, and as we will see, he was still able to place his formulations in the context of a dual instinct theory.

At this point, Freud returned to the sexual instincts, which are represented by the germ cells, and asked the question as to whether they seek the earlier state of the inanimate or whether they might be exceptions. He believed that they are exceptions, for two reasons: one, because they retain the original structure of living matter and, two, because after a certain point in time they detach themselves from the organism and start afresh and produce another organism. In this way they achieve immortality. But even here, Freud did not necessarily believe this means that they actually seek life; it could mean that they are merely lengthening the road to death.

Freud did not believe there is an instinct for higher development. Primitive life strives to remain primitive. The outer world, by its impingements, disturbs this clinging to the primitive and impels the organism to develop, which gives the deceptive appearance of a structuralizing life force. Freud here stated the paradox that the striving for life and higher developmental forces is a defense to protect the death instinct.

Still, Freud needed to preserve the dual instinct theory. Here he returned to a discussion of the germ cells, which because of their sexual activity, represent life instincts. If life, simply stated, is a defense to preserve the seeking of death, then there must be different levels: a defense, and that which is being defended against. A dual instinct theory, however, requires that the basic instincts belong to the same conceptual level. It is difficult to conceive of one instinct as representing a defense; it would have to have an independent origin to ensure its autonomy, in order to be considered basic.

In this section of *Beyond the Pleasure Principle*, Freud turned to various fascinating experimental findings and speculations which he imaginatively used to make some fundamental assumptions. Since he was dealing with the foundations of life and death, he turned to primitive living organisms—the unicellular protozoa.

According to Freud, Weisman reached conclusions from the biological frame of reference resembling those drawn from psychoanalytic speculation. Weisman separated the soma from the germ cells in the same manner discussed in the last section, but he felt that the death instinct was not a primal attribute of living matter. He believed the death instinct developed only in multicellular organisms. This, of course, would mitigate against the hypothesis of a basic death instinct.

Freud next discussed the work of the American, Woodruff, who studied over 3000 generations of Infusoria and concluded that these elementary organisms are potentially immortal: they reproduce by fission, and after 3000 such divisions are just as vital and energized as the first animalcule that divided itself. This would speak for the existence of a life instinct, not a death instinct.

Freud questioned whether experiments with simple protozoa are appropriate sources of data for the study of such complex phenomena as life and death instincts. Nevertheless, once he introduced these data, he had to pursue this line of inquiry in order to strengthen his argument. These experiments, which seem to contradict the existence of a death instinct, were conducted under very special conditions: the organism must be placed in a fresh solution after dividing or it will die. Thus, Freud concluded that the manufacturing of waste products leads to the death of the animalcule. It is important that these are the waste products of *that organism*. This means, according to Freud, that there are elements and processes within living matter that cause its death. If these unicellular organisms are placed in a media containing another species' waste products, they will continue to live.

Freud then called attention to other data regarding the life instinct. If two organisms coalesce (exchange cellular matter) just before senescence sets in, they will become rejuvenated. This phenomenon is called conjugation and is believed to be the forerunner of sexual intercourse. In any case, unification seems to represent a striving for life.

At first it seemed that manifestations of the death instinct in unicellular organisms might be concealed by life-preserving forces, something that would not occur in more complex multicellular forms. However, these findings from biological studies indicate otherwise. Even in the most primitive types of living matter, there are forces propelling the organism toward death.

Two kinds of processes, which pull in opposite directions, seem to be operating constantly in living matter: one "constructive or assimilatory, and the other destructive and dissimilatory" (Freud 1920, p. 49). These opposite tendencies can be conceptualized as life and death instincts.

Freud discussed an interesting metaphor (although I wonder if he considered it a metaphor) in which he endowed the individual cells of a multicellular complex organism with life and death instincts. Certain cells give up their life instincts to other cells in order to neutralize their death instinct. The germ cells are totally narcissistic in that their life instincts are revitalized by other cells. Freud further speculated that the germ cells require this fresh impetus of life instinct to prepare them for their immense task of reproduction. Malignant cells perhaps share this narcissistic feature, causing the destruction of surrounding cells.

Freud here reviewed the development of instinct theory and discussed some of the difficulties he encountered in maintaining a dual instinct theory. He first noted the difference between sexual instincts, which are directed toward objects, and other instincts, which are concerned with self-preservation. In 1910 (Freud 1910) he called the latter "ego instincts," which implies that they are different than the sexual instincts. This dichotomy was difficult to sustain. Freud discovered that libido flows toward both objects and the ego. In fact, he stated here as well as in his narcissism paper (Freud 1914), that the "ego is the true and original reservoir of libido," a statement he corrected in, "The Ego and the Id" (Freud 1923), in which he wrote that the id is "the great reservoir of libido."

Bibring (1941) emphasized the difficulty in maintaining a dichotomy between sexual and self-preservative instincts if both are cathected with libido. He traced the development of instinct theory, which Freud also did in this section but in an abbreviated form. I will now attempt to synthesize Freud's formulations and Bibring's reorganization of them.

Bibring divided Freud's instinct theory into four stages:

1. There is a division between sexual and ego (self-preservative) instincts, which corresponds to the basic needs of hunger and love.

2. The ego instincts, through the discovery of narcissism, are also fueled with sexual energy, and thus Freud found it difficult to maintain a dualism based upon sexual versus nonsexual. Consequently he introduced the dichotomy of ego libido and object-libido.

3. Still he could not dispel the idea of a nonsexual energy. Thus, he postulated a nonsexual component to ego instincts, which he called

interest. We could say that, at this transitional point in the development of instinct theory, he was postulating three types of instinct: ego-libidinal, ego-interest, and object-libidinal. He did not add object-interest instincts, that is, a primary nonsexual relationship to external objects. Freud's dualism was now being threatened more than ever. His next step was to push the concept of ego interest in the background and concentrate upon an instinct of mastery, the aggressive instinct known as sadism. Freud first considered sadism as a component instinct of the sexual instinct, but then he found a better solution for his task of formulating a dualistic instinct theory: he gave sadism a separate status and stated that the two fundamental instincts were libidinal and aggressive. Freud (1915b) did not define sadism as being initially characterized by the need to inflict pain; this occurs only after it becomes fused with sexual instincts.

In this monograph Freud emphasized that sadism represents an attempt at mastery. It is an aggressive adaptation. During the oral phase it leads to the destruction of the object and later, during genital sexuality, it accomplishes the satisfaction of the sexual instinct in the service of reproduction by subduing the sexual object. Freud drew the interesting conclusion that sadism or the aggressive instinct finds its way into the world through the sexual instinct.

There are two obvious objections to this theory. The more obvious one refers to the use of the aggressive instinct to master and subdue the sexual object. This is, of course, a chauvinistic masculine viewpoint in which the sexual instinct is restricted to males; females have to be subdued. Taken to its extreme, it would mean that females have no sexual needs of their own. The other objection relates to the theory's inconsistency. In the narcissism paper, Freud (1914) postulated the existence of anaclitic object relationships in which the sexual instincts "lean" on the dependent instincts. Although there he was writing about ego or self-preservative and sexual instincts, he discussed how sexual instincts follow nonsexual instincts on the pathway to object relationships; here he was emphasizing the reverse—aggressive instincts following the sexual instincts.

Ego interest, aggressive instincts, and self-preservative instincts become combined and constitute the aggressive instinct, which is set alongside the sexual instincts. Many psychoanalysts are content to remain with this formulation.

4. Freud was not, because he saw another problem and this constitutes the next stage. Now with the formulation of the aggressive drive, he was content to accept that the ego can relate to objects on a nonsexual

basis, that is, in terms of aggression, although it quickly offers itself for sexual mastery. How can the vicissitudes of such a drive be formulated?

First the development of sexual instincts can be briefly stated as follows:

Autoerotism→primary narcissism→secondary narcissism→
object relationships

A similar pathway for the aggressive instincts would necessitate the following sequence:

Auto-aggression→primary masochism→secondary masochism→
sadistic control of objects

I must again emphasize that sadism is not primarily associated with the infliction of pain. Rather, it concerns an aggressive form of mastery. The fusion of sexual and aggressive instincts occurs when they begin to be directed toward objects.

Freud never coined an expression for the energy of the aggressive instincts, which in his final instinct theory revision became the death instinct; just as the sexual instincts became the life instincts. Other analysts have suggested such terms as *mortido* and *destrudo* (Federn 1931; Weiss 1950), but since the death instinct has been so controversial, hardly anyone ever uses them.

A primary instinct of aggression directed toward the self in primitive stages of development would lead to the destruction of the organism, similar to the object of the oral instinct, food, being destroyed with the gratification of that drive. Thus, what began as an ego instinct, a self-preservative instinct, was modified into a basic aggressive instinct and finally into a death instinct. The progression of self-preservative instincts becoming death instincts is an interesting one.

The life instinct being the outcome of sexual instincts also presents an interesting paradox. The purpose of the sexual instincts (Freud 1905) is to lower the level of excitation. In this monograph as well as others, Freud equated this with the pleasure principle. Freud also viewed the lowering of excitation as a tendency toward death. If we follow this line of reasoning to its ultimate, it could be stated that the sexual instincts—the life instincts—seek death. This is clearly a contradiction.

Toward the end of this section, Freud stressed the life-seeking qualities of the sexual instincts. Conjugation, the forerunner of sexual intercourse, rejuvenates. The unifying forces of the sexual instinct, the coalescence of germ cells, and the production of a new organism operate on the basis of a life instinct, since they are constructive and strive for higher, more structured organizations. Freud referred to the writings of Plato, who believed that primeval human beings had four arms and legs and female and male sexual organs. They were split in two and became separated as man and woman. These separated beings tend to reunite, thereby restoring an earlier state. The sexual instinct is the underlying impetus to unite male and female. It re-establishes an earlier state, but it also joins, which is an attribute of life, not of death, which separates.

This section, as Freud admitted, is difficult to follow, and the arguments are frequently abstruse and convoluted. Freud was struggling to place speculation—for him very important speculation—on a solid scientific footing. I doubt that many of us would believe he succeeded, but we cannot help but admire the ingenuity of his reasoning and erudition.

VII

In this final section, Freud returned to a discussion of the pleasure principle, the aim of which is to abolish totally or diminish as much as possible the level of excitation. The psyche, however, is primarily involved in binding energy—converting unbound energy into bound, quiescent, tonic energy. This process transcends the pleasure principle. However, the binding of energy is not necessarily in opposition to the pleasure principle. It can be a preparatory activity which makes possible the operation of the pleasure principle.

Freud next raised the interesting question as to whether unbound and bound energy, that is primary and secondary process, can both produce feelings of pleasure and unpleasure. He concluded that primary process impulses lead to more intense feelings of pleasure and unpleasure. Still, the pleasure principle is more "restricted." By this he meant that it is more vulnerable to interruption. When energy becomes bound, the pleasure principle becomes stabilized.

In addition to feelings of pleasure and unpleasure we also perceive internal tensions, which may become either pleasurable or unpleasurable. Rather than the energy state, such as primary or secondary process, or the magnitude of the excitation, it is the change of cathexis in a certain unit of time that detemines the quality of the excitation.

The psyche is more sensitive to internal sensations, which are linked to the life instincts. They emerge as disturbers of the pursuit of life which is death. The death instincts are more or less silent and work unobtrusively. The pleasure principle, according to Freud, best serves the purpose of the death instincts. Freud was once again equating pleasure with the diminution or abolition of excitation, which also occurs with death.

To summarize, all of Freud's hypotheses in this monograph are based upon psychoeconomic, energic models. Nevertheless, he discovered certain principles that cannot be overstressed; the repetition compulsion and his understanding of self-destructive behavior have become crucial for the treatment of patients whom we formulate chiefly in terms of defects of psychic structure rather than in energic terms.

9

"The Ego and the Id" (1923)

SYNOPSIS

This monograph can be considered to be the last of a series of articles that culminate in the construction of the structural hypothesis. *Beyond the Pleasure Principle* (Freud 1920) represents the final step in Freud's development of instinct theory; "The Ego and the Id" furnished psychoanalytic theory with an anatomy of the psyche apparatus in which instinctual forces can be put in a proper context.

Freud reviewed the topographical hypothesis, emphasizing the significance of the dynamic unconscious. He outlined the path of inner and external stimuli as they attach themselves to word presentations and become conscious. At this point, Freud felt the need for a more precise classification of the psychic apparatus. He postulated that the ego develops from the unconscious, and includes perceptual consciousness and the preconscious, which embraces mnemic residues. Freud declared here that what is not ego is *id*, using the term, which he borrowed from Groddeck, for the first time.

There is no clear demarcation between the ego and the id; one gradually blends into the other. This stresses a continuum, and the fact that the ego has both conscious and unconscious parts solved a dilemma, in that previously Freud had been unable to explain how such organized functions as repression or complex feelings as guilt could be unconscious.

Though the ego has somatic components, it comprises a wide spectrum. It dips into the id, but it also includes the highest levels and represents the rational forces of the psyche. It may be driven by the id, but it also controls it. The ego gains structure by identifying with external objects. Freud postulated that the id becomes capable of giving up external objects when the ego identifies with them. Then the id can direct libido toward the ego.

Identification is an important process for the formation of psychic structure, and it is especially relevant for the construction of the superego or the ego ideal (Freud used these two terms synonymously). Around the age of 3, the little boy develops sexual wishes toward his mother. He then develops castration anxiety because he fears his father's retaliatory prohibition. Consequently, he internalizes the prohibition and identifies with his father, the superego being the outcome of this identification. Freud coined the word "superego" in this monograph. The superego is the heir to the Oedipus complex as incestuous feelings are repressed. Something similar occurs with a little girl, but Freud did not pursue the development of girls in this monograph. Freud also pointed out that there is a spectrum of identifications, depending upon how much of the father and how much of the mother is incorporated into the superego.

In addition to laying the foundations of the structural hypothesis in this monograph, Freud also wanted to further his formulations about instincts. By now, he had completely embraced the dualism of life and death instincts and discussed their roles in both regressive and progressive processes as well as their relationship to ambivalence. Still, he continued to make formulations in terms of aggressive and sexual drives. He viewed the fusion of these two drives as leading to progression and their defusion as regression. Ambivalence is the outcome of incomplete fusion. This ambivalence, similar to constitutional bisexuality, is an inherent part of the psychic from the beginning of its development. Love can be transformed into hate, as occurs in paranoia, and hate can also be transformed into love. However, the ego has at its disposal a neutral displaceable energy, which can cathect either the love or hate element of the fundamental ambivalence.

In the final section of this monograph, Freud stated that the superego owes its special position in the psyche to two factors: (1) the weakness of the ego at its onset, and (2) the fact that it is the heir to the Oedipus complex. It is particularly strong and harsh because it is closer to the id than consciousness.

Clinically, Freud formulated the unconscious sense of guilt and the negative therapeutic reaction on the basis of the harshness of the superego. Individuals with different neuroses react differently to the injunctions of the superego. Obsessive patients rebel. Their egos are concerned with overcoming the prohibitions or threats of the superego, or they give in to them. The egos of depressed patients are passive and acquiesce to the superego's accusations which cause them to feel miserable and unworthy. Hysterical patients' predominant defense against the superego is repression, and the sense of guilt remains unconscious.

The ego organizes perceptions, achieves reality testing, and orders time. It controls the drives by determining their access to motility. The ego serves three masters: outer reality, inner reality, and the superego. The task of psychoanalysis is to further the conquest of the id by the ego.

———

The editors of the *Standard Edition* wrote a scholarly and comprehensive introduction that represents the end or almost the end of a long, arduous struggle to define the conceptual basis of psychoanalysis. They traced Freud's concepts of the unconscious from a descriptive, dynamic, and systemic viewpoint from early papers to the present monograph. Rather than reviewing what they wrote, I prefer to deal with the historical evolution of psychoanalytic principles in the context of Freud's presentation.

Freud stated in the preface of "The Ego and the Id" that he considered this work to be a synthesis of ideas that he had begun to explore in *Beyond the Pleasure Principle*. He also maintained that his theories here did not have any predecessors who he would be obligated to acknowledge.

The Conscious and the Unconscious

Freud began this monograph by reviewing the topographic hypothesis, in which he divided the psyche into three parts: the conscious, the preconscious and the unconscious. This was discussed in detail in Chapter 1.

Freud had already outlined this hypothesis in the seventh chapter of *The Interpretation of Dreams*, but he repeated himself here in order to expand upon his earlier ideas.

The unconscious can be thought of as a descriptive term which tells us about quality—whether something is felt as conscious or not. Even in consciousness, elements do not retain the quality of consciousness very long. They are replaced by other perceptions, as consciousness is able to deal with only a very limited amount at one time. The sensations that leave consciousness, which are then thought of as unconscious, can, however, be easily brought back into the conscious sphere. They are latent thoughts or feelings.

There are other psyche elements that are not latent, in that their access to consciousness is barred. Here then we have two different groups that descriptively are both unconscious. However, only the group that cannot gain access to consciousness without special effort (as occurs in psychoanalytic treatment) is considered to be unconscious in a dynamic sense. Thus, the dynamic unconsciousness, at this point in the discussion, contains only repressed elements.

Freud was still meeting opposition about the existence of an unconscious. Postulating a dynamic unconscious strengthened his argument. He referred to dreams and hypnosis and indicated that there are forces within the mind that a person is not aware of. These forces produce ideas and actions that are conscious although their causes—these inner forces—are not (see Introduction and Chapter 1 for a discussion of post-hypnotic suggestion as an excellent illustrative example of the dynamic unconscious).

Freud also attacked his dissenters who insisted that everything that belongs to the realm of the psyche is conscious. Otherwise it is not psychic. His opponents added that the psyche—consciousness—can be conceptualized as consisting of different gradations ranging from very weak perceptions to very vivid ones. Freud replied that this was as absurd as saying there is no darkness, just different shades of light, or that there are only different intensities of life and no death. These ideas are trite, especially so today because we do not hear too many people (although there are some) arguing against the existence of the unconscious. Freud, however, was not content to stop here because he envisaged difficulties. Clinical experience had made him aware of the inadequacy of his concepts.

The aim of analysis, according to Freud, is to make the unconscious conscious by undoing repression. The patient opposes the analyst in this task—a phenomenon called resistance. The patient, however, is not aware that he is resisting and using repression. Freud believed that repressing forces originate within the ego.

From these data, we are forced to draw the following conclusions. All that is repressed is unconscious, but all that is unconscious is not necessarily repressed. The unconscious parts of the ego are not all latent, as is the situation with preconscious elements. Freud realized that to postulate so many different types of unconscious—descriptive, dynamic, latent and unconscious ego—must be confusing, so he here introduced to a new psychic model, the structural model.

The Ego and the Id

Here, Freud discussed the relationship between the conscious and the unconscious and asked how an unconscious idea or feeling becomes conscious. As he said in *Beyond the Pleasure Principle* (Freud 1920), consciousness is located on the surface of the psyche and is in apposition to the external world.

Freud raised the question as to how a thought is formed. Does it begin with an inner displacement of energy and proceed to the psychic system responsible for consciousness? Is this system, activated by the emergence of the thought? Or does consciousness move down to meet the thought? Freud did not believe that either theory was true, and introduced another possibility to explain the making of the unconscious conscious: for an inner sensation to become conscious, it has to connect itself with a word presentation (Freud 1915c) or, more precisely, become preconscious. The annexation of the word presentation determines whether a psychic element is preconscious or unconscious.

The word presentations are memory traces of external perceptions. This is confusing in that an external perception is usually thought of as being concrete, whereas words are abstractions. The internalization of an abstraction may be especially complicated. Here, we can state that the spoken word or auditory percept becomes incorporated within the ego and is then elaborated in terms of the secondary process. Apart from inner feelings, only percepts that have been at one time conscious can become conscious, according to Freud.

Memory traces are contained in a psychic system adjacent to consciousness so that cathexes can easily pass over into consciousness. This system is, of course, the preconscious. A memory is not experienced in the same vivid fashion as an external percept or an hallucination. In reliving a memory, the cathexis remains for the most part, in the memory system, whereas in both an external percept and an hallucination, the cathexis moves over in its entirety to the perceptual system.

These statements and those that follow can be confusing. I believe one reason for this is that Freud gave the impression that the perceptual system makes direct contact with the outer world and receives its cathexis without having become involved with other parts of the psyche. We know, however, that Freud did not believe this. In *The Interpretation of Dreams* (Freud 1900) he used what we call the picket-fence model, in which an impulse—a stimulus from the outer world—is received at the sensory end of the psychic apparatus and then travels through the pickets, which represent memory traces, until it reaches the motor end and is discharged. Although this is just a simple reflex model and does not highlight the role of consciousness, it is apparent that the stimulus may become conscious after having been fused or linked with the appropriate memory traces, which are memories of experiences that are similar to or can be associated with the stimulus.

Thus, an external stimulus activates a sensory system and first travels through a somatic pathway (sensory nerve fibers). Through these fibers it seeks to reach higher central nervous system centers. At lower levels it is simply a physical or physiological impulse, prementational or prepsychological in nature. It then enters the system unconscious and progresses to the preconscious if there is no resistance. There it cathects a memory trace, which enables it to proceed to its final destination, consciousness.

Even with this series of events, which agrees fairly well with the findings of neurophysiology, there are still difficulties in understanding how to distinguish an external from an internal percept. To repeat, Freud felt that either the stimulus remains bound to the memory trace or the memory trace is simply activated, that is, its cathexis is increased, with an internal stimulus. It does not transfer its cathexis to any large extent to the system perceptual-consciousness. The cathexis of the memory trace apparently is only transient with an external stimulus, and it proceeds into consciousness.

There are several factors that must be examined more carefully. For one, Freud emphasized that the act of becoming preconscious requires that the stimulus become attached to a word presentation. The latter develops from memory traces, which were formed from auditory perceptions. However, if the cathexis of the memory trace is passed completely to perceptual consciousness and becomes detached from that memory trace, then we can wonder how consciousness occurs. What determines the content of consciousness, since all that has happened to the system perceptual-consciousness is that it has become energized? There are, according to Freud, no memory traces in the sphere of consciousness.

To confuse things further, in the paper "A Note upon the Mystic Writing Pad" (Freud 1924), Freud stated that as an external stimulus enters the conscious sphere, the preconscious sends out "feelers" (cathexis) to meet it. This formulation ignored that sensory stimuli first enter the body at somatic levels and then undergo a hierarchal progression through which they ultimately reach consciousness.

Freud provided no theoretical resolution to these inconsistencies. Perhaps the best conclusion is that we are dealing with quantitative factors. An external percept may cathect a memory trace much more intensely than an inner feeling or whatever inner processes lead to the formation of thought. Freud implies that this may be an adequate explanation when he asserted that the hypercathexis of a thought causes a person to view that thought as if it were an external percept.

Pleasurable stimuli do not have an impelling force about them, in sharp contrast to unpleasurable feelings which press toward discharge and change. Pleasure and unpleasure are distinguishable quantitatively and once again, as he so often did, Freud repeated that unpleasure is the outcome of heightening of cathexis, and pleasure a result of lowering it.

These fluctuations of levels of cathexis—the feelings of pleasure and unpleasure—behave in the same way as repressed impulses. The resistance, that is, the obstacles barring them from consciousness, have to be removed if either pleasure or unpleasure are to be felt. In this instance, however, the attachment to the word cathexis does not occur, or if it does, it has no effect on becoming conscious. There is no participation of the preconscious. Feelings are either conscious or unconscious. Objections to the concept of unconscious feelings were discussed in Chapter 1.

Freud returned to a description of the ego to provide a more comprehensive synthesis of this psychic system. He stated "It starts out, as we see, from the system *Pcpt.*, which is its nucleus, and begins by embracing the *Pcs.*, which is adjacent to the mnemic residues" (Freud 1923, p. 23). Freud had earlier stated that the mnemic residues were adjacent to *Pcpt-Cs* and contained in systems (the preconscious) that are adjacent to *Pcpt-Cs*. I believe that Freud's imprecision may be explained by the fact that he was just beginning to think in terms of a structural hierarchy.

Freud was trying to refine his concepts and required an appropriate terminology. "I propose to take it into account by calling the entity which starts out from the system *Pcpt.* and begins by *Pcs.* the 'ego' and by following Groddeck in calling the other part of the mind, into which this entity extends and which behaves as though it were Ucs., the 'id'" (Freud 1923, p. 23). (The impersonality of this deeper layer of the psyche is emphasized by a literal translation of the German word for id, which is *Das Es. Es* means "it.") There are no clear separations between psychic levels. The ego gradually dips into the id. The repressed also merges with the id. It is, however, cut off from the ego by the resistance of repression.

Freud drew a diagram, on the left side of which he placed a "hearing cup", which sits askew on the surface near the preconscious. This is analogous to the auditory lobe and emphasizes that external perceptions and memory traces are primarily acoustic.

Freud summarized by stating the ego is that part of the id that, through the perceptual-consciousness system, has been modified (more precisely, structuralized) by the influence of the outer world. Since perceptual-consciousness is on the surface of the psychic apparatus, the ego represents a surface differentiation, but also penetrates deeper, attempting to influence adherence to the pleasure principle and substituting the reality principle instead. Freud had already discussed this in "Formulations on the Two Principles of Mental Functioning" (1911), but he was more precise here, using his concept of ego consistently.

The ego is the fount of reason, whereas the id is immersed in unreasoning passions. The ego is connected with the soma and controls motility. Here Freud introduced an analogy that has since become famous. He compared the relationships of the ego to the id with a man on horseback. The man can control the horse and make him do his bidding in spite of the horse's superior strength. To carry the analogy further, the id can direct the ego and the ego acts as if it were by choice rather than compulsion, much in the same way a horse will lead the rider, who will not try to oppose the animal if he wants to remain in the saddle.

The formation of the ego is stimulated by both inner and outer forces. The outer forces, as has been emphasized, are experienced through the influence of perceptual-consciousness; the inner forces spring from the soma. The surface of the body receives both inner and outer stimuli. Touch, for example, produces two types of sensations, and one is experienced as if it had an internal source. The ego is derived from bodily sensations, much in the same fashion as pain makes us aware of the particular organ or part of the body. Here we encounter one of Freud's most famous quotations: "The ego is first and foremost a bodily ego; it is not merely a surface entity, but is itself the projection of a surface" (Freud 1923, p. 26).

On a scale of values, ego elements would rate higher than the products of the id. The distance from consciousness of a mental function ordinarily defines where it fits in our social or ethical scale. Still, as evidenced by dreams, there are subtle, integrative, and delicate mental operations that can occur at unconscious levels. Freud cited as an example how a difficult problem may be worked over in a dream so that the person awakes with the solution in mind. Freud was definitely asserting that complex intellectual activity can occur during the sleep or dream state. This has subsequently been questioned. Freud himself stated that such activity occurs in a preconscious state and then enters the dream (Freud 1900); however, this activity is not produced de novo in the dream. Then he stated that intellectual activity does not occur in dreams, but he also stated the opposite in the same book. The example that comes to mind is Kekulé's dream of a snake swallowing its tail and rolling down a hill. On awakening, Kekulé was able to formulate the benzene ring, but it is clear that he had worked very hard and very long on the problem before the dream.

Nevertheless, Freud stressed that higher-level, well-integrated processes can occur at unconscious levels. He had already discussed repression, which originates in the ego but is unconscious as being one of these processes. He now added that a sense of guilt may determine a person's behavior although that person is not consciously aware of feeling guilty. The two phenomena, repression and the unconscious sense of guilt, caused Freud to elaborate the structural hypothesis.

The Ego and the Superego (Ego Ideal)

As can be seen from the title of this section, Freud did not yet distinguish between the superego and the ego ideal. In his narcissism paper (Freud 1914), he spoke of the ego ideal as the ideal state which one strives to achieve. These strivings represent an attempt to regain the lost narcissism of childhood. The superego is different in that it is a judgmental self-critical agency, the outcome of a differentiation within the ego. Freud felt the novel aspect of his formulations in this monograph was his assertion that the superego is less firmly related to consciousness.

It is interesting that Freud earlier attributed the function of reality testing to the superego (Freud 1921). He now corrected himself; stating that the ego, because of its relationship to the perceptual system, has the task of reality testing. He also stated that the perceptual system is the nucleus of the ego, although earlier (Freud 1920) he had formulated that the unconscious part of the ego represents such a nidus, whereas later (Freud 1926) he postulated that the superego was its nucleus. The latter is difficult to understand because the superego is a later developmental acquisition, "the heir to the Oedipus complex," and this would be a contradiction to it being an early kernel for the formation of the ego, a developmental level that leads to the acquisition of mentation.

Freud now considered how the ego is constructed. He viewed it as the outcome of identifications. As occurs in melancholia, the lost love object is set up again in the ego. Object cathexis is given up and replaced by identification. These identifications contribute heavily to the structure of the ego.

During the oral phase, object cathexis and identification cannot be differentiated. I assume that Freud meant that the external cathected object is food. Food is internalized (eaten) and becomes part of the self. Freud was discussing the psychological representation of the nurturing substance that becomes part of the ego as a nurturing matrix, and that later structuralizes to a memory trace of a gratifying relationship.

Freud conjectured that identification might be a necessary process, a condition permitting the id to give up external objects and thus causing the ego to achieve higher levels of cohesion and structure. In this context he made a statement that is frequently quoted by psychoanalysts: ". . . the character of the ego is a precipitate of abandoned object-cathexes and it . . . contains the history of those object-choices." Freud carried these formulations one step further when he stated that a condition for giving up objects is an alteration of the ego, as occurs with character changes and identification.

The transformation of an erotic object choice into an ego alteration is also a way in which the ego gains dominance over the id. It is as if the ego forces itself upon the id and insists, to quote Freud, "See, you can also love me, I am the same as the object." This is an example of anthropomorphization of abstract concepts, something not particularly unusual in Freud's writings.

Freud next equated sublimation with desexualization. An instinct is tamed by transforming its sexual aim into an aim that is more socially acceptable. Again he emphasized the role of the ego, stating his belief that this socialization of an instinct (which represents a structural advance) cannot occur without the mediation of the ego.

Up to now, Freud's formulations of psychopathology depended primarily upon instinctual conflicts and the dominance of one instinct over another. The instincts could war with each other in the ego, or they retreat into the id to continue their battles. Here, Freud introduced another factor, in that the ego itself can be responsible for certain clinical syndromes. For example, he explained that patients with multiple personalities had made conflicting identifications. Since these identifications determine how the character is formed, their vicissitudes are examples of characterological psychopathology.

I do not mean to imply that Freud was concentrating upon structural rather than psychodynamic factors or that he was becoming an object relations theorist. He still emphasized instinctual forces and wrote about their fusion and defusion. However, in this section he focused upon the development of character in that he discussed the acquisition of psychic structures, the superego in particular. In turn, the superego has a regulatory and modulating function that permits the ego to integrate acceptable experiences with external objects so that it can make further identifications.

Since this monograph represents a beginning attempt to construct an ego psychology, the use of certain terms is imprecise. Freud had always used the word ego in a very loose fashion. Here he sharpened his definition by discussing the ego in terms of process and function, and operational approach. However, he continued to use the concept of identification very loosely, applying the term to primitive types of incorporation as well as to the process of character formation, as we do today.

Freud did not de-emphasize the importance of instincts. He investigated the ego's structuralizing processes and identifications in terms of sex by tracing how masculine and feminine characters are achieved. First he mentioned a structural given, constitutional bisexuality. The strength of the masculine and feminine component is important in determining the final outcome of what today we would call the sexual component of the self-representation. However, he did not ignore the role of object relations. Indeed his formulations about the construction of the superego, a psychic structure with both id and ego elements, are based upon the cathexes of external objects. In this case, these are the triangular object relations of the Oedipus complex.

The preliminary discussion of internalization of objects leads to the formulation of the superego, this monograph's most important contribution. He chose to emphasize the boy's development although he saw a parallel development in little girls. In later papers he viewed the female oedipal phase as being somewhat more complicated.

The little boy directs his libidinal wishes toward his mother. They follow dependent impulses, as occurs in an anaclitic object choice (Freud

1914). The child identifies with his father. As his sexual wishes intensify, the father is viewed ambivalently inasmuch as he is perceived as dangerous. The boy fears his father will castrate him because of his incestuous impulses. Freud conjectured, however, that ambivalence toward the father is there from the beginning but becomes reinforced with the upsurge of sexual feelings.

Freud remarked several times in this section that identification with, and ambivalent attitudes toward, the father are there from the very beginning of life, that is, before there are any actual object relations. He was discussing an inherited attitude from a prehistoric period in which there is a primal hatred of the father. He was espousing a Lamarckian hypothesis in which feelings toward external objects and primitive identifications are carried through generations. During the oedipal phase of libidinal impulses toward the mother and ambivalence toward and fear of the father, these primal feelings strengthen what has been constructed during the course of emotional development. Freud had combined a constitutional viewpoint with an object relations perspective.

Freud continued explaining what happens with "the demolition of the Oedipus complex." The boy has to give up his wish to possess the mother. He can either identify with her or with his father, the latter being a normal outcome.

Freud made a clever observation that was motivated by maintaining conceptual consistency. He stated that according to his theory, we would expect a boy to identify with his mother rather than his father, because the giving up of object cathexis occurs mainly through identification, that is, by internalizing into the ego the relinquished object. In the English translation, the editors refer to abandoned objects which implies an active rejecting reaction. Freud used the word *aufgegebende*, which literally means "given up" and which need not connote rejection and imply intentionality in a hostile sense. Freud's lesser view of women was once again expressed when he next stated that girls more easily demonstrate the process of identification when giving up their attachment to their fathers by developing a masculine character.

Still, the complete Oedipus complex results in both masculine and feminine identifications, the intensity of each being determined by the constitutional bisexuality. Freud generalized the existence of the Oedipus complex in both normals and neurotics, but he did not pursue the idea of its universality although he implied it. He postulated a spectrum from a negative Oedipus complex, characterized in the boy by a mother identification and a longing for the father, to the positive Oedipus complex, characterized by identification with the father, the mother representing the sought-after object. Between these poles are varying degrees of mother and father identifications and object cathexes. These identifications and object cathexes cause an alteration of the ego. Freud viewed them as forming a precipitate within the ego, set apart from other psychic elements. Today we would state that identifications lead to character consolidation and form new psychic structures. This precipitate or new structure constitutes the superego. As previously mentioned, Freud did not distinguish the superego from the ego ideal.

Freud clearly stated that the superego arises de novo with the repression of the Oedipus complex. It does not allow for forerunners. Phenomena commonly observed even in children of less than 1 year of age demonstrate inner restraints and self-punishment. Some theorists place the origin of the superego around the anal phase. Melanie Klein believed the child is born with a superego. This theory is in accord with the Catholic doctrine of original sin.

Freud added that the superego consists of more than just identifications and a residual of the id's object choice; it also contains a reaction formation against them. For example, in the father-identification, the child's superego includes strivings to be like the father as well as prohibitions against such strivings. Identification with certain traits is acceptable, but other traits, such as the possession of the mother, are the father's prerogatives and are not to be shared. The superego maintains the repression of the Oedipus complex. The father's prohibition of the child's oedipal wish for the mother strengthens the infantile ego, enabling it to achieve repression of the Oedipus complex inasmuch as it incorporates this prohibition.

Freud was somewhat obscure here. The essence of his discussion is that the ego's incorporation of the father's prohibition creates the superego. Thus, in the process of formation, the superego achieves repression of the Oedipus complex, but it also owes its existence to that repression. We can conceptualize this inner play as a reinforcement. As the oedipal wishes push forward as a return of the repressed, the superego becomes strengthened and further consolidated, also strengthening repression.

Freud believed two general factors are responsible for the formation of the superego. First he referred to the relatively long biological helplessness of mankind, which is related to infantile sexuality. This brings us to the second point, the existence of the Oedipus complex, which ushers an interruption, the latency period of psychosexual development.

He compared the latency period to geological development which included a glacial epoch. Ferenczi (1913) wrote about and discussed these fanciful and obscure ideas with Freud. Freud stated that the repression of the Oedipus complex represents a heritage of the effect of the ice age on cultural development. Obviously this is vague in terms of psychic inheritance. The comparison seems to be a metaphor in which the ice age on a global scale represents the latency period of the developing child. Freud seemed to believe that the experience of the glacial epoch somehow became incorporated into the individual psyche and led to a modification of psychosexual development, manifested as the latency period.

Freud now had an opportunity to assert that psychoanalysis concerns itself with the higher side as well as the lowest side of mental life, inasmuch as the latter is changed into the former through the formation of the superego. The analysis of the ego permits us to look at the higher nature of the psyche which children attribute to their parents as they admire and fear them. They also identify with these attributes. "The ego ideal is therefore the heir of the Oedipus complex and thus it is also the expression of the most powerful impulses and most important libidinal vicissitudes of the id" (Freud 1923, p. 36). He added that with the construction of this ego ideal (or superego, as we prefer), the ego masters the Oedipus complex but it places itself in subjection to the id aspects of the superego.

The reader could easily become confused here, because Freud stated merely that the ego becomes subjected to the id. The reader has to infer the role of the superego, and his inferrence is supported by the next sentence. Here Freud postulated that the ego is the representative of the external world, whereas the superego reflects the internal world of the id. This is also confusing, because there are other id elements that are not at all related to the superego.

The remainder of this section is concerned with hereditary factors as they enter into the formation of the superego. Freud continued to discuss the higher and lower sides of the psychic apparatus, but the original German minimizes any value judgments about what is primitive within the developmental scale or psychic hierarchy. Freud used the word *tiefsten*, which is better translated "deepest," rather than "lowest" as it appears in the English translation (p. 36). He acknowledged again that the ego ideal involves the higher nature of man and "contains the germ from which all religions evolve" (Freud 1923, p. 37). Pursuing briefly his formulations in "Totem and Taboo" (Freud 1913a), he discussed the phylogenetic factors in the development of the ego ideal.

Freud was, in essence, a Lamarckian. He believed in the inheritance of acquired traits, but he questioned how this occurs in terms of the psychic structure he hypothesized. He concluded that the ego's experiences, after being repeated generation after generation, eventually become incorporated into the id and thus become part of the race's heritage. These now are constitutional elements, which contribute to the formation of the superego. The original prohibitions, as exemplified in primitive taboos, are incorporated into the modern superego. In view of the ego aspect, Freud postulated that the superego may be "reviving shapes of former egos and be bringing them to resurrection."

Although the modern theory of evolution rejects the Lamarckian view, Freud's ideas are nevertheless interesting. Modern genetics has far from exhausted which environmental factors may affect the DNA code. Freud's ideas may be fanciful, but the study of the superego through the analysis of patients suffering from primitive mental states frequently reveals such archaic qualities that we can reasonably wonder whether they are the outcome of ontogeny or phylogeny.

The Two Classes of Instincts

Up to this point Freud had developed the structural hypotheses. Now he returned to instinct theory, as he wanted to point out the relationships between the newly postulated psychic structures and the instincts. He again compared the relationship of the ego to external perceptions with the id's relationship to the drives. This is not absolute, because the ego is also connected with the drives since it is a differentiated part of the id.

These relationships have relevance to current concepts about early developmental stages. At first, the infant is primarily concerned with inner sensations, that is, impulses and needs that disturb homeostatic equilibrium. We can interpret the neonate's state as being drive-dominated and we can assume that the psyche is primarily id. However, the id differentiates into the ego as external stimuli impinge upon it, and as the id reacts to drives the developing ego is related to external percepts in an analogous fashion. Still, insofar as the infant's boundaries are not established, there is very little distinction between the inner and outer world. Internal needs are not yet well differentiated from external stimuli. The equations of drive to id and external world to ego are somewhat obscure. Actually, the instincts, which are incorrectly viewed as synonymous to drives (Freud 1915b), are part of the content of the id. Similarly, one of the functions of the ego is to act as the site in which stimuli from the external world are perceived.

Freud once again stressed dualism, as he did in *Beyond the Pleasure Principle* (Freud 1920), here distinguishing between the life and death instincts. His purpose was to extend the concepts he postulated in the earlier paper. He described how, in the process of structuralizing unicellular organisms into multicellular organizations, the death instinct is neutralized by the life instinct, which is dominant. This constitutes fusion, but if fusion occurs then defusion is also possible.

Fusion is part of the growth process and leads to structured psychic states. Instincts become tamed and sublimated through neutralization, which is the outcome of the fusion of libidinal and aggressive drives, a point that some modern ego psychologists have stressed. This formulation, however, is incomplete. It is difficult to understand how the fusion of two instincts can create states of higher integration. Instincts operate on the basis of the primary process. The fusion of two primary process elements cannot result in a secondary process structure. Other structuralizing processes are required for the elevation of primitive instincts to higher-reality attuned structures. Psychic development cannot be understood only in terms of instincts interacting with each other. It is a complicated process involving instincts, ego systems, internalizing processes, and nurturing and soothing object relations.

Freud added that the regressive process is characterized by instinctual defusion. The reduction to basic instincts is related to a regression from structured to primitive mental states. Perhaps ambivalence can be explained on the basis of such a regression, as an example of instinctual defusion leading to the release of love and hate toward the same object, whereas previously the subject related to the external object on the basis of a fusion of love and hate, each held in check because of the ensuing neutralization. Freud questioned his formulation, reminding himself that ambivalence is a fundamental attitude in that it is a primal orientation based upon a racial characteristic as he discussed in his Lamarckian viewpoints at the end of the last section of *Beyond the Pleasure Principle*. However, even if we were to accept this fanciful hypothesis of an inherent constitutional ambivalence, this does not necessarily mean that the psyche could not advance from this position and then regress back to it. Freud's final conjecture was that ambivalence may represent an incomplete fusion.

The justification for differentiating two classes of instincts requires supportive data. This section is very difficult to follow because the translation is inexact and the original German is extremely cumbersome. Freud referred to the polarity between love and hate as he did in "Instincts and Their Vicissitudes" (Freud 1915b). He discussed various attitudes and changes of feelings toward the external object that do not necessarily require a dual instinct theory. He cited paranoia, in which the beloved person becomes the hated persecutor, and postulated a stage in which love is transformed into hate. The opposite may also occur. Analyses investigating the origin of homosexuality or desexualized social feelings show that powerful aggressive feelings of rivalry are overcome and replaced by affectionate feelings or lead to an identification with the external object. These phenomena can be explained on the basis of a transformation of hate into love.

Freud offered another explanation to support his dual instinct theory, returning to his concept of a primal ambivalence present from the beginning of mental life. The dominance of hate over love he explained on the basis of displaceable energy. For example, the erotic impulse is decathected and the aggressive tendency is further energized. When the opposite occurs, this is frequently a matter of expediency. The child, because of his dependency and weakness, cannot discharge his aggressive impulses. Consequently the other side of his ambivalence is cathected, reinforcing the loving attitude.

These formulations do not require the assumption that love is transformed into hate or vice versa. However, they do require another assumption. Freud postulated the existence of a freely displaceable reservoir of neutral energy. He did not know whether it resides in the id or the ego. Freud's indecision is interesting because, as the appendix to this monograph discusses, he was not consistent as to where he located the reservoir of libido. In earlier papers he placed it in the ego; here, he stated that it belongs to the id. In later papers he referred again to its position in the ego. In any case, this neutral energy can augment the intensity of either libidinal or aggressive impulses. This energy comes from narcissistic libido, that is, libido that has been withdrawn from objects back into the ego (secondary narcissism), and that has become desexualized as the outcome of sublimation.

Freud ended this section by bringing the death instinct into the foreground, as he had in *Beyond the Pleasure Principle* (Freud 1920). By desexualizing libido, the ego is working at cross-purposes to Eros. Freud jumped to the conclusion that in that case (sublimation), the ego is siding with the death instinct. The aim of the sexual act is to discharge germ cells, which from a psychological viewpoint is equivalent to the discharge of Eros. With less Eros in the psyche, the death instinct can take over. That is why, according to Freud, each orgasm can be considered a momentary death.

The Dependent Relationships of the Ego

This final section of "The Ego and the Id" is both theoretical and clinical. Here Freud focused upon the special importance of the superego for character structure and psychopathology.

According to Freud the superego owes its special position within the ego the two factors: (1) the weakness of the ego at the time of its formation and (2) its status as heir to the Oedipus complex. He was referring to the dominance and strength of the superego. A stronger, more mature ego could better resist the critical onslaughts of the superego. The strength of the superego is due in part to being closer to the id than consciousness. Compared to the anatomical homunculus of the brain, the superego is standing on its head.

Freud became involved here with important clinical issues, in which the superego plays a major role. He described patients who responded to analytic progress and to the temporary relief of symptoms by getting worse. Every improvement is followed by a marked worsening of the illness. This could partly be explained by rebellious attitudes toward the analyst and narcissistic fixations, but even after these attitudes have been analyzed, the same intolerance for improvement persists. Freud called this the negative therapeutic reaction, and today it is recognized as an important treatment impasse and a characteristic of special types of psychopathology. Current formulations of the negative therapeutic reaction emphasize that the patient will not improve because he is then beholden to and thereby vulnerable to the analyst. Or, as Melanie Klein believed, getting well means destroying internal objects toward which the patient feels both greed and envy. To Klein, the negative therapeutic reaction represented a reparative activity.

Freud continued to prove himself an astute clinician. He distinguished a type of negative therapeutic reaction that is not as obstinate as others he had encountered. In this reaction the patient has identified with another person's unconscious sense of guilt. The sense of guilt that has been taken over as one's own is not rigidly integrated into the character structure, but operates as a foreign body and is somewhat more accessible to analysis.

This is not a true identification in modern terms. Actually, Freud wrote of "borrowing" the external object's guilt.

This type of interaction can display itself strikingly in other clinical entities. For example, we occasionally encounter patients who have all the florid symptoms of a psychosis. Still, when we examine their past history and general level of functioning, they do not seem to be seriously impaired or at least as impaired as their symptoms would indicate. Similarly, in treatment, they do not demonstrate the difficulties anticipated in the therapy of severely disturbed patients. In analysis, these patients reveal that their psychoses are the outcome of an identification with an emotionally significant person, more precisely an identification with that person's psychosis. This entity has in the past been referred to as an hysterical psychosis. In view of psychic processes, this situation is the same as Freud described as the borrowed unconscious sense of guilt.

Moving on to other clinical areas, Freud next described the role of the superego in the production of obsessive neuroses and depressions. In the obsessive neurosis, the ego rebels against the harsh injunctions of an unusually severe superego. The compulsive ritual, as Freud had already explained in his discussion of the Rat Man (Freud 1909b), represented both an attempt to express the forbidden impulse and the prohibition against it. Freud broke down obsessive defenses into several components that are at the mercy of the patient's intense ambivalence: the ego can overcome the prohibitions and threats of the superego, or it may give in to them. The Rat Man's behavior with the stone in the road is a classic example. The Rat Man noticed a stone in the road. He reasoned the stone was dangerous, because when his lady friend drove down that road in her carriage the wheel could hit the stone, the carriage could topple over, and she could be seriously hurt. To prevent this he kicked the stone to the side of the road. Next, he reviewed the situation and concluded this was all ridiculous, so he kicked the stone back into the middle of the road. His initial fears returned and the ritual of kicking the stone was repeated over and over. The patient was alternately responding to hostile destructive impulses expressed by kicking the stone in the middle of the road and to superego prohibitions expressed by removing it to the side.

The ego of the depressed patient remains passive. It acquiesces to the accusations of the superego and the patient feels miserable and unworthy. This also occurs through the process of identification, in this instance, with an external object toward whom the patient has an intensely ambivalent relationship. Usually there has been a separation from this object, which is retained in the psyche by identifying with it. There may be an actual loss through death, but not necessarily. Freud described these processes in considerable detail in "Mourning and Melancholia" (Freud 1917).

It is interesting that Freud emphasized the harsh, cruel superego. Its constructive elements, its role in acquiring values and ideals as the character is consolidated were understressed. He attributed to the superego the function of determining how the personality will be constructed inasmuch as it represents the first and most important identification.

Freud, however, was more interested in understanding psychopathology than pyschic development in terms of structural theory. Furthermore, in viewing character formation as beginning after the repression of the Oedipal complex he ignored all the formative experiences occurring during the first year of life. Freud's work at this juncture represents a transition point at which structural factors are gaining in importance over id psychology. I believe that modern psychoanalytic theory directly derives from these early formulations about incorporative processes. The developmental timetable has been pushed back considerably, somewhere between what Freud postulated here and what Melanie Klein later conceptualized. (As stated, Klein viewed the superego as being present from the beginning of life.)

Continuing with his clinical formulations, Freud stated that the hysteric's predominant defense against the superego is repression, a mechanism that is, of course, typical of the hysterical patient. The sense of guilt remains unconscious, but, to some extent, this is true of everybody.

Heretofore, psychoanalysis concentrated upon the baser passions, but with the formulation of the superego it began to be concerned with the moral side of human nature. The psychoanalytic viewpoint has discovered that human beings are both more immoral and more moral than had been previously assumed.

Psychoanalysis must also be credited with the discovery that some criminals commit their crimes because of an overly severe superego rather than a lack of conscience. They commit their crimes so that they will be caught and punished. They seek punishment to appease their superego or, as Alexander (1961) said, to bribe it. This harshness of the superego is also a significant factor in determining masochistic behavior. The superego is relatively independent from the ego and, to repeat, is closer to the id. It is, nevertheless, accessible to consciousness, but here Freud again became confusing. He stated that the superego undoubtedly contains verbal prohibitions, admonitions and lectures, internalizations of experiences with the outer world as it represents a part of the ego, but that these only become cathected by energy emanating from the id. He did not explain the significance of the localization of energy. We can surmise that he was emphasizing the primitive elements of the superego and trying to reconcile them with higher psychic structures, which have to be involved in both the sense of guilt and morality. According to Freud, the melancholic patient's superego rages mercilessly against the ego. It is a pure culture of destructiveness. He believed that the melancholic's superego houses the death instinct which aims toward the patient's self-destruction. By contrast, the obsessional patient has a guarantee against suicide.

Clinical experience does not support Freud's reasoning. Obsessional patients sometimes commit suicide. True, often their defenses have failed them and they have regressed. In other instances, however, their rituals are acted out in such a fashion that the patient may hurt or even kill himself. To the observer, this may appear to be an accident, not an intentional suicidal attempt. In addition, Freud's clinical formulations do not seem consistent. He wrote that the pure culture of death instinct in the melancholic's superego leads to self-destruction. The obsessive patient is protected from suicide because he directs his destructiveness toward an object. The depressed patient also reacts toward an object. I suppose the essential difference is that the obsessional patient has the ability to view the object as external and as separate from the self, whereas the depressed patient cannot effect a separation between himself and the object. Consequently the destructive impulse is directed toward the self-object and can lead to suicide.

The superego consists of desexualized Eros. Instinctual impulses are sublimated. In the melancholic, there is a defusion; Eros is no longer able to bind destructive impulses. The balance between Eros and destruction is different in the superego of the obsessional patient. According to Freud, the obsessive patient regresses to the anal-sadistic phase, at which point sadism is released toward the external object. The ego is sufficiently alert that it institutes defenses, mainly reaction formation, to protect the object. Apparently, Freud believed that the release of sadism through regression is different than the defusion that occurs in the superego of the depressed patient. This is difficult to understand. We can speculate that Freud was discussing differences between regression to developmental stages that are not severely psychopathologically disrupted. During the course of ordinary development, the anal phase contains a moderate amount of sadism which is directed toward maintaining control and organization. It is structure promoting and not fused with Eros. I suppose that in this context fusion is a defensive activity. Eros controls destructive sadism rather than structure-promoting sadism, or to be more exact, structure-promoting aggression.

The question remains whether sublimation, a normal adaptation, should be distinguished from fusion as a psychopathological defense. Freud formulated that the death instincts can be controlled in various ways—they can be fused with erotic instincts or directed toward the outer world. He added, however, that this process may not be sufficient to hold the death instinct in check; this happens with melancholia.

Returning to the formation of the superego, Freud added that in addition to identification, sublimation is involved. Eros becomes desexualized, thereby losing its power to neutralize. This also constitutes a defusion and again releases quantities of death instinct. Such formulations create further theoretical difficulties because, in essence, Freud was postulating that a normal developmental process is inevitably followed by psychopathological consequences. I conjecture that Freud would not have agreed that the release of death instinct is necessarily psychopathological. Freud did not pursue these distinctions further. Today few clinical theoreticians would be concerned about these issues since, in their conceptual system, instinctual forces are superseded by structural considerations.

The ego has many important functions. Due to its connection with the perceptual system, it organizes perceptions, thereby achieving reality testing and an ordering of time. It controls the drives by determining their access to motility. However, this is more apparent than real, and Freud once again demonstrated his deftness in constructing metaphors. He compared the ego to a constitutional monarch who has to give his approval to any law passed by congress, but who is still very careful before he dares impose a veto.

Experiences with the outer world enrich the ego. Now, Freud was beginning to enter the area of object relations theory. Experiences with the outer world are structure-promoting. Id cathexis is withdrawn from external objects and directed toward the ego. Id content can reach the ego in two ways: (1) It can proceed directly from the id to the ego. This was discussed in some detail in "The Unconscious" (Freud 1915b). (2) The id can also gain access to the ego through the superego.

In these formulations, the ego is not the same passive agent as it was in previous papers. It has developed from a psychic agency at the mercy of drives to an organizing force that masters and inhibits primary process-oriented instinctual activity. The task of psychoanalysis is to further the conquest of the id by the ego.

Freud, as was frequently his custom, presented abstruse concepts in a melodramatic fashion, the above being an example. He emphasized a battle between the id and ego in which the latter was the conqueror. He viewed the analyst as a participant in that struggle. Such anthropomorphic constructs simplify matters and have explanatory value. Still, their importance goes beyond didactic exposition. Freud's concepts of a raging battle, dominance and submission, conqueror and vanquished, contribute to his clinical orientation and philosophy. He envisioned treatment as a battle between analyst and patient. The analyst is constantly struggling with the unconscious and trying to make it conscious, that is, to force it into ego territory. He is fighting the resistance the unconscious erects. The analyst recommends himself to the id as a libidinal object, thereby attempting to deflect libido upon himself. Undoubtedly Freud was referring to how transference enables treatment to achieve its task of broadening the ego's domain and increasing its power over the id.

This is not exactly how some analysts now view treatment. Rather than being a power struggle, psychoanalysis is conducted as a cooperative endeavor. The id is not an evil force that has to be conquered, and its constructive adaptive elements are focused upon instead. True, treatment may be stormy and the patient may fight and rebel against the analyst, but this is viewed as a repetitive expression of infantile constellations that have to be understood and not reacted to. Furthermore, the patient may experience considerable relief from projecting the hated parts of the self into the analyst. Instead of treatment consisting of an active struggle between antagonists, the analytic setting creates a holding environment in which infantile elements can emerge and transference develop. The analyst's receptivity allows this regression to occur in a manageable and nondisruptive fashion. Various parts of the psyche are not judged and evaluated relative to each other.

Freud's position was that the ego serves three masters: outer reality, inner reality as depicted by the id, and the superego. It is, so to speak, in a central position and tries to appease them all. It may be manipulative and even deceitful in its endeavor to maintain intrapsychic peace.

In the short space remaining in this monograph, Freud opened up a new area—anxiety theory, which he pursued in his next major monograph, "Inhibitions, Symptoms and Anxiety" (Freud 1926a). Again he placed the ego in a central position, facing dangers threatening from the same three areas, the id, superego, and reality. Each danger leads to a specific type of anxiety. He did not describe specific types of anxiety extensively, although he discussed some thoughts about them. Basically he described, without specifically acknowledging it, an hierarchal concept of anxiety. He also included various psychic elements and external objects in his different categories of anxiety.

To begin, he once again emphasized that anxiety is generated in the ego as a reaction to danger. This leads to "flight," meaning that the dangerous object is decathected. The ego also feels threatened when it loses its cathexis or when it is no longer loved as occurs when the superego hates it. These formulations are relevant to our understanding of characterological psychopathology. In many schizophrenic patients as well as other primitively fixated personalities, there is practically no self-esteem. The self-representation is depleted in that it has no cohesion. This can be explained in energic terms as a loss of cathexis, which leads to the terror of psychic dissolution. Existential anxiety and the loss of identity are the inevitable outcomes of the crumbling of the self-representation. The type of anxiety associated with an unloved or decathected ego is what Freud called *Todesangst*, the fear of death. He did not conceptualize the self-representation as an ego subsystem so he could not locate exactly where the loss of cathexis or self-esteeming love occurs.

Freud then described what is easily recognizable as separation anxiety. In this instance anxiety occurs when the external object can no longer be cathected. However, this is another example in which the loss of love is the essential factor. Instead of libido ceasing to flow to the ego from the id, the ego finds itself abandoned by an external object.

Freud postulated a connection between these various types of anxiety which established an hierarchal sequence. At the primitive end of the spectrum we have *Todesangst*, in which the ego feels abandoned; there is no libido directed toward it, and it is therefore vulnerable to the non-neutralized death instinct. This occurs because of the loss of an external object or the hateful onslaughts of the superego, a characteristic situation in melancholia. At the higher level *Todesangst* is replaced by a fear of conscience which can be thought of as a bound, tamed version of *Todesangst*. Because of secondary process organizations, the primitive fear of death is elevated to the fear of conscience, a moral dread. Both *Todesangst* and the fear of conscience are the products of the working over of castration anxiety. The sense of guilt is the outcome of a strengthening of these various anxieties, which are the products of a clash between the superego and the ego.

This is confusing if we do not specify which psychic levels correspond to these three types of anxiety, that is, which belong to the higher, more organized levels and which are characteristic of primitive psychic structures. Freud listed the following sequence—castration, conscience, and death anxiety. It would have been clarifying if he had explained that castration anxiety belongs to the oedipal level, which leads to the formation of the superego. As development proceeds in a progressive direction, conscience anxiety develops. If regression occurs, death anxiety develops.

Freud ended this monograph by once more stressing the importance of the death instinct. The id can only express love or hate toward the ego, since it has no unifying principle to modulate feelings. (This can only occur in the ego.) In the id Eros and the death instinct are constantly battling with each other. The death instinct is mute in that its manifestations are covert rather than overt as it attempts to silence the peace-disturbing life instinct under the aegis of the pleasure principle, which seeks a lowering of energy levels.

10

"Inhibitions, Symptoms and Anxiety" (1926)

SYNOPSIS

In the first section of this monograph, Freud distinguished between inhibitions and symptoms, the former referring to the restriction of a function and not necessarily associated with psychopathology. However, if an inhibition is the outcome of an internal conflict, it can also be a symptom. Freud enumerated various types of sexual and nonsexual inhibitions, such as those affecting nutrition, locomotion, and work. However, a nonsexual activity can also be erotized and thereby result in an inhibition. Freud cited the example of a writing inhibition in which the pen becomes a symbol for the penis and the ink represents semen.

By contrast, symptoms are reactions to instinctual impulses that create unpleasure. What is pleasurable at one level is unpleasurable at another. The ego achieves its dominance by repressing unpleasure and inhibiting instinctual impulses. Freud asked how this comes about, phrasing the question in the context of energic distributions and the production of anxiety.

The ego attempts to regulate excitations according to the dictates of both the pleasure and reality principles. It creates a "signal of unpleasure" when it has to oppose an instinctual impulse because of the reality principle. The energy for this "signal of unpleasure" comes from the decathected instinctual impulse but is produced in the ego. Freud once again emphasized that the ego is where anxiety is produced, clearly a contradiction of his first anxiety theory.

The process of symptom formation is initiated by failure of repression; the forbidden instinctual impulse seeks gratification through a substitute formation, which constitutes a symptom. The ego attempts reconciliation by synthesizing and integrating. Its synthetic function is the outcome of the unifying qualities of Eros. The ego acquired such a function before its energy was neutralized. The ego also tries to incorporate and synthesize the symptom into its organization, but it may fail. The symptom may be experienced as a foreign body, and the ego may set up a secondary defensive struggle against it. In that case the symptom may be dissociated from the main ego current. If it is incorporated the ego may exploit the symptom for its secondary gain.

Freud explored these concepts in a clinical context by discussing Little Hans and the Wolf Man. Little Hans was afraid of horses; this is a symptom. He was unable to walk on the streets for fear of encountering a horse; this is an inhibition. The phobia, the fear of horses, represented Hans' attempt to resolve his ambivalence toward his father. The Wolf Man was similar to Little Hans in that they both had phobias which involved oral aggression—the fear of being bitten by a horse and the fear of being eaten by a wolf. The fear of being devoured was a manifestation of the Wolf Man's regressively expressed tender feelings toward his father.

Freud's discussion of these cases led him to conclude that there are other defenses beside repression—in this instance, regression. Regression is more powerful than repression inasmuch as the repressed impulse remains intact whereas the regressed impulse is "damaged," having undergone a regressive denigration.

The Wolf Man, according to Freud, was considerably sicker than Little Hans. Freud formulated that the Wolf Man's passive homosexual longings toward his father were much stronger than those of Little Hans, which were hardly discernible. The basic fear behind the two phobias was that of castration, which was regressively expressed by the fears of being bitten by a horse and eaten by a wolf. Because of the strength of passive homosexual impulses, this fear was experienced in different ways. Little Hans was afraid that his father would cut off his penis in retaliation for his incestuous feelings toward his mother. The Wolf Man, because of his homosexual longings toward his father, had to adopt a feminine attitude toward him, which meant that he had to be castrated. From these formulations, Freud concluded once again that anxiety is created in the ego rather than being the manifestation of repressed libido.

Next, Freud discussed the obsessional neuroses and placed their symptoms into two categories: (1) those arising from the superego and consisting of prohibitions and restrictions, and (2) those arising from the id and striving for the discharge of instinctual impulses by seeking substitute gratification and displacements. During the formative phases of the neuroses the first group of symptoms is usually dominant because of the strength of the superego, but with the passage of time the repressed impulses become stronger as they press toward discharge and overcome the repressive barrier. Because of the ego's tendency to synthesize, there is an impetus to combine these two groups of symptoms, which results in compromise formations. Freud, however, paid particular attention to the defense mechanisms of undoing and isolation.

Freud constructed a hierarchy of defenses. Repression is characteristic of genital feelings, whereas other defenses, such as isolation and undoing, are associated with the anal-sadistic phase. The fundamental danger that the ego has to defend itself against is castration anxiety. Anxiety is emitted as a signal to set defenses in motion to protect the ego against the danger of castration.

Freud wrote about two types of anxiety. (1) The first type is a response to mounting excitation, a situation of emotional vulnerability and helplessness. (2) As the child begins to recognize the mother's capacity to nurture and soothe him, he transforms what was essentially a discharge phenomenon into a mode of communication. Anxiety as a signal has become adaptive. These two types are in keeping with the progression from the first to the second anxiety theory.

Symptoms are constructed to avoid anxiety as well as danger. They also provide substitute modes of gratification. Danger, as is true of any psychic element or response, can also be viewed in terms of a hierarchy. For example, during early childhood, the infant cannot master large amounts of either inner or outer excitation. He fears the loss of the nurturing and protective mother. As he develops emotionally, he comes to fear his father because he perceives him as a rival for his mother's love. Still later, he becomes afraid of his superego as he begins to experience social anxiety.

These formulations are relevant to the understanding of psychopathology, primarily the neuroses. Freud struggled with the problem of the choice of neurosis and postulated three factors in the predisposition to neurosis: biological, phylogenetic, and psychological. The biological factor is the outcome of the long period of total dependence in human beings, compared to that of other animals. The phylogenetic factor concerns the diphasic nature of sexuality as it peaks around the age of 4 or 5 at the culmination of the Oedipus complex, and then again during puberty. The psychological factor is based upon imperfections of the psychic apparatus; because of certain dangers in the outer world certain drives become dangerous.

This monograph, in essence, ends with the above formulations, but Freud also wrote an addendum, in which he covered such important clinical topics as resistance and anticathexis, repression, and defense, and made some supplementary remarks about anxiety.

Although Freud wrote many more important papers, this seminal monograph completes a conceptual continuum. Many of his other papers deal with extensions and elaborations of ideas found in papers in this volume. "Inhibitions, Symptoms and Anxiety" contains Freud's most mature thinking about anxiety, as *Beyond the Pleasure Principle* and "The Ego and the Id" completed his ideas about instinct theory. All of these works also deal with many other related and fundamental issues important to the clinician.

The editor's introduction to this monograph emphasizes the wide range of topics Freud addressed. However, the problem of anxiety was the main theme; indeed, when this work was reprinted as an article by the Psychoanalytic Quarterly Press, it carried the title "The Problem of Anxiety."

We have discussed Freud's first anxiety theory, which emphasizes an accumulation of libidinal tension, in his early paper, "On the Justification for Detaching a Particular Syndrome, from Neurasthenia under the description 'Anxiety Neuroses'" (Freud 1895). He referred to this theory in several papers, but as early as 1897 in a letter to Fliess (Freud 1950, letter 75) he indicated that anxiety is *not* related to the production of libido. The editors of the *Standard Edition* pointed out that this is an "isolated recantation." In "Inhibitions, Symptoms and Anxiety" he did not entirely repudiate the first anxiety theory, but was able to retain it in the context of postulating a hierarchy and intensity of trauma.

Freud distinguished anxiety from fear, the latter being realistic anxiety, (Freud 1915c). If one cannot flee from a dangerous situation, that is, if the danger cannot be influenced by withdrawal or flight, then presumably the danger is internal, and the accompanying affect is identified as neurotic anxiety. The editors pointed out that there are significant difficulties in distinguishing between anxiety as a direct response to trauma and anxiety as a signal to the danger of a threatening trauma. Freud emphasized that the occurrence of trauma is the fundamental factor in generating anxiety, whereas the anticipation of trauma leads to the formation of a warning signal.

This explanation raises several questions. How much affect is involved in the generation of a signal? If a person contemplates or is alerted to the possibility of facing danger, are we justified in thinking in terms of anxiety? The realistic appraisal of the consequences of an external event produces thoughts with shifts of low cathexis. Furthermore anxiety has been defined as referring to internal, unrealistic dangers. The differentiation between external and internal sources of anxiety cannot be precisely made. External stimuli activate internal conflicts, which are perceived as threatening, and the blurring of ego boundaries makes the distinction of inside and outside even more difficult.

Freud continued to view the traumatic state as one in which the ego feels helpless and vulnerable in the face of accumulated libidinal tension that cannot be discharged. Jones (1927) coined the expression *aphanisis* to describe this state of helpless vulnerability—a state of complete impotence and loss of sexual feeling, accompanied by a feeling of inchoate terror. However, if we think in terms of structural factors, such a vulnerable ego is so precariously held together that it does not have sufficient integration and cohesion to generate organized feelings. In Freud's model, accumulated tension which entails an accumulation of libido, causes disruption and loss of integration so that that same lidido can no longer be experienced in a structured fashion.

An affect expresses itself in a way considered characteristic of that affect. This is a tautology. If a patient describes himself as hyperventilating, has an increased pulse, has beads of perspiration on his forehead, and is suffering from other vasomotor disturbances, we would not hesitate in asserting that he is suffering from anxiety. If the patient states that he has no feelings or does not feel anxious, we consider this unusual and assume that he has repressed his feelings.

Very early in the development of his ideas, Freud (1895) called attention to the similarity of the physiological concommitants of anxiety and sexual excitation, which supports his thesis that anxiety is the outcome of dammed-up libido. This raises the difficult question as to how dammed-up sexual feelings are related to life-threatening dangers, which also cause the subjective experience of anxiety and its accompanying sequelae. As this monograph beautifully illustrates, Freud was well aware of the complexities involved in understanding the many subtle facets of the ubiquitous affect of anxiety. He approached the problem from many angles and he went far beyond his initial formulations about dammed-up libido. He moved more and more in a structural framework, as evidenced by the importance he attributed to the role of the ego. Freud had already postulated that the ego is the site of anxiety before he wrote this monograph. Here he further emphasized, as he did in "The Ego and the Id" (Freud 1923), that the ego feels threatened by separation, abandonment, and loss of love. Consequently, according to Freud, the first experience of anxiety occurs at birth, which represents the first separation—that from the mother's body. The baby's crying, which marks the beginning of life, is also an expression of anxiety. Again this formulation would be difficult to reconcile with the concept of accumulated sexual tension.

Freud's ideas about birth were different from those of Rank, who gave very special importance to the act of birth. Rank felt birth to be the prototypical trauma relived in all later anxiety experiences. Freud did not go that far; he merely noted certain phenomenological similarities in the baby's reactions and the anxiety attack.

I

Freud began this monograph by examining phenomena that he had discussed throughout his writings. (In view of his more sophisticated outlook, he had to re-evaluate the mechanisms of mental processes, which are fundamental to psychopathology.) He focused here upon inhibitions and symptoms, and began by pointing out the obvious. Inhibitions and symptoms do not have the same implications. An inhibition refers to the restriction of a function, and is not necessarily a sign of psychopathology. A symptom, on the other hand, is much more complicated, representing a compromise between an impulse and repressive forces. An inhibition may be the consequence of internal conflict and, therefore, a symptom. However, it may also be the result of the rational appraisal of reality testing.

As we continue to study and treat patients suffering from ego defects, we are becoming increasingly aware of how inhibitions represent some of the most important manifestations of these disorders. Whatever the level of fixation or developmental distortion the patient will eventually suffer from an inability to function due to a defect in the ego's executive system.

As we would expect, Freud was concerned about the sexual function. He explained that in men inhibitions may involve impotence, or a lack or diminution of the libido when sexual excitation occurs. Disturbances in sexual performance, such as premature ejaculation, well illustrate the connection between a symptom and an inhibition. In women, according to Freud, this connection is particularly well established; in women who are afraid of sex, sexual impulses cause anxiety and are therefore repressed (inhibited). Freud then outlined various manifestations of disturbances of the sexual function, such as deflection of libido, poor performance, attaching conditions to sexual activity, and other defensive measures.

Freud briefly mentioned inhibitions that affect nutrition, locomotion, and work. Disturbances and inhibitions of locomotion (as occur in hysterical paralyses) are no longer common. Eating disorders, including anorexia and bulimia, and work inhibitions, which when extreme lead to complete functional paralysis, are frequently seen in patients fixated at early developmental levels.

After he established these seemingly nonsexual inhibitions, Freud returned to sex. First he discussed how a function can become erotized, and by virtue of its symbolic representation of the forbidden sexual act, become inhibited. He cited the example in which a pen may represent the penis and the ink the ejaculatory fluid. Consequently, the neurotic's sexual conflict is manifested by an inability to write. The more a modality of the ego's executive system becomes erotized, the less is the capacity to exercise that modality or adaptive technique.

This is not the first time that Freud had written about erotization. Here, however, it is tied more specifically to the ability to function and the causes of inhibition. Clinicians have observed that erotization can serve as a defense or as an adaptation. Erotization also occurs in severely disturbed patients, those who suffer from states of disruptive agitation in which no psychic content can be discerned. I have called this level of regression prementational (Giovacchini 1979), as it involves regression to a neonatal stage of development in which there is as yet no capacity to feel and organize in terms of psychological configurations. A state of primitive disruption and terror can occur in a relatively unstructured ego. This state of inchoate tension can be erotized, a process that gives it some organization and reduces agitation. I believe many impulsive sexual encounters that we hear about between therapists and patients can be explained on such a basis. The therapist may have absorbed the patient's disruption, or because of his own ego defects, the therapist may have regressed to such an amorphous painful psychic level. He exploits the patient sexually to gain relief for himself. I believe that anger can be used in a similar fashion.

At the end of this section, Freud discussed the phenomenon of a general inhibition. If a person is struggling with a difficult internal problem, such as mourning, there is very little energy left over for external object relationships or other reality related endeavors. Many patients show low energy levels associated with general inhibitions rather than inhibitions that have a specific intrapsychic focus. Further investigation frequently reveals that an early traumatic environment caused the ego to develop in a fragmented rather than a cohesive fashion. The ego is not able to integrate external percepts with inner structure efficiently. It is what we call a "weak" ego and appears inhibited because it is poorly integrated. As a result, it does not have the capacity to cathect persons or situations that would help it achieve gratification or make creative contributions. The borderline patient is a prominent example of someone who functions at such a low level.

II

Freud briefly returned here to a discussion of symptoms. He stated that a symptom is a reaction to an instinctual impulse that creates unpleasure. To Freud, the notion of the gratification of an instinctual impulse causing pain was a contradiction. We can wonder why Freud found this formulation unusual.

By referring to different psychic levels, Freud explained how a symptom can cause unpleasure. The instinct can be pleasurable at one level and create pain at another, but the ego finds it unacceptable. Modern psychoanalysts find this explanation almost self-evident, but we must remember that Freud had introduced the ego concept just a few years earlier, having previously laid stress predominantly upon the id.

Thus the ego, which has frequently been described as weak and helpless against the onslaughts of the id, now can be viewed in terms of its power and ability to control the id. The ego achieves its dominance by repressing the unpleasure producing instinctual impulses. Freud posed the question of how this comes about so that he could explore energic distributions and the production of anxiety. He said that the ego is connected to the perceptual system and receives stimuli from both the internal and external world. It attempts to regulate these excitations according to the dictates of the pleasure and reality principles. The latter leads to the creation of what Freud called the "signal of unpleasure" when it causes the ego to oppose an instinctual impulse.

Freud had pointed out many times that the ego takes over the cathexis of the instinct, and then uses the energy to repress that same instinctual impulse. In this monograph, however, he revised this formulation. In formulating the first anxiety theory, Freud had also postulated that instinctual cathexis is directly transformed into anxiety. Here he admitted that this was a phenomenological description rather than a metapsychological explanation. He revised these formulations by first considering how the ego reacts to an external danger. It flees from the danger, decathecting the threatening object or situation. We can add that the ego does not form an established memory trace of that danger and does not attach the withdrawn cathexis to such a memory trace. The ego uses that energy to remove itself from or defend itself against the external trauma. An internal threat is handled in a similar fashion: the dangerous instinctual impulse is decathected, and that energy is used to create the "signal of unpleasure" in the ego. This signal produces a modicum of anxiety and is known as the anxiety signal. To repeat, it uses instinctual energy but the signal is created in the ego. As Freud (1923) had discussed previously, the ego is the site where anxiety is produced.

The decathexis of the instinctual impulse means that it is repressed. To achieve preconscious or conscious representation, the impulse has to be cathected and hypercathected (Freud 1915b). Freud asked, ". . . how is it possible, from an economic point of view, for a mere process of withdrawal and discharge, like the withdrawing of a *preconscious ego-cathexis*, to produce unpleasure or anxiety, seeing that, according to our assumptions, unpleasure and anxiety can only arise as a result of an increase in cathexis (Freud 1926, p. 93; emphasis mine)?" He implied that hypocathexis is the result of "the withdrawing of a preconscious ego cathexis." He also implied that this is a contradiction, inasmuch as the achievement of consciousness and the production of a feeling are the outcome of hypercathexis. What is puzzling is why Freud considered that a hypocathexis exists. True, he wrote of a withdrawal of a preconscious cathexis, but presumably this meant a decathexis of an instinctual impulse that has reached the preconscious; the energy that is liberated from this withdrawal causes a hypercathexis.

Anxiety is not created de novo each time an internal danger occurs; rather, the mnemic trace of a previous but similar trauma is activated. The psyche apparently registers traumatic experiences and the accompanying anxiety affect. When an event occurs that stimulates internal dangers associatively connected with these traumas, the already constructed anxiety emerges in the form of what we might call a memory trace (Freud's mnemic residue), and is felt as a signal of unpleasure. This does not mean, however, that Freud believed as did Rank, that every anxiety experience represented an attempt to master the trauma of birth.

Freud mentioned in passing that anxiety episodes might be the normal prototypes of hysterical attacks, which he implied were rather recent acquisitions. This is another instance in which Freud, in a very short space, said something very important that requires elaboration. First of all, was it true that hysterical attacks were rather recent occurrences in Freud's time? Freud did not document this conclusion, but in the literature of antiquity there are descriptions of states that could easily be hysterical attacks, most likely psychotic in origin. The seventeenth century handbook of witchcraft, the *Malleus Malleficarum*, reports many such examples. Unquestionably there is a relationship between the cultural milieu and the manifestations of psychopathology. As we know, the so-called classical hysteric attack is very rare today.

A second point of Freud's theory that requires clarification is the connection between anxiety and hysterical attacks. We can postulate a continuum, at one end of which the patient experiences primarily anxiety. The patient has a paucity of other symptoms, stressing the recurrent and episodic nature of disruptive feelings and the physical concommitants of anxiety. This situation can be considered the core from which other neuroses develop. Rather than discussing specific defenses that are constructed as a response to anxiety and that lead to symptom formation, we can trace a group of defenses in which, in a manner of speaking, anxiety is shifted to different locations and produces specific neuroses. This was discussed in Chapter 2, but it is worth mentioning again in this context. First anxiety is moved into the somatic part of the ego. This results in conversion hysteria. As the anxiety moves outward, it reaches the external world and is attached to an object or situation, causing the formation of a phobia.

As Freud repeatedly stated, all neuroses are based upon repression. Can repression exist before the formation of the superego? The superego does not develop until fairly late in childhood. It is unlikely, however, that there are no repressive forces operating before the age of 3, and Freud himself was well aware of clinical data indicating that repression operates much earlier. He once again divided repression into two types, primal repression and after pressure, which in other papers he has called secondary repression (Freud 1915a). When excitations break through the protective shield (Freud 1920), they cause intense anxiety. Primal repression, he believed, occurs very early and represents an attempt to deal with these primitive states of terror. However, he was careful to point out that the protective shield is only concerned with external stimuli. Repression occurs in two situations: (1) when an external percept stimulates a dangerous internal impulse and (2) when an instinctual impulse is excited without external stimulation. Secondary repression, however, occurs only after the formation of the superego.

Freud had thus constructed a hierarchy of repression and was also hinting at a hierarchy of anxiety, which he developed later in this monograph. Here he distinguished an early state of anxiety, a painful tension that somehow leads to primal repression. Freud does not explain how this occurs, but presumably the psyche is not sufficiently structured to modulate anxiety into a signal of unpleasure. Most likely, as we will see later, Freud believed that the inability to bind sexual excitation leads to anxiety as he had postulated in his first anxiety theory, in which excitations are directly transformed into anxiety. He did not specify however, whether libido is involved in the situation of the helpless and vulnerable infant.

If repression is complete we cannot know about it. Only when repression fails does it cause manifestations that can be studied. In the first page of this section, Freud briefly discussed symptom formation. He stated that because of the failure of repression, the forbidden instinctual impulse finds a substitute, presumably a symptom. We can assume from this sequence that repression is partially undone as a symptom is established. Repression in this context, requires elaboration. Some theoreticians teach that defenses are instituted to maintain repression. The return of the repressed excites a series of psychic processes that reinstitute repression. The defenses that are utilized manifest themselves somatically, affectively, or behaviorally, as symptoms that are a compromise between the repressed impulse and the repressing forces. Perhaps this compromise may be considered a sign of incomplete repression.

Freud previously had used the concepts of repression and defense interchangeably. In an addendum to this monograph, however, he formulated a viewpoint that is still considered valid: that repression is a particular type of defense.

Freud wrote that the substitute, which has to be a symptom, does not have access to motility, and thus cannot achieve discharge. Freud added that if it is impossible to prevent discharge, the substitute ". . . expends itself in making alterations in the subject's own body and is not permitted to impinge upon the external world. It must not be transformed into action" (Freud 1926a, p. 95). The substitute expending itself in the body indicates some kind of affective reaction, since Freud defined affects as internal discharges.

We can question Freud's insistence that substitute formations or symptoms are not transformed into actions. Obsessive actions and compulsive rituals are manifestations of ego defenses such as isolation, reaction formation, and undoing. Still, they very definitely express themselves in action. An example is the Rat Man (Freud 1909b), who was involved in complex, energy-consuming rituals. We can modify what Freud said by stating that although the symptom is sometimes manifested in action, it does not achieve the same amount of discharge as does an unrepressed instinctual impulse. If our theoretical viewpoint does not include hydrodynamic energic factors, then we can state that the symptom is not experienced as gratifying; it is an adjustment, an adaptation, but not a particularly satisfactory one.

Freud concluded this section in a curious manner, stressing that the ego controls access to both motility and consciousness. Freud recognized that this evaluation of the ego contradicted many of his previous statements about this psychic agency. He had repeatedly stressed that the ego is weak and vulnerable to the onslaughts of the id and the sadism of the superego. He called attention to these two descriptions and then lamented that many analysts had been one-sided in adopting his position about the ego's weakness. However, he did not reconcile these contradictory viewpoints; he simply stated them.

III

In this section Freud reviewed further the strength or weakness of the ego. Even though the ego can repress id derivatives such as instinctual impulses, this is not necessarily a sign of strength. Freud hinted at the interesting point—one strongly subscribed to today—that these two psychic agencies may work in collaboration. Since the ego is a differentiated layer of the id it is expected that there need not be a fundamental opposition between id and ego. Nevertheless, Freud continued to explore the ego's battles against other psychic elements. The instinctual impulse fights the ego so that it is not destroyed by the repressive process but continues to exist within the symptom, which Freud first viewed as residing outside the ego organization.

In their present form these conclusions are bewildering. If the symptom is not in the ego, then where is it? It would make no sense to place it in the id. The symptom is adjacent to the ego, according to Freud, and interacts with it as a foreign body that stimulates reactions in the surrounding tissue. This explanation is plausible if the symptom is considered to be dissociated from the main ego current; it is split off, but the split-off portion is still part of the ego.

Freud acknowledged that in some instances the instinctual impulse loses its impelling force when a symptom forms. He believed this occurred in conversion hysteria. More frequently, however, the ego and the symptom become involved in a secondary defensive struggle, while the instinctual impulse continues to be active.

Still, the ego is an organization fueled by desexualized or sublimated energy. Freud emphasized here the importance of sexuality in his subsequent formulations of ego functions. The ego has the task of reconciliation; it is supposed to bring into harmony different psychic systems. As we now stress, it has a synthetic and integrative function. Freud knew this and pointed out that the synthesizing qualities of the ego can be attributed to its origins before its energy has become desexualized. The function of the sexual instincts is to bring various elements together into a unified whole.

The ego also tries to incorporate and synthesize the symptom into its organization. The clinician would view this incorporation as an attempt at character consolidation. If the symptom is maladaptive—as to some extent all symptoms are—it may indicate a character neurosis, which can be contrasted to a symptom neurosis, in which the symptom is dissociated, or partially dissociated, from the main ego current. Freud had something similar in mind when he formulated that the ego adapts to the symptom as it does to the external world. In fact, symptoms may become so adaptive that the ego exploits them. This is what is known as the secondary gain of symptoms. However, Freud warned the reader not to confuse secondary gain with the etiology of neurosis. The neurosis is not created because of the advantages the symptoms may eventually bring. These advantages, however, make resistance to analysis more intense than it would have been if there had been no secondary gain. This can be a serious treatment problem.

The ego can either incorporate the symptom into itself or repress it. This seems strange, because we have learned that the symptom is formed in response to defenses that are attempting to maintain repression. Now the manifestations of that very defense, the symptom, can be repressed. The symptom represents a compromise. Freud was still writing about a secondary defensive struggle. According to him, the impulse may not choose to abide by the terms of the compromise, but instead continue to seek satisfaction through discharge by action into the outer world. Then the ego has to renew its struggle against the impulse. This may happen in different ways, so Freud decided to examine specific cases, those of Little Hans (Freud 1909) and the Wolf Man (Freud 1918).

Freud's writing style continues to be notable. He repeatedly uses metaphors that refer to battles and struggles. The psyche seems to be composed of parts that are in a constant power struggle with each other. Adaptation occurs in a combative camp.

IV

Little Hans was afraid of horses. Freud stated that this fear could be considered a symptom and the accompanying inability to go out on the street an inhibition, an ego restriction that prevented the outbreak of anxiety. However, matters were not so simple. Freud discovered that the fear of horses was more specific than it seemed at first. Little Hans had an Oedipus complex; he wanted to possess his mother and was jealous and hostile toward his father. Hans was ambivalent, however; although he wanted to get rid of his father, at the same time he loved him. Hans' phobia represented an attempt to resolve this conflict. Freud knew that there were other methods by which the psyche might deal with such a conflict. The hostile feelings might be replaced and repressed by intensifying affection, which would be exaggerated and compulsive, thereby betraying its defensive origin. Freud (1909a) thoroughly discussed this mechanism of reaction formation in the case of the Rat Man.

Little Hans did not use this defense mechanism. He repressed his hostile feelings toward his father, but rather than using reaction formation he used phobic defenses. Hans once reported having seen both a playmate and a horse fall down and hurt themselves. Analysis demonstrated that he had wished his father would also fall down and hurt himself. There was other evidence that Hans wished to get rid of his father, such as his desire that his father move out of the house.

Freud recognized that he still needed to explain the phobia, and his incisive use of metaphor helped to clarify the situation. He described a hypothetical household in which the young male servant falls in love with his mistress. It would be natural for the servant to fear that the master of the house might find out about it and severely punish him for his infatuation. Freud recognized that Hans was in a similar position; if he had been simply afraid of his father, he would not have developed a neurosis. It is the use of the mechanism of displacement, by which Hans replaced his father with a horse, that defined the existence of a neurosis. Freud, with his usual astuteness, asked why it should be the *reaction* to an impulse that is defended against. Presumably he meant, Why not deal with the hostile feelings directly so that no fear has to be experienced?

Hans would also not have had a neurosis if he had directed his hostility toward horses instead of his father. To some extent he did this, but his anger was not particularly in the foreground. This meant that only the object of the anger had changed, while the drive remained unchanged.

Little Hans' phobia required further elaboration, especially in reference to his fear of being bitten by horses, but before discussing Little Hans further, Freud introduced the Wolf Man. As we would expect, the Wolf Man had a fear of wolves. Little Hans' father had played games with him involving horses; the Wolf Man's father pretended he was a wolf who would eat his son. This was made clear by his associations to a dream in which seven wolves were on a tree. Freud also cited a third patient here, an American who did not have a phobia but did have a recurrent fantasy similar to these phobias, of an Arabian chieftain who hunted the Gingerbread Man. According the Freud, the chieftain represented the patient's father, and the Gingerbread Man was the patient himself. The theme of being devoured was dominant in all three patients.

Freud considered the fear of being devoured to be a manifestation of a regressively expressed, passive, tender feeling toward the father. The sexual component of such feelings is well hidden when it is expressed in the language of the sadistic libido organization (the anal-sadistic stage). Freud questioned whether this was a regressive method of expressing a feeling, or whether the impulse had regressed from a genital to a pregenital phase. This question is puzzling because we would expect that the method by which an impulse is expressed would depend on the associated ego state.

Freud seemed to be concentrating here on distinctions between relatively mild and severe psychopathology. Though both Little Hans and the Wolf Man had phobias, Freud believed that the Wolf Man was by far the more disturbed. He expressed this by concluding that the Wolf Man suffered from an instinctual regression, whereas Little Hans was involved only with a regressive manifestation of ambivalent impulses toward his father and the ensuing castration anxiety.

Freud once more emphasized that repression is not the only defense against a forbidden and disruptive instinctual impulse. Here he referred to regression as a defense that is, in a way, more powerful than repression, inasmuch as it damages the defended-against impulse—it has undergone a regressive denigration, whereas the repressed impulse remains intact. He apparently thought that in regression the impulse loses its higher-level organization and assumes forms characteristic of earlier levels of psychosexual development. During repression this does not happen; presumably such feelings are barred from consciousness but remain intact. In "The Unconscious" (1915c), Freud discussed the question of the status of unconscious mental content. He then thought that an affect could only exist in consciousness as a feeling. An unconscious affect has the potential of becoming an affect but does not yet have the organization that would allow it to be felt. If we carry this line of thought further, we can conclude that repressed psychic elements must to some extent also undergo a "regressive denigration." In any case, regression is another defense which Freud added to his list. He pointed out that, in many cases, once the regressive process is set in motion, repression occurs.

Both the Wolf Man and Little Hans had hostile feelings toward their fathers, which became repressed and were then transformed into their opposites. Thus, their destructive feelings toward their fathers were replaced by fears based upon their fathers' supposed revenge against them. This constitutes interplay between regression and repression. Their hostility was located at the anal-sadistic stage and did not have far to regress to the oral phase, which was expressed by the phobia of being bitten by a horse or devoured by a wolf.

Still, more than one instinctual current is involved. In addition to hostile feelings, both Little Hans and the Wolf Man, had passive tender feelings toward their fathers. These feelings were also repressed and had an influence in determining the content of the phobia. Although their affectionate feelings toward the mother were also repressed, this had no effect on their phobias. In fact, all the components of the Oedipus complex were drawn into the regressive current and the repressive process.

Freud recognized that no neurosis is particularly simple, meaning that more than one repression is always involved. He also saw certain important differences between these two patients. He concentrated upon the Wolf Man's tender feelings toward his father, that is, passive homosexual longings. Freud doubted that such longings were particularly operative in Little Hans, perhaps they were there to some extent and had a hand in repressing hostile feelings, but they were not strong enough to set repressive forces in motion.

It is interesting that Freud considered Little Hans a normal boy because he had a positive Oedipus complex. Certainly Hans gave considerable evidence of having feelings that were characteristically oedipal and, from Freud's viewpoint, of positive Oedipus. However, the subsequent history of Little Hans does not indicate a weak homosexual tendency; Little Hans grew up to be a musical stage director. He apparently had various sadistic relationships with women and was rumored to have had homosexual affairs. Whatever the actual facts, he had a reputation bordering on notoriety, which is not a normal outcome of a positive Oedipus complex in a normal boy.

Considerably more is known about the follow-up of the Wolf Man. In view of the obviously severe nature of his psychopathology and the severe traumas he had to endure throughout his life, it is surprising that he did as well as he did. Freud felt that the Wolf Man's passive homosexual orientation toward his father was particularly intense, but that it had regressed sufficiently so that it was not detectable in the fear of being devoured by wolves. The common denominator in these two phobias was a basic fear of castration, which underwent regressive expression in the fears of being bitten by a horse or eaten by a wolf. However, because of differences in the strength of their homosexual feelings, there are differences in how castration anxiety was experienced and which impulses were dominant. Hans feared that his father would cut his penis off in retaliation for his sexual feelings toward his mother. The Wolf Man, by contrast, unconsciously wanted a passive homosexual relationship with his father. In other words, he wanted to adopt a feminine attitude toward him. But to do this he had to be castrated so that he could become a woman. To achieve what he desired would cause him to lose his penis. Although for very different reasons, this fear produced anxiety in both patients.

Freud implied that the prospect of castration is a terrifying experience, even when, as was the case with the Wolf Man, it is a means of achieving instinctual gratification. He linked fear of castration with fear of annihilation, which is a regressive degradation of castration anxiety. Still, there are enough examples of self-castration occurring among psychotics to indicate that anxiety, even the fear of annihilation, can be delusionally denied.

Castration anxiety is transformed into an animal phobia and becomes a realistic danger. It is not the outcome of repressed libido or the repressive process. Rather, it is derived from the repressing agency. Freud acknowledged that this formulation is radically different from what he had previously postulated in stating that anxiety is created when libido cannot be discharged. These are antithetical formulations: in the more recent hypothesis, anxiety is created by the ego and leads to repression, whereas previously Freud thought that anxiety stems from the id and is the result rather than the cause of repression.

However, Freud did not relinquish old theories too easily. He observed that there is usually some anxiety present after repression has occurred. This could be explained on the basis of his first anxiety theory. He also called attention to the data that led him to formulate the theory, that repressed libido is converted into anxiety. He described a variety of situations in which sexual tension cannot be discharged, such as coitus interruptus and forced abstinence. Freud believed that his ideas about anxiety were correct descriptions rather than metapsychological formulations. He felt that the phobias unequivocally placed the production of anxiety in the ego, but other clinical data do not permit absolute conclusions.

V

In this section, Freud pursued further the formation of symptoms and their relationship to the ego. He started by stating cryptically that phobics are not particularly good subjects for study, since the anxiety which dominates the clinical picture obscures the problem. Then he turned to hysteria (conversion hysteria), in which, he emphasized that anxiety is absent. Furthermore, patients with chronic symptoms do not feel pain. He stated that the ego behaves toward symptoms as though it has nothing to do with them. With intermittent symptoms the situation is different. We can question whether our clinical experience confirms these observations; however the manifestations of some emotional illnesses may have changed drastically throughout the generations.

To explore these questions further, Freud turned to the obsessional neuroses. They have two groups of symptoms: (1) those representing prohibitive precautions or atonement, what he called negative symptoms and (2) symptoms that are designed to gain instinctual satisfaction through various psychic mechanisms such as displacement or through symbolic gratification. In the obsessional neuroses, the prohibitions are initially dominant because of the strength of the superego. However, instinctual forces eventually gain the upper hand. In the struggle between the repressed and repressing forces, the repressed gradually asserts itself.

Again, Freud mentioned the ego's tendency to synthesize, which enables it to combine the prohibition with instinctual satisfaction. This formulation emphasizes the compromise formation of symptoms. We can conceptualize symptoms as the mentational and behavioral manifestations of defensive processes. They are defensive in character, but they are also adaptive in that they give expression to what is being defended against.

Obsessional symptoms are diphasic. Freud meant that they followed a temporal sequence in which an action aimed at gaining instinctual satisfaction is followed by another one that stops it even to the point of carrying out an opposite action. Freud's example of the Rat Man kicking the stone is a classic example of this sequence.

The interplay between forces striving for satisfaction and prohibitions against them can be most striking in the obsessional neuroses and need not involve diphasic temporal sequences. The behavioral manifestations of the defense of reaction formation are prominent examples. The patient who washes his hands fifty times a day to ensure absolute cleanliness is constantly preoccupied with dirt. The gentle soul who abhors all forms of cruelty displays a maddening saccharin orientation. Some of the letters that antivivisectionists have written in support of their cause could have been written by the judges of the Spanish Inquisition. Both the prohibition and the underlying impulses are contained in the symptoms formed by reaction formation, but the id component is what we primarily feel.

Freud clung to the view of the fundamental role of the Oedipus complex in the formation of symptoms. The instinctual forces consist of oedipal wishes, and the opposition is characterized by castration anxiety. As has already been discussed, Freud felt that repression worked fairly effectively in hysteria and acknowledged the existence of other defense mechanisms in other neuroses.

Freud had noted as early as 1896 in "Further Remarks on the Defence Neuro-Psychoses," that there is a relationship between hysteria and the obsessional neuroses. Here, he considered this relationship further by asking the question as to whether obsessional neurotics suffer from a fixation at the anal-sadistic stage, or whether they have regressed to that stage from the Oedipus complex. He decided on the latter. During the Oedipus complex there is a fusion of erotic and aggressive impulses. In regression there is a defusion of these instinctual components.

From the above, we could conclude that Freud was emphasizing id strivings and intrapsychic conflicts and was excluding structural considerations. However, this is not entirely true, inasmuch as he stressed that the obsessional neurosis is a caricature of the normal. Adaptive character traits such as conscientiousness, neatness, and frugality become exaggerated, often turning into crippling symptoms. These symptoms, the products of reaction formation, are the outcome of a severe, strict superego. Freud believed that these defensive measures are designed to prohibit the practice of infantile masturbation. This struggle can produce a series of symptoms in the form of time- and energy-consuming ceremonials and rituals.

Ordinarily, destructive impulses are replaced by substitute impulses when they reach ego levels. If they appear directly, the thought content reaches consciousness without any affect. Freud discussed this phenomenon in terms of the defense mechanism of isolation.

Freud made an especially interesting connection in this context. Even when the ego has successfully excluded objectionable impulses, it may still feel guilty because the superego is savagely attacking it. Without emphasizing the obvious anthropomorphization, Freud stressed certain structural connections: the superego, in spite of its dipping into the id, is produced relatively late in the process of psychic structuralization, and it represents what we can call a higher structure. In this sense it is closer to the ego than to the id, and primary-process–oriented defenses such as repression thus do not have the same force in these higher spheres and are less capable of appeasing the superego.

When primary process defenses are, so to speak, transported to higher levels, as occurs in making the unconscious conscious, they may be converted into an ego function. Freud remarked that defenses, in some instances, gradually become vehicles of gratification. However, the ego may also become completely paralyzed—in a paralysis of will as Freud called it—caught between the dictates of the superego and the id.

VI

Here Freud delved further into obsessional mechanisms, specifically the defenses of undoing and isolation. Undoing in German is *ungeschehenmachen*, which is literally translated as "to make unhappen." This is related to defenses that cause the individual to take precautionary measures to prevent the occurrence of the feared event. Undoing has a magical quality, cultivating the false belief that nothing has ever happened. It is a way of rewriting history. Freud made an interesting connection between undoing and repetition, a frequently encountered obsession. He stated, "When anything has not happened in the desired way it is undone by being repeated in a different way. . . ."

Isolation is also a typical obsessional defense and can be compared to the repression of hysterics. In hysteria an impulse is totally repressed, whereas in isolation it is divested of its affect, but the thought content remains in consciousness. Its connections with other related and associated currents of thinking may also be broken off, so the thought is, in fact, isolated. It stands alone and is thereby devoid of meaning and force. Freud described how the obsessional patient may embark on a certain course of behavior, then stop, and do and think nothing, afterwards resuming what he had started. This is a form of isolation in which there is a break in continuity.

This break in continuity seems different from the repression of affect, a form of isolation often referred to as intellectualization. Freud did not explain how these two phenomena are connected. A thought sequence, the outcome of repression of affect, is interrupted. In some instances a segment of thought is removed from the mainstream during the interruption. This thought is in a sense isolated. Some analysts have referred to such an event as temporal isolation.

Another common obsessional symptom that Freud discussed is the fear of (taboo against) touching. He made a clever formulation: touching is a way of expressing love—an erotic activity. At the same time to touch someone is destructive—in the unconscious, as we often find when we uncover the fantasies of obsessional and schizophrenic patients, touching means contaminating. Here Freud was referring to the conflict between libidinal and aggressive impulses.

In the final paragraphs of this section, Freud reiterated that symptom formation in hysterics, phobics, and obsessionals is based upon the Oedipus complex and castration anxiety. He did not know exactly how castration anxiety operates in women since he believed they are already castrated. He concluded that women must have other motives for repression, and that they can only be said to have a castration complex, rather than castration anxiety.

VII

Freud now continued his discussion of phobias and obsessionals, restating some general principles that might be challenged today. He stated emphatically that a neurosis is based upon sexual conflicts or, as he put it here, ". . . against the demands of the libido and not against those of any other instinct that the ego is defending itself." He arrived at this conclusion after he had raised the question of whether Little Hans, who had a positive Oedipus complex, was dominated by his erotic feelings toward his mother or his aggressive feelings toward his father. He acknowledged, however, that there was much more to learn about this topic. I was particularly struck by the following statement: "If we cannot see things clearly, we will at least see clearly what the obscurities are."

When aggressive impulses seem to be dominant, they are, nevertheless, connected with libidinal feelings. Freud had worked this out when he developed the concept of narcissism (Freud 1914). Repression, he stated, is a defense mechanism characteristic of the genital phase of development. Earlier levels are associated with other defenses. He continued to assert that castration anxiety is the fundamental danger against which the ego has to defend itself. He formulated that anxiety is emitted as a signal to set defenses in motion to protect the ego against the danger of castration anxiety. This signal anxiety does not phenomenologically or subjectively differ from realistic anxiety, which is the fear of an external rather than an internal danger.

Freud made an interesting concession at this point in his discussion. He admitted that he was aware of complex cases of phobias in which impulses other than just sexual ones are repressed. He added, however, that these impulses join the "main current of the neurosis at a later stage". This is a very interesting formulation, because Freud implied that later experiences, as well as infantile ones, could become involved in the creation of a neurosis. He also implied that etiology may involve factors in addition to the sexual.

At this point Freud briefly discussed the dynamics of agoraphobia. Patients suffering from agoraphobia supposedly undergo a temporal and apparently very deep regression to the fetal stage, in which their mother's womb protected them against external dangers. Some agoraphobics can walk the streets only if they are accompanied by someone they trust. The few cases of agoraphobia I have seen had an underlying psychotic core. I recall a young lady suffering from severe agoraphobia who managed to come to my office only if she were driven there by her father. After a year of treatment she developed a somatic delusion, believing that her nose was ugly and deformed. Actually it was a fairly average nose. Finally she revealed a basically paranoid orientation with delusions and auditory hallucinations.

Freud also discussed the fear of being alone. He apparently felt it was self-evident that this fear was the outcome of the temptation to masturbate. I believe that we would now view this somewhat differently. Some patients experience being alone as terrifying because it recapitulates the fear of abandonment and ego dissolution.

By contrast, everything in the obsessional neuroses is internalized. There is no projection, and the main problem is the ego's fear of the superego. But even here castration anxiety plays the dominant role. The father, according to Freud, becomes depersonalized into the superego, the castrating father abstracted into *Gewissensangst*, which literally means conscience anxiety.

Freud's concept of castration anxiety was broad; he considered any separation from the body to be a form of castration. For example the loss of feces is regressively experienced as castration anxiety. The superego serves a protective function, and the ego fears being abandoned by it. Freud had already discussed these processes in the context of the traumatic neuroses when the protective shield is broken into in *Beyond the Pleasure Principle* (Freud 1920).

Freud finished this section with an unanswered question. Reactions to separation are pain and mourning, not anxiety. Why is this so, and why is mourning painful?

VIII

Precisely what is anxiety, and how does it differ from other affects? Freud asked these questions and realized that they had not yet been adequately answered. He pointed out three characteristics of anxiety: (1) it is unpleasurable; (2) it is an act of discharge; and (3) it is a perception of (1) and (2). The last two qualities distinguish anxiety from other affects. Thus anxiety consists of increased excitation, which creates unpleasure and seeks relief through discharge. To my mind, this represents a return to the first anxiety theory, which Freud attempted to replace in this monograph. However, he was concentrating on a thesis that Darwin developed—that the expression of emotions had an adaptive meaning in the prehistoric past. Freud referred to the act of birth as a prototypical example of an increase in excitation leading to discharge. He believed that anxiety states had the same discharge pathways as the trauma of birth, but did not believe, as did Rank, that every future episode of anxiety basically represents the birth trauma.

Freud continued to concentrate upon adaptive features. All affects are reproductions of earlier meaningful experiences. Anxiety is a reaction to a danger and is reproduced whenever danger occurs, but it is an expedient reaction in that it leads to protective actions. Freud drew an interesting parallel, which helps unite his two anxiety theories. He repeated that affects in the pasts of both the individual and the race were adaptive. "The innervations involved in the original state of anxiety probably had a meaning and purpose. . . ." For example, the discharge phenomenon at birth—crying—prepares the lungs for breathing and accelerates the heart rate, helping to rid the blood of toxic substances. Later, when anxiety occurs, it may no longer be functionally adaptive.

Now Freud turned to the second anxiety theory. Anxiety can once again become adaptive if the danger is recognized and if anxiety warns of its impending approach. Freud struck some modern notes in this section that are compatible with recent findings of neonatal research. Freud postulated that Rank's birth theory of anxiety was incorrect because the capacity to feel anxiety as an organized affect does not develop until later in the course of emotional development, a conclusion which has been confirmed by neonatal research.

Freud formulated that the child cathects what he calls the mnemic image of the longed-for person, the caretaker. It may reach hallucinatory intensity but does not furnish the satisfaction the actual object would have supplied. Hallucinating a caretaking person does not work, because eventually the child experiences the discomfort of unmet needs. In terms of the psychoeconomic hypothesis, this is equivalent to an increase of excitation that cannot be mastered psychically or discharged, a situation Freud felt was analogous to the birth process. These economic conditions constitute danger. These points are based upon certain fundamental economic assumptions that many do not find useful. However, if these assumptions are accepted, Freud is consistent.

The child realizes early that a caretaking person—the mother—can protect him from this danger by ministering to his needs. She modulates his excitation by soothing and nurturing him. The infant now knows that he can obtain relief, and the loss of the mother becomes the dangerous situation. Freud put it succinctly: ". . . the content of the danger it fears is displaced from the economic situation onto the condition which determined that situation, viz., the loss of the object." The child is no longer at the mercy of his needs. He can now intentionally reproduce anxiety as a signal to bring his mother to him.

Freud distinguished two types of anxiety, which correspond to the first and second anxiety theories. The first type is an automatic response to mounting excitation. Freud referred to this as a mental helplessness analogous to biological helplessness. The mother, by ministering to the child's needs protects and gratifies him so he no longer feels helpless. Thus anxiety, rather than being an abreaction, becomes a signal to obtain relief and satisfaction. In this early period the mother is the child's chief adaptive modality.

Freud did not abandon the important position he had given to castration anxiety; he viewed it as an upward hierarchal extension of the loss of the caretaking object. The separation of the penis from the body is a type of separation, and incestuous wishes, for the boy, represent an attempt to reunite with the mother.

Freud claimed that he was no longer particularly interested in economic concepts, although from the above it would seem that he was. However, he was emphasizing the signal theory of anxiety. He still viewed the energy that causes the affect of anxiety as being derived from repressive forces but he did not feel this was important. Id anxiety, he stated, makes no sense as such, since anxiety is something that is felt and therefore can only occur in the ego. The id may create conditions that will stimulate the ego to produce anxiety.

Regarding the significance of castration anxiety in girls, he now asserted that the motive force behind the production of anxiety is loss of love. This fits well with his basic formulations about the importance of separation, as it represents danger. With further psychic structuralization, the fear of loss of love in girls is equivalent to the fear of castration in boys.

IX

In this section, Freud explored further the connections between symptoms and anxiety. He concluded, after reviewing several clinical situations such as agoraphobia, that symptoms are constructed to avoid anxiety. He noted that if a symptom, such as hand-washing compulsion, is hindered, the patient will have an anxiety attack. It may not be necessary to feel much anxiety in order to form symptoms; anxiety could be minimal in intensity and serve as a signal. Symptoms are also produced to avoid danger, and they represent substitute formations—that is, they seek alternate modes of gratification. They are also analogous to flight from danger, in that the ego seeks to avoid an external threat, which stimulates inner impulses that are also perceived as dangerous.

Freud anticipated the objection that the fundamental danger of loss of love is an external threat like the animal involved in a phobia. However, he wryly pointed out that the wolf, for example, will attack irrespective of one's feelings toward him. The child fears loss of love and castration because of his inner destructive feelings. Therefore these inner feelings are dangerous and are responsible for the dangers perceived in the external world. In the phobias, as Freud had repeatedly pointed out, inner danger is attributed to an external danger, whereas in the obsessive neuroses the feared object is the superego, an endopsychic danger. Different phases of life are associated with specific danger situations. During early childhood, the infant cannot master large amounts of excitation either from the inner or the outer world, and fears the loss of the protective mother. Later, he fears the father, as he begins to perceive him as a rival for his mother, toward whom he has developed sexual feelings. Still later as he forms social relationships, he begins to fear the superego as he experiences social anxiety.

Freud compared the affect of anxiety to pain. It is normal for the girl to cry at 4 when her doll is broken, at 6 when her teacher scolds her, at 16 when her boyfriend slights her, or at 25 when her child dies. Most of these painful situations run their course, but the effects of the loss of a child are retained for the rest of one's life. These are, according to Freud, normal reactions whereas, if a grown woman cries over the loss of something worthless, she is behaving as neurotics do. Neurotics, although they know that they will not be punished by being castrated, still behave as if they were in real danger. They cling to infantile, anxiety-producing dangers. However, although there are many phobias and rituals during childhood, indeed so many that they can be considered normal, they do not often persist in adult life in the form of a neurosis. Every adult neurosis can be connected with an infantile neurosis, but the reverse is not true. There is some truth in the cliché that the child will outgrow the phobia.

Toward the end of this section Freud raised the question of why the conditions that produce anxiety do not always disappear as the psyche proceeds to higher developmental levels. This is another way of asking about the choice and cause of neuroses, questions that he felt had not been answered. To this day there is much to be answered about these questions.

X

Freud pursued the question of choice of neurosis further, in terms of predisposition to anxiety. Adler proposed an innate organ weakness, which creates feelings of inferiority that lead to vulnerability and anxiety. Freud dismissed this theory out-of-hand because it was not based upon psychoanalytic principles. He then returned to Rank's birth theory, which he believed belonged in a psychoanalytic context. Freud was referring essentially to economic factors, exemplified by the process of abreaction, but he no longer believed in the importance or the therapeutic efficacy of abreaction. He explicitly stated that the frequent and intense repetition of anxiety by neurotic patients does not lead to symptom improvement or resolution. Furthermore, there is no proof that hard and traumatic labors and birth are associated with a higher incidence of emotional illness. Freud finally concluded that it is unlikely that there is a single and "ultimate cause" of neurotic illness.

What follows is especially interesting and is relevant to understanding the emotional rigidity seen in so many patients today. I believe Freud was discussing characterological fixations, although he spoke of them in terms of instinctual impulses. He postulated that when an impulse is driven out of the ego sphere into the id by repression, the ego gives up part of its "sovereignty." The impulse acquires independence from the ego and now obeys the laws of the id.

When a new impulse arises that is not perceived as dangerous by the ego, it follows the same path as the old repressed impulse. In effect, Freud stated that the id strives to maintain repression, whereas the ego is willing to give it up. Certainly we see constrictions and inhibitions in our patients that are confined to specific impulses. Freud emphasized the compulsion to repeat as a fundamental characteristic of id processes which dominate the entire psyche. Furthermore, the psyche can relate to the external world only in a limited fashion, and this we attribute to structural defects.

Although the choice of neurosis remains unanswered, Freud had some ideas about predisposition. He pointed out three predisposing factors: biological, phylogenetic, and what he referred to as purely psychological. The biological factor refers to the child's basic helplessness. Compared to other animals, the human gestation period is relatively short. At birth, the neonate is completely helpless, facing a dangerous outer world and being totally dependent upon nurturing and protective caretakers.

The phylogenetic factor involves the diphasic nature of human sexual development, which Freud formulated at the very beginning of the development of psychoanalysis. Infantile sexuality reaches its peak at around age 5, followed by a latency period until puberty, when there is a second efflorescence of sexual feelings, this time biologically impelled. Freud believed that this was a recapitulation of geological sequences in which the development of the earth was interrupted by a glacial epoch. He was heavily influenced by one of his most loyal followers, Ferenczi, who first suggested these ideas. Because of the prematurity of infantile sexual impulses, they are perceived as dangerous. Later sexual feelings, as has already been discussed, are also considered threatening. Freud compared the biological with the phylogenetic factor; the former is based upon a premature contact with the external world and the latter a similar premature contact with sexual drives.

The psychological factor in the predisposition to neuroses is the outcome of the imperfections of the psychic apparatus. Freud was referring to the interconnections between the id and the ego. Because of the inherent dangers in the outer world, certain drives also become dangerous. However, Freud did not explain how this occurs. I would assume that if a person tried to gratify all his inner wishes, he would meet opposition from his environment, and if his inner drives were hostile, he might encounter destructive retribution. In any case, the ego tries to construct defenses against such drives, and these lead to symptoms and neurotic suffering.

XI

This section is an addendum in which Freud pulled together some loose ends. He remained conflicted about replacing his earlier views with different hypotheses. As much as possible he tried to maintain a continuum between the first and second anxiety theories, but he also modified his concepts about several other important psychic processes and mechanisms.

Resistance and Anticathexis

I will outline the sequence of Freud's thoughts upon these important issues. Repression requires a continuous expenditure of energy. It is not just a one-time repressive impact that keeps the forbidden impulse outside the ego sphere. The energy that maintains repression is called anticathexis; during analytic treatment it is manifested as resistance. It is also the outcome of certain alterations in the ego.

Once more, Freud made formulations in terms of character structure. This anticathexis is easily recognizable in the obsessional neurotic whose ego has acquired certain traits, that is, character adaptations, that protect it from aberrant instinctual impulses. Anticathexis is produced by reaction formations, which are a major part of the obsessive's character. In hysterics, anticathexis and characterological changes are not as obvious. Freud believed that hysterics nevertheless could also be thought of in terms of alterations of psychic structure. This is interesting because Freud based his early id psychology and psychodynamic hypothesis almost exclusively on the study of allegedly hysterical patients. Here he briefly mentioned subtle character changes. A hysterical woman, for example, may repress her murderous wishes toward her child by being overly affectionate, but this type of reaction formation is not generalized—she does not display any particular love for other children.

Hysterics frequently direct their anticathexis toward the outer world. Segments of the external world, because they stimulate dangerous inner impulses, become threatening. Therefore these segments are avoided. Freud borrowed a term coined by Laforgue (1926), *scotomization*, to describe this situation. Phobias are another example of anticathexis toward the outer world. Obsessives, however, direct their repressive energies inward. This distinction caused Freud to make the following puzzling statement: "It suggests that there is an intimate connection between repression and external anticathexis on the one hand and between regression and internal anticathexis (i.e., alteration in the ego through reaction formation) on the other." I suppose repression and external cathexis refer to hysterical anticathexis. Regarding internal anticathexis, Freud had discussed reaction formation as a character alteration which kept dangerous internal impulses repressed. Regression must be connected with the characterological type of anticathexis. Freud probably thought of such a character change as a form of regression. He had postulated that these reaction formations were caricatures of normal character traits, and in this sense he may have conceived of them in terms of regression.

As has been repeatedly noted, resistance was a key topic for Freud, especially in the discussion of technical treatment principles. Because of its connection with the repressed, resistance is often unconscious. Even when conscious during psychoanalytic treatment, it can still persist in its tenacious effects. Freud revealed his personal analytic style when discussing this subject. He spoke of urging the patient to give up his resistance, to cajole him, to speak of the rewards that would follow and the premiums to be gained; in other words, he was stressing manipulation, a method that may now seem to be antianalytic.

The tenacity of resistance, even after the ego is willing to give up repression, is explained by the force of the id. Freud referred to the resistance of the id, which is based upon the repetition compulsion. The id tends to repeat infantile sequences and adaptations in spite of the ego's willingness to allow drives to emerge and be satisfied through transactions with the external world.

Freud postulated five types of resistance:

1. Resistance due to repression, which has already been discussed.
2. Transference resistance, which is a variation of resistance due to repression. The patient renews his repressions as he directs infantile feelings toward the analyst, feelings that otherwise might have been recollected.
3. Resistance due to the secondary gain of the illness. This, as we remember, Freud had discussed in "The Ego and the Id" (Freud 1923).
4. Resistance of the id, which is maintained by the repetition compulsion.
5. Superego resistance, which is discussed in "The Ego and the Id" in terms of the unconscious sense of guilt and the negative therapeutic reaction.

Anxiety from Transformation of Libido

Freud has already discussed most of the points he made in this section elsewhere in this monograph. Here, however, he further separated anxiety from libido, and explicitly stated that anxiety is created by the ego and consists of desexualized energy. Still, at the end of this section, he wrote that there are "two modes of origin to anxiety in later life." The first occurs when there is an involuntary, automatic production of anxiety brought about by the dangerous situation analogous to birth. He was describing an organism, in a state of basic helplessness, being overwhelmed by uncontrollable excitation. The second situation is one in which anxiety is produced by the ego whenever a dangerous situation, such as that just described, threatens to occur. In another ingenious analogy, Freud compared the latter situation to a self-administered innoculation, "submitting to a slight attack of the illness in order to escape its full strength."

Repression and Defense

This is a short but compact section. Here, Freud briefly reviewed his development of the concept of defense, a crucial concept of clinical psychoanalysis. He used the term in "The Neuro-Psychoses of Defence" (Freud 1894) but then quickly moved on to the process of repression. He had been concentrating upon hysteria. He saw the main task of the ego in hysteria as excluding unacceptable sexual impulses. This is the essence of repression.

Later, studying the obsessional neurosis, Freud noted that the aberrant impulse was "isolated." The content remained conscious but the affect was repressed. He also described undoing. He understood these mechanisms as having similar functions to repression but also as being different in their dynamics. He was, of course, formulating that the ego has many defenses at its disposal, repression being a particular type of defense. This is all well known, but Freud first explicitly made these formulations in this section. He said that regression is a defense in the obsessional neurotic. As the ego regresses to earlier developmental positions, instinctual demands also change and become compatible with the more primitive ego state. Freud conjectured that specific defenses are characteristic of particular developmental stages as well as specific types of psychopathology. These have proven to be valuable clinical insights.

Supplementary Remarks on Anxiety

Freud continued to wrestle with the question of distinguishing realistic from neurotic anxiety. In ordinary usage the reaction to a real danger is usually called fear (*Furcht*), anxiety (*Angst*) being reserved for neurotic reactions. Fear is easily understood and has a definitive quality. It is a reaction that we might all expect to have under similar circumstances. The lack of such a reaction, in itself, could be considered a sign of neurosis. Anxiety, by contrast, is indefinite and vague and cannot be easily explained. Realistic and neurotic anxiety can occur together. This is usually manifested by an exaggerated reaction to a real danger. According to Freud, an unknown instinctual danger is attached to the real danger.

What is the essence of the dangerous situation? Freud's pithy response to this question was most illuminating. The victim feels physically helpless in the face of real danger, whereas with instinctual danger he feels psychically helpless. The helpless state represents the traumatic situation. Freud summarized as follows. The original reaction to the traumatic state of helplessness is anxiety, which is passively experienced. Later when an associatively similar situation threatens, anxiety is produced as a signal that recalls the initial helplessness. The ego now repeats actively the traumatic situation in a weakened version in order to master it. This has its prototype in the repetition compulsion, in which something that was passively experienced is now actively repeated in order to master it. Freud's example of his grandson throwing the spool as a symbol of mother's leaving him is a classic example (Freud 1920). The same process is also seen in play.

Freud commented that there is a danger of spoiling the child by overestimating the value of the person who the child fears losing. Presumably he would have advocated not catering to the child's need to be constantly with his mother. Still he viewed the disruptive reaction to the loss of the nurturing object as a natural, instinctive phenomenon.

Human infants, unlike the young of other species, do not have an inherent appreciation of external dangers. Unless protected they can seriously hurt themselves. Freud believed, however, that some phobias, such as the fear of thunder, small animals, and so on, might be "vestigial traces of the congenital preparedness to meet real dangers which is so strongly developed in other animals." If these phobias become fixed and persist into adult life, then they have become attached to inner conflicts and constitute a neurosis. The intrapsychic state is always in some way connected to a basic feeling of helplessness, which would cause some clinicians to think in terms of structural defects.

Anxiety, Pain, and Mourning

Freud raised some very difficult questions in this final section that, to a large measure, still remain unanswered today. The loss of the object leads to anxiety but it can also lead to mourning. It is self-evident that the loss of an object should be painful. Therefore, when does such a loss lead to anxiety or mourning or just pain by itself? Freud made a distinction, which does not seem to be altogether clear. He stated that if the infant has a need that only the mother can satisfy, her absence will be felt as a traumatic situation rather than a danger. I had always thought of traumatic situations as being dangerous, a point which was emphasized by Freud when he discussed the traumatic neuroses (Freud 1920), especially the war neuroses. Perhaps, he was distinguishing once again between internal and external. An unmet need is felt as disruptive undischarged excitation from the vantage point of Freud's psychoeconomic hypothesis, whereas a danger is an external assault that breaks through the protective shield.

The traumatic situation of birth is not associated with the loss of an object, because at this earliest of stages there are no objects. Anxiety that occurs at this stage has to be more primitively organized than later anxiety reactions and is based upon internal tension states rather than on feelings of being isolated, unprotected, and abandoned. The latter reactions are too sophisticated for this early presymbiotic period.

As the child develops and recognizes how the mother produces comfort and supplies nurture, he begins to feel threatened by her absence. He longs for her because she is capable of satisfying his needs and protecting him from danger. Implicitly, Freud traced a developmental hierarchy of the affect of anxiety. He postulated that the initial situation of a trauma before the recognition of an object creates anxiety, whereas intense longing is felt as pain. Pain is a response to the loss of the object, whereas anxiety is a reaction to danger that occurs without the protection of the object.

Freud drew an interesting parallel between physical and mental pain. As we have learned from several of his papers, Freud believed that pain was the outcome of increased cathexis. If a part of the body is painful, we are very much aware of it, whereas ordinarily we do not focus upon it. The mental representation of that aspect of the soma is cathected or hypercathected. If our interest is diverted elsewhere we are likely to "forget" about our pain. Painful longing for a lost object is a similar process, which Freud compared to a shift from object cathexis to narcissistic cathexis. Object cathexis is transferred to the soma, which becomes hypercathected and painful. When the object returns, the cathexis is transferred back to it and non-painful equilibrium is restored. If the object does not return, the ego has to decathect the imago of the lost love object, this constitutes the painful process of mourning.

This monograph not only represents the final development of anxiety theory but also introduces concepts that are still clinically relevant to the treatment of patients who Freud repeatedly stated were untreatable by the psychoanalytic method. As so often happens when we study Freud, we find that he seriously explored many ideas which are strikingly modern in their import and relevance. Much of what we consider new today can frequently be found in Freud's writings, and often he developed these theses in a more comprehensive and comprehensible fashion than have many modern psychoanalytic investigators.

Course Outline and Bibliography

I General Introduction

   A Freud's passage from neurophysiology to phenomeno-logical therapies to an etiological approach.

   B Justification for the concept of the dynamic unconscious. (All Freud references will be found in *Standard Edition*, 24 Vols., Hogarth Press, London, or *Collected Papers of Sigmund Freud*, Vols. I–IV).

     Reference: "The Unconscious," (Freud 1915c).

   C Early Clinical Studies

     Reference: Studies on Hysteria (Breuer and Freud 1895).

      1. "On the Psychical Mechanisms of Hysterical Phe-nomena" (Breuer and Freud).

      2. "Anna O." (Breuer).

      3. Theoretical Section, "Hypnoid States" (Breuer).

      4. "The Psychotherapy of Hysteria" (Freud).

II Psychodynamic Theory

   A Defenses

   B Nosology

     Reference: "Further Remarks on the Defence Neuro-Psychoses" (Freud 1896).

III Anxiety Theory (First)

    A (Some elements of the Second Anxiety Theory are considered here with more detail to be supplied later).

    B Nosology is also discussed in the context of anxiety theory. *Reference:* "On the Grounds for Detaching a Particular Syndrome from Neurasthenia under the Description 'Anxiety Neuroses'" (Freud 1895).

IV Instinct Theory

    A General Aspects of Instincts and the First Instinct Theory. *Reference:* "Instincts and Their Vicissitudes" (Freud 1915).

    B Sexuality
    Reference: Three Essays on Theory of Sexuality (Freud 1905).

    C Narcissism
    Reference: "On Narcissism: An Introduction" (Freud 1914).

    D Later Developments in Instinct Theory up to 1920
    Reference: Beyond the Pleasure Principle (Freud 1920); "The Development and Problems of the Theory of Instincts" (Bibring 1941); International Journal of Psycho-Analysis, Volume 22.

V Introduction to Structural Hypothesis and the Second Anxiety Theory
    Reference: "The Ego and the Id" (Freud 1923). "Inhibitions, Symptoms and Anxiety" (Freud 1926).

References

ALEXANDER, F. (1961). *The Scope of Psychoanalysis*, New York: Basic Books.

BERNARD, C. (1895). *An Introduction to the Study of Experimental Medicine*, Schurman, 1949.

BOYER, L. B. and GIOVACCHINI, P. L. (1980). *Psychoanalytic Treatment of Characterological, Borderline and Schizophrenic Disorders*, New York: Jason Aronson, Inc.

BREUER, J. and FREUD, S. (1895). Studies on Hysteria, *Standard Edition*, Vol. 2, pp. 1–307, London: Hogarth Press, 1962.

BIBRING, E. (1941). The development and problems of the theory of instincts, *International Journal of Psycho-Analysis*, Vol. 22, pp. 102–132.

CANNON, W. B. (1932). *The Wisdom of the Body,* New York: Norton.

ELLENBERGER, H. (1970). *The Discovery of the Unconscious*, New York: Basic Books.

FEDERN, P. (1931). The reality of the death drive, *Almanach der Psychoanalyse*, pp. 6–28.

FERENCZI, S. (1913). *Thalassa*, Albany, New York: The Psychoanalytic Quarterly Inc., 1938.

FREUD, S. (1877a). Über den Ursprung der hinteren Nervenwurzeln im Rückenmarke von Amnocoetes, *S.B. Akad Wissenschaft*, Vienna, III Abt. 75 (1), pp. 15–27.

—— (1877b). Beobachtungen über Gestaltung und feineren Bau der als Hoden beschriebenen Lappenorgane des Aals, *S.B. Akad Wissenschaft*, Vienna, I Abt. 75 (4), pp. 419–431.

—— (1893). A case of successful treatment by hypnotism, *Standard Edition*, Vol. 1, pp. 115–129, London: Hogarth Press, 1966.

—— (1894a). The neuro-psychoses of defence, *Standard Edition*, Vol. 2, pp. 41–62, London: Hogarth Press, 1962.

—— (1895). Project for a scientific psychology, *Standard Edition*, Vol. 1, pp. 281–392, London: Hogarth Press, 1966.

—— (1895a). On the justification for detaching a particular syndrome from neurasthenia under the description "anxiety neurosis," *Standard Edition*, Vol. 3, pp. 85–116, London: Hogarth Press, 1962.

—— (1896). Further remarks on the neuro-psychoses of defence, *Standard Edition*, Vol. 3, pp. 157–187, London: Hogarth Press, 1953.

—— (1900). The Interpretation of Dreams, *Standard Edition*, Vols. 4 and 5, London: Hogarth Press, 1953.

—— (1901). The Psychopathology of Everyday Life, *Standard Edition*, Vol. 6, London: Hogarth Press, 1966.

—— (1904). Fragment of an analysis of a case of hysteria, *Standard Edition*, Vol. 7, pp. 1–123, London: Hogarth Press, 1953.

—— (1905). Three Essays on the Theory of Sexuality, *Standard Edition*, Vol. 7, pp. 123–244, London: Hogarth Press, 1953.

—— (1906). My views on the part played by sexuality in the aetiology of the neuroses, *Standard Edition*, Vol. 7, pp. 269–281, London: Hogarth Press, 1953.

—— (1909). Analysis of a phobia in a five-year-old boy, *Standard Edition*, Vol. 10, pp. 1–148, London: Hogarth Press, 1955.

—— (1909a). Five lectures on psycho-analysis, *Standard Edition*, Vol. 11, pp. 1–56, London: Hogarth Press, 1957.

—— (1909b). Notes upon a case of obsessional neurosis, *Standard Edition*, Vol. 10, pp. 151–319, London: Hogarth Press, 1955.

—— (1910). The psycho-analytic view of psychogenic disturbance of vision, *Standard Edition*, Vol. 11, pp. 209–219, London: Hogarth Press, 1957.

—— (1910a). The future prospects of psycho-analytic therapy, *Standard Edition*, Vol. 11, pp. 139–153, London: Hogarth Press, 1957.

—— (1911). Formulations on the two principles of mental functioning,

Standard Edition, Vol. 12, pp. 213–227, London: Hogarth Press, 1958.

—— (1911a). Psycho-analytic notes on an autobiographical account of a case of paranoia (dementia paranoides), *Standard Edition*, Vol. 12, pp. 1–85, London: Hogarth Press, 1958.

—— (1911–1915). Papers on technique, *Standard Edition*, Vol. 12, pp. 85–172, London: Hogarth Press, 1958.

—— (1912). The dynamics of transference, *Standard Edition*, Vol. 12, pp. 97–109, London: Hogarth Press, 1958.

—— (1912a). A note on the concept of the unconscious in psycho-analysis, *Standard Edition*, Vol. 12, pp. 255–267, London: Hogarth Press, 1958.

—— (1913). The predisposition to obsessional neurosis, *Standard Edition*, Vol. 12, pp. 311–327, London: Hogarth Press, 1958.

—— (1913a). Totem and taboo. *Standard Edition*, Vol. 13, pp. 1–162, London: Hogarth Press, 1955.

—— (1914). On narcissism: an introduction, *Standard Edition*, Vol. 14, pp. 67–105, London: Hogarth Press, 1957.

—— (1914a). Remembering, repeating and working-through, *Standard Edition*, Vol. 12, pp. 145–157, London: Hogarth Press, 1958.

—— (1915). Repression, *Standard Edition*, Vol. 14, pp. 141–159, London: Hogarth Press, 1957.

—— (1915a). On the history of the psycho-analytic movement, *Standard Edition*, Vol. 14, pp. 1–67, London: Hogarth Press, 1957.

—— (1915b). Instincts and their vicissitudes, *Standard Edition*, Vol. 14, pp. 109–141, London: Hogarth Press, 1957.

—— (1915c). The unconscious, *Standard Edition*, Vol. 14, pp. 159–205, London: Hogarth Press, 1957.

—— (1916). Introductory Lectures on Psycho-Analysis, *Standard Edition*, Vol. 16, pp. 241–478, London: Hogarth Press, 1963.

—— (1917). Mourning and melancholia, *Standard Edition*, Vol. 14, pp. 237–259, London: Hogarth Press, 1957.

—— (1918). From the history of an infantile neurosis, *Standard Edition*, Vol. 17, pp. 1–123, London: Hogarth Press, 1955.

—— (1920). Beyond the Pleasure Principle, *Standard Edition*, Vol. 18, pp. 1–65, London: Hogarth Press, 1955.

—— (1920a). The psychogenesis of a case of homosexuality in a woman,

Standard Edition, Vol. 18, pp. 145–173, London: Hogarth Press, 1955.

—— (1921). Group psychology and the analysis of the ego, *Standard Edition*, Vol. 18, pp. 65–145, London: Hogarth Press, 1955.

—— (1923). The ego and the id, *Standard Edition*, Vol. 19, pp. 3–63, London: Hogarth Press, 1961.

—— (1923a). The infantile genital organization of the libido, *Standard Edition*, Vol. 19, pp. 141–149, London: Hogarth Press, 1961.

—— (1924). A note upon the "mystic writing pad," *Standard Edition*, Vol. 19, pp. 227–235, London: Hogarth Press, 1961.

—— (1925). Negation, *Standard Edition*, Vol. 19, pp. 235–241, London: Hogarth Press, 1961.

—— (1926). Fetishism, *Standard Edition*, Vol. 21, pp. 147–159, London: Hogarth Press, 1961.

—— (1926a). Inhibitions, Symptoms and Anxiety, *Standard Edition*, Vol. 20, pp. 75–175, London: Hogarth Press, 1959.

—— (1933). New Introductory Lectures on Psycho-Analysis, *Standard Edition*, Vol. 22, pp. 1–183, London: Hogarth Press, 1964.

—— (1950). *Origins of Psycho-Analysis: Letters to Wilhelm Fliess, Drafts & Notes, 1887–1902*, Ed. by Marie Bonaparte et al., Tr. by Eric Mosbacher & James Strachey New York: Basic Books, 1954.

GIOVACCHINI, P. L. (1958). Some affective meanings of dizziness, *Psychoanalytic Quarterly*, Vol. 27, pp. 217–225.

—— (1967). Methodological aspects of psychoanalytic critique, *Bulletin of the Philadelphia Psychoanalytic Society*, Vol. 17, pp. 10–25.

—— (1979). *Treatment of Primitive Mental States*, New York: Jason Aronson, Inc.

GLOVER, E. (1930). Grades of ego differentiation, *International Journal of Psycho-Analysis*, Vol. 11, pp. 1–12.

JONES, E. (1927). Early development of female sexuality, in *Papers on Psychoanalysis*, pp. 438–451, London: Balliere, Tindall and Cox, 1950.

—— (1955). *The Life and Works of Sigmund Freud*, Vol. 1, New York: Basic Books.

KNIGHT, R. (1953). Borderline patients, *Bulletin of the Menninger Clinic*, Vol. 19: 1–12.

LAFORGUE, R. (1926). Verdrängung und skotomisation, *International Zeitschrift für Psychoanalyse*, Vol. 12, 54.

LOEWALD, H. (1960). On the therapeutic action of psychoanalysis, *International Journal of Psycho-Analysis*, Vol. 41, pp. 16–34.

REICHARD, S. (1956). A re-examination of *Studies on Hysteria*, *Psychoanalytic Quarterly*, Vol. 25, pp. 155–177.

ROTHGEB, C. (1973). *Abstracts of the Standard Edition of the Complete Psychological Works of Sigmund Freud*, with an introduction on reading Freud by R. R. Holt, New York: Jason Aronson, Inc.

SCHLESSINGER, N. *et al.* (1967). The scientific style of Breuer and Freud in the origins of psychoanalysis, *Journal of the American Psychoanalytic Association*, Vol. 15, pp. 404–422.

SIMMEL, E. (1918). *Kriegneurosen und "Psychisches Trauma,"* Munich.

TARACHOW, S. (1963). *An Introduction to Psychotherapy*, New York: International Universities Press.

TAUSK, V. (1919). On the origin of the influencing machine in schizophrenia, *Psychoanalytic Quarterly*, Vol. 2, pp. 510–556.

WEISS, E. (1950). *Principles of Psychodynamics*, New York: Grune and Stratton.

WINNICOTT, D. W. (1953). Transitional objects and transitional phenomena, in *Collected Papers*, pp. 229–242, New York: Basic Books.

———— (1960). Ego distortion in terms of true and false self, in *The Maturational Process and the Facilitating Environment*, pp. 140–153, London: Hogarth Press.

Index